CONFRONTING
ENVIRONMENTS

GLOBALIZATION AND THE ENVIRONMENT

This AltaMira series publishes new books about the global spread of environmental problems. Key themes addressed are the effects of cultural and economic globalization on the environment; the global institutions that regulate and change human relations with the environment; and the global nature of environmental governance, movements, and activism. The series will include detailed case studies, innovative multisited research, and theoretical questioning of the concepts of globalization and the environment. At the center of the series is an exploration of the multiple linkages that connect people, problems, and solutions at scales beyond the local and regional. The editors welcome works that cross boundaries of disciplines, methods, and locales, and which span scholarly and practical approaches.

SERIES EDITORS:

Richard Wilk, Department of Anthropology, 130 Student Building, Indiana University, Bloomington IN 47405 USA or wilkr@indiana.edu

Josiah Heyman, Department of Sociology & Anthropology, Old Main Building #109, University of Texas at El Paso, 500 West University Avenue, El Paso, TX 79968 USA or jmheyman@utep.edu

BOOKS IN THE SERIES

1. *Power of the Machine: Global Inequalities of Economy, Technology, and Environment*, by Alf Hornborg (2001)
2. *Confronting Environments: Local Environmental Understanding in a Globalizing World*, edited by James G. Carrier (2004)

CONFRONTING ENVIRONMENTS

Local Understanding in a Globalizing World

EDITED BY
JAMES G. CARRIER

ALTAMIRA PRESS
A Division of Rowman & Littlefield Publishers, Inc.
Walnut Creek • Lanham • New York • Toronto • Oxford

AʟᴛᴀMɪʀᴀ Pʀᴇss
A division of Rowman & Littlefield Publishers, Inc.
1630 North Main Street, #367
Walnut Creek, CA 94596
www.altamirapress.com

Rowman & Littlefield Publishers, Inc.
A wholly owned subsidiary of The Rowman & Littlefield Publishing Group, Inc.
4501 Forbes Boulevard, Suite 200
Lanham, Maryland 20706

PO Box 317
Oxford
OX2 9RU, UK

British Library Cataloguing in Publication Information Available

Library of Congress Cataloging-in-Publication Data

Confronting environments : local understanding in a globalizing world / edited by James G.
Carrier.
     p. cm.—(Globalization and the environment ; 2)
     Includes bibliographical references.
     ISBN 0-7591-0562-6 (alk. paper) — ISBN 0-7591-0563-4 (alk. paper)
     1. Human ecology—Philosophy. 2. Nature—Effect of human beings on. 3. Human beings—
Effect of environment on. 4. Environmental policy. 5. Globalization—Environmental aspects.
6. Tourism—Environmental aspects. I. Carrier, James G. II. Title. III. Series.

     GF21.C66 2004
     304.2'8—dc22   2004017883

Printed in the United States of America

♾ᵀᴹ The paper used in this publication meets the minimum requirements of American
National Standard for Information Sciences—Permanence of Paper for Printed Library
Materials, ANSI/NISO Z39.48-1992.

CONTENTS

Preface

IN ANTHROPOLOGY, in cultural studies, and to a degree in the more social side of geography, works on people's understandings of and relations with the environment have been something of a boom industry in the past few years. Although the disciplinary spread of this interest is fairly broad, the primary background of the contributors to this collection is anthropology, and it is anthropology of the environment that is my main concern here.

While there is a growing body of work in that field of inquiry, overall that work has left me faintly dissatisfied. I lay out some of this dissatisfaction in properly judicious academic terms in the introduction. Here, I want only to say that it has been marked by more analytical and empirical simplification than I would like. There are, of course, important exceptions to a generalization this broad, but the common analytical models have been more uniformitarian than I had hoped and the empirical focus has been restricted, perhaps inevitably, to the natural environment.

While there was a wave of interest in environment in anthropology in the late 1960s, especially following the publication of Roy Rappaport's *Pigs for the Ancestors* (1968), the recent disciplinary interest in sociocultural aspects of the environment rests on a markedly different set of foundations, and so it is reasonable to treat it as relatively new. And simplification is, perhaps inevitably, a characteristic of this sort of novelty. Clarity and simplicity of vision can be both attractive and motivating. Equally, it is perhaps characteristic that, after a while, the simplicity gives way to more complex understandings of the world (see Hyman 1959). This collection might best be taken as part of the generation of those understandings.

This effort to extend those understandings is signaled in the collection's title. "Confronting environments" points to the fact that people confront more than just the natural environment, what we commonly call "nature." Rather, they confront a number of environments. This is so in two senses, which I explore in the introduction but want to mention here. First, the material surroundings that we confront extend beyond what can loosely be called the natural, to include a landscape shaped by humans and even the built environment. Second, and perhaps more important, our relationship with and understandings of those surroundings occur in the context of social environments, which means other people, beliefs, and values, social and political institutions, and the like. If, then, we are to make sense of people and the material surroundings, we have to recognize the importance of these social environments as well. This is hardly a novel observation, but it needs to be stressed, and one goal of this collection is to stress it.

The origin of this collection is a panel that I organized at the conference held at the University of Aberdeen in April of 2001, "Space, culture, power." The organizers, Phil Withington and Peter Kirby, were generous with conference time and meeting rooms, allowing six of us to present our ideas. The seventh contributor was recruited on the advice of Paige West, at Barnard College, in order to fill in some gaps with the work of an interesting scholar, and Josiah Heyman agreed to write a concluding chapter. Richard Wilk suggested that this collection might be part of a series on anthropology and the environment that he was organizing with Josiah Heyman. The result is what you see.

I want to thank Paige West and Richard Wilk for their help and encouragement. I also want to thank Josiah Heyman for writing his concluding chapter in the face of the demands on his time caused by a move to a different university and by his taking up the duties of department head. I also want to thank the contributors, who have tolerated what must, at times, have seemed an inordinate stream of e-mails while they all were busy with the rest of their lives and work. They had the good sense to ignore the wrongheaded suggestions and focus on the worthwhile essentials.

James G. Carrier
January 2004

References

Hyman, S. E. 1959. *The tangled bank: Darwin, Marx, Frazer and Freud as imaginative writers.* New York: Atheneum.

Rappaport, R. 1968. *Pigs for the ancestors.* New Haven, Conn.: Yale University Press.

Introduction

JAMES G. CARRIER

I N THE PAST DECADE AND MORE, there has been a growing public concern for the relationship between people and the environment, witnessed by the increasing salience of environmental issues in public debate. This has been reflected in scholarly work, as indicated by the growth of anthropology of the environment (e.g. Ellen and Fukui 1996; Fairhead and Leach 1996; Milton 1993, 1996; Croll and Parkin 1992; see Kottak 1999; Little 1999 for reviews), of a concern with the environment and environmentalism in geography and cultural studies (e.g. Guha and Martinez-Alier 1997; Macnaghten and Urry 1998), and of political ecology (e.g. Bryant and Bailey 1997; Escobar 1996) (see generally Brosius 1999). Contributors to this collection address issues that fall within the scholarly study of the environment and they address environmentalist topics. However, at the outset I want to raise a question about the idea of the environment as a distinct object of study in the social sciences. That concern springs from the connotations of "environment."

Perhaps inevitably, the term carries with it the idea of the natural. This is certainly the idea associated with "environmental conservation" and "environmentalist," and if the term were to be distinctive, I doubt that it could have any other meaning. The concept "nature" is complex, and Raymond Williams (1976, 219) says that it "is perhaps the most complex word in the English language." However, I think it is fair to say that, in the context of conceptions of the environment, natural states and processes are understood as those that would exist without conscious human intervention, and arguably without any human intervention at all. Such an idea may have utility as a hypothetical standard or an ideal state, rather like a perfect vacuum or a point mass in physics. However, considered in practical terms, I doubt that many of us have noticeable contact with the natural world in this sense. Rather, what we confront is a set of surroundings that reflect, and hence embody, human action, whether material or symbolic.

My point that the idea of a pristine "nature" is a peculiar construct is hardly novel (e.g., Cronon 1995; Escobar 1999; Ingold 1993). It does, however, indicate that it may be worthwhile situating this collection in a broader frame than the study of the environment. Some of the people described in this collection may confront something that they would call a "natural environment." However, the fact that they might call it that does not oblige us to accept their nomenclature, does not mean that we should adopt it for our own use, rather than treat that nomenclature as something to be understood (in addition to those considered in this introduction, influential attempts at such understanding include Beck 1992; Douglas and Wildavsky 1982). In part because of the problematic connotations of "environment," I prefer to take as a frame for this collection something that is less redolent with meaning, the study of people's relationships with their surroundings (see Milton 1996).

What is in the category of people's surroundings? To begin with, what some people call the natural environment is included. In addition, landscape is included, for the study of landscape in the social sciences revolves around the ways that people understand and portray their material surroundings, as shaped by human activity but not as wholly constituted by it (e.g., Abramson and Theodossopoulos 2000; Bender 1995b; Hirsch and O'Hanlon 1995). It is worth extending the term "surroundings" to include more than this, however, for the frankly built environment is important as well. People may distinguish conceptually the world that they have built from the natural environment and from landscape. However, it shares with them an externality and facticity. For each of us, the built environment is not much less of a given than is the natural world. It is true that people have created the built environment, but once it is created, we are constrained by it and seek to make sense of it (e.g., Bender 1995a; Edholm 1995) in ways that do not seem to distinguish it very much from the natural environment and landscape.

It should be apparent that my concern with the idea of "environment" is not just a quibble. It is true that people may divide their surroundings into distinct categories like "nature" and "the city," and it is true that those divisions may themselves be significant for people's thoughts and actions. However, if we become beguiled by these divisions, we run the risk of ignoring two important points. One point is that, by people's own definitions, the existence of secure dividing lines between nature, the landscape, and the built environment may be untenable. Consider common Western uses of these terms. The "nature" that one sees as one passes through the Appalachian Mountains in the United States or the Black Mountains in Wales is something that has experienced human activity for millennia and shows the signs of that activity. The landscape that one sees or that is portrayed in a Turner painting contains objects and structures that people have built. The built environment contains elements of landscape and even things that people call "nature." And to come full circle, Tilley and Bennett (2001) suggest that some people see what we would call naturally occurring objects as being human artifacts. On inspection, then, nature, landscape, and the built environment blend into one another, so that the existence of those categories and dividing lines should be seen as a question to be addressed and explained, rather than a framework to be adopted.

There is a second point that we run the risk of ignoring. Common usage may see the substance of nature, landscape, and the built environment as being different. However, the ways that people deal with them are not very different, as is demonstrated in Read's (1996) description of people's relationship with different aspects of their surroundings (see also Gupta and Ferguson 1997). We stand in similar dialectical relationships with each. We act with regard to and even upon each of them, so that we shape each of them, turn them all into human artifacts, albeit in different degrees. We are constrained by each of them, materially and culturally, and so are shaped by each of them, albeit in different degrees. We bestow meaning upon each of them, and as part of our cultural baggage we receive meaning from each of them, albeit in different degrees: they all are what Kenneth Burke calls "second nature," characterized by the fact that cultural meanings and the social relations associated with them are "first *ascribed* to nature, then 'derived' from it" (Burke [1935] 1965, 278n). Certainly the degrees differ, but they are all implicated in the same human social and cultural processes.

In the preceding paragraphs I have sought to justify my combining these three categories into the encompassing concept of "surroundings" in a general analytical way. The contributors to this collection justify that combining in more concrete and ethnographic terms. Some contributors write of an aspect of people's surroundings that would fall under the rubric of "natural environment"; some write of what would be "landscape"; and some write of "built environment." But the social and cultural processes and issues that concern them are similar. I turn to some of those processes and issues now.

Dealing with the Surroundings

People and organizations act with regard to their surroundings, for different reasons and in different ways. Some act to conserve aspects of those surroundings, some act to exploit them; some are concerned with nature, some with landscape, some with the built environment. But none act naively. Rather, the situations in which they have found themselves in the past lead them to understand their surroundings in the present in particular ways. Of course, while this process can be pointed to in a simple way, it is not itself simple, and an example will help indicate the sorts of complexities that can be involved.

Veronica Strang (1996, 1997) has described cattle stations in Far North Queensland. Among the people she studied are the young men who work as stockmen, particularly during the seasonal mustering of stock. These young men understand or think about the stock and the station in particular ways, ways that can be considered their understandings of their surroundings. What are the elements that can be expected to shape and help account for those understandings? In any given case there will be a host of idiosyncratic elements. However, Strang indicates that there are also some elements that are likely to be relatively common.

Among these is the fact that for many of these young men, their work is temporary, and understood as part of their transition to adulthood, from being youths to men. So, one of the elements that shapes their understandings of their surroundings is their understanding of masculinity and maturity, and of themselves as more or less mature males. It is also the case that these young men often come from relatively urban areas. So, another element that shapes their understanding of their surroundings is their understanding of the differences between rural and urban Australia, between the more natural and the more artifactual, which itself intersects with notions of masculinity and maturity. A further element springs from the fact that these young men are Australians working in Far North Queensland. Culturally this territory is seen to be much more clearly Aboriginal than are the more urban parts of the country from which these young men generally come. So, their understandings of their surroundings and their work on these stations are shaped as well by their understandings of Aboriginal and white Australia, as these are reflected in the spatial distribution of Aboriginals and whites in that country. And, of course, these in their turn are shaped by Australian history: the imperial and colonial social, political, and economic impulses and practices that shaped that history in its early stages; and the national social, political, and economic impulses and practices that shaped its later stages, and that have even started to reverse some of the results of these earlier impulses (see Strang 2000).

What I have said of Strang's discussion of stockmen on cattle stations in no way does justice to the quality of her work, because my purpose is not to present in any detailed way the case that she has studied. Rather, I have invoked aspects of her work only to illustrate my simple, general point: people do not think about or act toward their surroundings naively; rather, their sociocultural backgrounds will shape those thoughts and actions.

While I have invoked Strang's work to illustrate my general point, I have done so only in static, systemic terms. I have, if you will, put our young stockman on a cattle station but have kept him in suspended animation, idly contemplating what he sees around him in terms of the cultural values that are likely to be part of his background. But this suspended animation is unreal; our stockman acts, and does so in the context of and with regard to his surroundings. He rides a horse, patrols fences, musters cattle, and all the rest. In doing these things, he does not simply contemplate his surroundings. Rather, he engages with them in terms of his own projects, interests, and relationships, and these engagements are important.

These engagements can take many forms, material and mental. But whatever their form, they link our young stockman to the particular cattle station where he is, to the specific parts of that station where significant events occur, and to the particular people with whom he works. When this happens, as Strang notes, our stockman comes to look, just a little bit, like the other set of people she describes, the indigenous Aborigines who live in the area. That is, particular places become infused with particular experiences and memories, and so come to take on particular meanings. With this transition, the significance of the surroundings takes on an important complexity. My earlier description of the background factors affecting our stockman's understandings of his cattle-station surroundings was generic. That is, in principle it applied to all cattle stations, to all stock work, and so has a distinct air of the universal. However, with the beginnings of engagement with the surroundings, these generic understandings are complemented by specific understandings. The universal is complemented by, and perhaps displaced by, the particular: not cattle stations, but *this* cattle station; not stock work, but *my* stock work.[1]

Abstract Nature

This mixture of the universal and the particular is apparent generally in people's relationship with all aspects of their surroundings. However, the cultural construction of "nature" common in Western thought makes this complexity especially apparent in people's relationships with what they take to be their natural environment. And appropriately, the focus of many of the chapters in this collection is the natural environment, as something to be exploited, protected, or conserved.

The environmentalist movement has generated a mass of arguments to make conservation appear important. Perhaps reflecting the fact that "the natural environment" and "nature" are abstract concepts, overwhelmingly these arguments are abstract and general. That is, they reflect and embody a logic and set of assumptions that tend to transcend particular places and times. Thus, even though they may be invoked in particular situations to further particular ends, notions like biodiversity and biomass, pollution and environmental health, all speak of factors and processes that are taken to apply to every place (on biodiversity, see Escobar

1998). In this abstraction they resemble what Ingold (1993) says is the characteristically modern understanding of the natural environment as globelike. This denotes a perspective that sees the natural environment as a separate thing that stands distinct from and opposed to people and their lives, "a world divorced from life, that is yet complete in itself" (Ingold 1993, 35; for the sort of resonances this view of nature can have, see Berglund 1998, 101–10). Arturo Escobar makes a similar point when he describes what he sees as the capitalist view of the natural environment. For him, the core of the capitalist view is an objectification of "nature" linked to the spread of patriarchal capitalism and the commodity form. This produces a distanced view of the natural environment, a realm to be apprehended through the frame of capitalist rationality and control (Escobar 1999, 6).

Ingold and Escobar point to the sort of view of people's natural surroundings that Macnaghten and Urry (1998, 1) call "environmental realism," a conception that sees the environment as "essentially a 'real entity' . . . substantially separate from social practices and human experience." They point also to the way that the natural environment is understood in abstract terms, as something that follows its own general laws and exhibits its own regularities. In this, "nature" is construed as a realm that has existence and even meaning in the absence of human engagement and the particularities that shape and that flow from it. Put differently, it is a realm that is construed in terms that are distinct from those that inhere in the people engaged with it.[2] In its abstraction, this construction resembles the construction that a typical young stockman would put on his surroundings when first and idly contemplating them. Each is an abstract construction, because each is concerned with general principles and properties. Each is different from the particular construction that comes from a person's experiences in a place, the particularity that complements "cattle stations" with "*this* cattle station," "the environment" with "my farm" and "my neighborhood."

This abstraction, this encompassing of the engaged construction by one of a higher and more general order, is not, of course, an all-or-none matter. An encompassing concept like "rain forest" does not stand opposed only to "where I live." To a degree it also stands opposed to "Peruvian rain forests," as well as to other intermediate levels. And of course "rain forest" itself is encompassed by other concepts, like "forest" and "nature." These different levels invoke or entail different sets of people and different levels of experience, and hence different degrees of distance from engaged people's perspectives. While these differences indicate that abstraction and generality are matters of degree, it is important to keep in mind that any talk of "rain forests" is different from "where I live." To speak of rain forests, even if in fairly localized ways, is to identify a place in terms of its general properties as a rain forest, itself an abstract concept, just as "cattle station" is relatively abstract, identifying a place in terms of its general properties. On the other hand, "where I live," whether I live in a rain forest or on a cattle station, speaks of a place in terms of particular people's experiences with it, speaks in terms of the particularities of those people's biographies and social relations, memories and values, circumstances and desires.

People's biographies and all that goes with them are particular. However, they are not wholly idiosyncratic, because people do not live their lives alone any more than they rely only on their own invention. Their dealings with and understandings of their surroundings reflect the fact that people live social lives, so that those dealings and understandings are shaped by their social setting, and to a degree are common and collective. Our young stockman, after all, carried with him a set of beliefs and assumptions that Strang indicates is relatively common among white Australians, and he is engaged in a set of relationships and practices that appear to be relatively common among Australian cattle stations. While social life and practices and beliefs may in fact be fairly common in a place like Australia, the perspectives on the surroundings that spring from that social life appear idiosyncratic. At least, conventionally we have had fairly few effective ways of talking about those perspectives in generalist or abstract terms.

The ability to talk in such terms is important, and its lack is a disadvantage. Many of those who seek to conserve the surroundings, like many of those who seek to exploit them, speak in abstract terms. The tract that talks about saving the environment, holding it in trust for our children's children's children, construes the environment in abstract terms when it invokes a perspective and frame of meaning that transcend the biographies, lives, and desires of this or that set of people. Likewise, the resort developer's tract or the government policy directive construes the pertinent parts of the world in abstract terms when it talks about global market forces, how growing free trade creates the need for new sources of foreign exchange (Carrier 1997; Greenberg forthcoming). Those who urge exploitation and those who urge conservation may have opposed goals, but they resemble each other when they use abstract frames, and despite their many differences they jointly stand opposed to those who lack such frames. From the perspective of the conservationist and the developer, to be opposed to or unable to invoke such frames is to be merely parochial (Carrier 2001b). In terms of conservation and protection of the environment, of landscape and of the built environment, those who are unable to express their objections to intrusions in their surroundings in abstract, general terms are NIMBYs. Their objection to a waste site, a bypass, or a new office building is reduced to "Not in my back yard." They are easily portrayed as self-centered hypocrites (see Luloff, Albrecht, and Bourne 1998).

The ability to use such frames and to oblige others to use them is the exercise of what Steven Lukes (1974; see also Jameson 1991, 263–64) says is one of the most potent forms of social power. That power is the ability to impose the terms of debate, in this case terms that speak of universal properties and processes, whether they are said to exist in an abstract nature or a global free market. And this is a power, because those terms define what is serious and what is not, what is a problem and what is not, what might be a solution and what is not, what is sensible and what is not. And just as the terms of debate define *what* is serious and what is not, so the ability to invoke and manipulate those terms defines *who* is serious and who is not, who needs to be listened to and accommodated and who does not.

As I said, when speaking of the surroundings the most powerful terms of debate are abstract, even universal. These universal terms subsume us all. And in doing so, they define us in universal terms, deny our individual and even our group particularities, make us all alike and so subordinate us to their compelling imperatives (cf. Scott 1998). And as I also said, the use of these terms is not one-sided. The universal imperatives of globalization can be opposed by the universal imperative to save the planet for our children's children's children; the logic of preserving a natural environment that is valued in itself (e.g., Durman 2000) can be opposed by the inexorable logic of market-based demand. To repeat, the invocation of one imperative against the other does not challenge the underlying universality of the terms of debate, a universality that denies significance to our individual and local experiences, similarities and differences.

While conventionally we have few effective forms to counter these abstract, universal forms of talk, late in the twentieth century one such form of talk began to gain legitimacy. That is the talk of tribalism, an intentionally provocative term I invoke to refer to ethnic and racial identity of a certain sort, coupled with the claim that those with that identity have a distinct and autochthonous way of seeing the world. In New Zealand, Maoris have increasingly been able to invoke their frame of meanings as Maoris to define their surroundings in ways that mark them as a legitimate exception to universalism (see e.g., Dominy 2000, ch. 7); in Australia, Aboriginals have increasingly been able to do the same (e.g., Weiner 1999); likewise in Canada and the United States (Clifford 1988, ch. 12). And it is pertinent that tribal groups not only have a distinct and autochthonous identity, but also have a distinct relationship with their surroundings, one that is construed as radically different from the Modernist view of the world (some of the complexities of this relationship are considered in Kirsch 2001).

In practice, the apparent success of tribalism in defending some of the groups involved against unwanted intrusion has led to efforts by others to loosen the criteria for what might count as an appropriate group (for a strong and early statement of this view, see Maffesoli 1996). So, groups that appear patently distinctive from their opponents in physical and cultural terms—like Maoris, Australian

Aborigines, and Amazonian Indians—come to be joined, however tentatively, by groups that are less distinct. The people of Trinidad who claim to be Carib Indians, for instance (see Forte 2000), are not noticeably different from the surrounding population. Increasingly, the pertinent mark of distinction is a claim of indigenous status, which often reduces to a claim to some degree of descent from those who have been in a place a long time. This is coupled usually with a claim of a special relationship with the surroundings. This claim may be based simply on custom and usage of the sort embodied in stories and myths (e.g., Basso 1996), though often it is based on a history of practical engagement, such as farming. An extreme case of this is the sheep farmers of the highlands of the South Island of New Zealand that Michele Dominy (2000) describes or the cattle ranchers in Queensland that Veronica Strang (1997) describes. These people are descended from European migrants, but the longevity of their and their forebears' residence and the practical nature of their engagement with their surroundings gives them a distinct air of being indigenous, quasi-tribal. These examples drive home Phil Burnham's (2000) point, that being indigenous is a relative term, that sets of people who are defined ancestrally as incomers in one context can be defined as indigenous in another.

This concept of tribalism is problematic for other reasons as well, and I want to mention two, both of which spring from its mixture of essentialism and abstraction. Firstly, it elides differences within a group that can claim to be tribal or indigenous. To speak of a tribal or indigenous frame is to be more particular than to speak of universal frames. However, such a way of speaking ignores what may be consequential differences among, for instance, Melanesians or Aboriginals (e.g., Gewertz and Errington 1995; Weiner 1999; see also the exclusions contained in the idea of Puerto Rican identity, in Duany 2000). That is, such a way of speaking still invokes a general frame, in terms of a Maori or Melanesian view of land. In this generality it resembles more what our stockman sees when first idly contemplating a cattle station than it does what he sees after he has lived there, a living that complements "cattle station" with "where I live." And in so doing, it makes it difficult to see how his background and experiences may produce a perspective that differs in important ways from the supposed general tribal view.

The second way in which it is problematic is more subtle. The idea that a set of people are entitled to a tribal view of their surroundings is likely to involve what Scott (1998) calls legibility, rendering their local and context-dependent concerns and understandings in terms that are comprehensible to important others, and especially those who can decide whether that particular group is entitled to tribal or indigenous status. Drawing on Scott, Errington and Gewertz (2001) argue that this leads to "generification," their term for turning those understandings and concerns and the people who hold them into generic cultural types. In effect, they are saying that the term "tribal" itself entails abstraction, rendering this or that set of people in terms of a universalistic frame. They show, for instance, the ways that dealing with government and other bodies lead the people they studied in Papua New Guinea to reduce the specificities of their understandings and values to something that conforms to the general category of "traditional culture." This reduction strips those understandings and values of their local context and efficacy, making of them just another example of a type, to be understood in typical terms, subsumed under what Richard Wilk (1995) calls structures of common difference, structures that define what is allowed to be different (here, tribal or indigenous), and how.

Thus, whether or not the tribal category expands, whether or not the legitimacy of the tribal view becomes more widely accepted, that view still resembles the more purely universalistic ways of talking that I have mentioned. It does so because it entails invoking a view that is characteristic of the tribe in question, a view which is likely to be relatively uniform compared to the particularities of individual views of members of the tribe. It does so also because it is likely to entail invoking that tribal view in terms that make it recognizable to important others as a tribal view, the abstracting process of generification. Because of these corollaries, those who seek to invoke a tribal view confront the same general problem as others who seek to invoke more abstract forms of talk, what I call the problem of translation. I turn to that problem now.

The Problem of Translation

To understand the problem of translation, it is necessary to go back to the difference between people's particularistic relations with and understandings of their surroundings on the one hand, and on the other hand the abstract and generalist frames of meaning that are accorded legitimacy and authority in public talk.[3]

The particularistic is based on people's actual experiences with their surroundings. These experiences are likely to be shaped by complex and subtle aspects of a person's biography in the context of the larger social and cultural setting. Our stockman, for instance, is motivated to become a stockman in the first place for reasons having to do with his understanding of what it means to be a man and of a mental geography of Australia, itself marked by the rural and the urban and by the Aboriginal and the white, and of his sense of himself in terms of these understandings. Also, he is likely to be motivated by his relations with family and friends, and by a range of other and more idiosyncratic aspects of his personal life. And, of course, he may simply need some money and think that this would be an interesting way to get it. Once our young man becomes a stockman, his understandings of his surroundings will be shaped by all of these factors in his background, as well as by the experiences he has in his work, experiences that will center on aspects of his surroundings and on the people with whom he works. Whatever the result of these factors and experiences, the understandings of his surroundings that develop are going to be personal and affective, and even if they may resemble the understandings of a set of similar young Australian men, in his mind they will be bound up with his personal life.

I have recapitulated some of what I have said already in this introduction to drive home a single point: though others may understand their surroundings in like ways, this young man's understandings are rooted in his own life and experiences. It is from that life and those experiences that he comprehends his surroundings and is moved to act with regard to them.

One thing that his personal experiences may motivate our young man to do is protect those surroundings, and it is at the point where he seeks to engage others in that protection that he confronts the problem of translation. Whatever experiences may have led him to think about his surroundings in the ways that he does, whatever experiences may have led him to want to protect his surroundings, in seeking to engage others he will need to persuade them to protect his surroundings, or at least need to explain or justify his desires. To do any of these things, he will be obliged to socialize his desires, turn them into a form that is effective in terms of the social setting in which he finds himself.

The problem of translation, then, is the problem of socializing the motives that spring from his personal experiences, turning them into an acceptable, which is to say persuasive, public language (this is addressed in a different context in Carrier 2001a). Bluntly, our young man is unlikely to persuade others to work to block the upgrading of a dirt track into a proper road by saying that he fell out with his girlfriend in Sydney when he was nineteen, and that as a result of this he decided to take a job as a stockman for a while to try to figure out his life, and that is why it should stay as a dirt track. People might empathize with his tale, but they are likely to see it as too personal and too happenstance to justify their trying to block the upgrading of this dirt track, rather than any other in North Queensland (on the problem of translation to the terms of environmentalist groups, see Berglund 1998, 59–60). In socializing his desires, of course, our young man comes to take a new perspective on his surroundings, comes to see them in more universal terms. His understanding of his surroundings is thus affected by the process.

The problem our young stockman confronts demonstrates that "abstraction" is not just a thing, as in "an abstraction." It is also a process (the points here are discussed at length in Carrier 2001b). One aspect of this process is removing an object from the context in which it had existed previously. For our hypothetical stockman, the object is the dirt track and the context is his experience as a stockman. This decontextualization is matched by a recontextualization, placing the object in a different context, in this case a model of the natural environment in Queensland and the processes that shape it. Neither of these contexts is independent of human practice and experience, so in this sense Ingold's Modernist globe orientation and Escobar's capitalist nature are no more independent of practical engagement than are the alternatives. However, they reflect different forms of engagement and experience: stock work, the Sydney girlfriend, and all the rest for our stockman; perhaps scientific research, political activities, experience with government agencies for someone with a more general environmentalist orientation. To hark back to a point I made earlier, this indicates that the process of abstraction is political, for it involves the imposition of one set of people's contexts in preference to those of another set of people.

I have illustrated the problem of translation by having our young man seek to persuade other individual people to help him achieve his goal. However, individuals of this sort are not the only others who present him with that problem. If he is successful in the early stages of pursuing his goal, he will come to confront government and other agencies and bodies, as he seeks regulation, legislation, funding, official support. And these agencies and bodies reflect the bureaucratic rationality that pervades officialdom, a rationality that, reasonably enough, constrains them to act with regard to general principle rather than individual circumstance and desire. More insistently than the individuals that our young men sought to persuade, these agencies and bodies will demand that he socialize his desires, translate them into plans and proposals that are justified by abstract and general logic and arguments.

This introduction of official agencies and bodies and their bureaucratic rationality indicates the insistence of the problem of translation. If our young man would be unwise to try to persuade individuals with the tale of his girlfriend's departure when he was nineteen and living in Sydney, he would be positively foolish to tell that tale in a funding application. One consequence is that the problem of translation requires not only translating personal experience and motivation into persuasive public terms; it also requires our young man to elide those personal experiences when he explains or advocates his goals. He must silence the personal to speak to the public.

This invocation of official agencies and bodies also indicates that what I have said about frames of meaning and ways of talking is not just words about talk. Rather, it drives home Lukes's point that we are in the realm of power. The ability to use the appropriate forms of talk, the ability to translate the personal into abstract and general terms, is important, whether we are looking at our young man trying to persuade the Queensland government to leave it as a dirt track or at a New Zealander trying to persuade a government body that hers is a Maori relationship with an aspect of her surroundings. Those forms of talk are important because they are intended to persuade others, ultimately states and organizations. They are intended to move levers of power.

There is more to moving the levers of power than being able to invoke abstract or tribal forms of talk. As Theodossopoulos (2000) has shown, the more mundane skills of handling official forms can be important, as can a host of other factors, ranging from having the time available to work on moving those levers and having the financial resources necessary to secure specialists, to having the social and political resources necessary to make those levers more responsive. So, I am not saying that these levers can always be moved by the right form of talk. Perhaps it would be better to say that the right form of talk is crucial in a negative sense. If our young man concerned with the dirt track is unable to socialize his desires, he will not even get a hearing. He will be one of those people who are not taken seriously.

In formal terms, then, the ability to invoke the right form of talk is a necessary condition for his success, but not a sufficient one. And I want to stress that the right form of talk is not sufficient, in order to forestall the assumption that meaning is all. It may be reasonable to see abstract or tribal talk as an "ensemble of texts" (Geertz 1973, 5, 452) or the webs of meaning on which we stand. However, we need to remember that some are better able than others to spin those webs, just as some are more likely than others to become ensnared in them; we also need to remember that those forms of talk need to be supplemented by, just as they confront, political, social, and economic resources.

In the preceding paragraphs I have taken a constructivist view of people's surroundings. That is, I have attended to the ways that people think about their surroundings, and have tended to ignore those surroundings themselves, treating them as a neutral backdrop. A constructivist approach is common in scholarly writing on the surroundings. However, it is not, of course, the way things are, and it is important to recognize this. It is perhaps easiest to make this point in terms of the natural environment, which is appropriate given the focus of many of the chapters in this collection. To take a constructivist view of the natural environment, the sort of approach illustrated in Ingold's and Escobar's work, may be useful for showing how different sets of people think about what is often called "nature." However, in focusing on constructions, this approach can make it harder to see that there is a natural environment, however much the boundaries and meanings of it are constructed. Put more bluntly, perceptions of the changing frequency of snappers, for example, in a given body of water may be a cultural matter, and the significance of that change certainly is. However, it is also the case that snappers are organisms with an anatomy and physiology independent of our thought processes. Regardless of how we construe "nature" or "the environment," snappers are out there, being snappers. And being snappers, they can be affected by people's activities. I do not introduce this point only to dispel the thought that how people perceive their surroundings is all that is important. I introduce it as well to make the point that the sort of localism that I have been describing is not necessarily more desirable than the abstractions to which I have opposed it, whether those be abstract environmentalist constructions of nature or the bureaucratic abstractions of the state or the commodity abstractions of the market.

Attention to local, concrete orientations to the natural environment is important for making us sensitive to how people see the world around them, which can help us to make sense of why they do what they do. It is, at heart, important if we are to take people seriously. In making this point, however, I do not mean that local orientations are the only ones that matter. Localities are, after all, situated in a larger context, one that has properties of its own, regardless of whether these properties are seen as "natural" or as being shaped by human action, and regardless of whether that larger context is seen in terms of balance or of discontinuity and instability (see Scoones 1999). Our attention to local contexts, then, needs to be complemented by an awareness of their relationship with larger contexts, and hence indirectly with other local contexts.

In pointing to the existence of linkages between local and broader contexts, I mean to challenge the notion that the two are not just distinct, but even opposed. This notion is implicit in the criticism of NIMBYism, a criticism that makes the claim that local orientations and interests are illegitimate because they run counter to broader orientations and interests. Doubtless this conflict between local and broader contexts exists often enough. At the same time, however, conflict is not inevitable. A local orientation can easily lead to the desire to prevent or halt actions that are harmful generally as well as locally.

The fact that NIMBY is commonly a term of abuse, then, indicates only that labeling an interest as local is a common rhetorical device. And the fact that it is a common device points to the importance of political and economic conflict over the shape and future of our surroundings. It also points to the fact that powerful actors in that conflict, and those who would be powerful, seek to claim high ground by associating themselves with the orientation that is culturally and institutionally valued, the more abstract orientation.

About the Chapters

The contributors to this collection concern themselves with a range of places and aspects of people's surroundings. And in describing these places and aspects, they illustrate and exemplify the points that I have made in the preceding paragraphs, adding flesh to what is necessarily a somewhat schematic presentation. The opening pair of chapters presents cases that show what can be involved when we talk about people's understandings of and relationships with their environs. They do so by describing places where those understandings and relationships are challenged, places that point to the importance of power when people confront their surroundings.

The first of these chapters is Donald Macleod's "Selling Space: Power and Resource Allocation in a Caribbean Coastal Community." Macleod describes an area on the south coast of the Dominican Republic, centered on the village of Bayahibe. Originally an area primarily of small-scale fishers and agriculturalists, in the 1970s it began to be opened to tourism, and by 2000 there were more than half a dozen hotels in the area open or under construction. In his presentation of the changing situation of the villagers, Macleod shows how the appearance of tourism marked the appearance in villagers' lives of new sets of meanings of and expectations concerning their surroundings.

Those meanings and expectations reflected the orientations of the tourists who came to those resort hotels, orientations shaped by understandings of ludic leisure. These were, after all, people who were on vacation, expecting release from the responsibilities and norms of their regular lives. They sought, then, to be entertained in a relatively unconstrained setting of sun, sand, and sea. These tourists' expectations were impressed on the surroundings of Bayahibe by the powerful outside commercial interests that sought to cater to and profit from them, with the result that the people of Bayahibe found that they and their surroundings had a new set of meanings and uses imposed upon them. What had been fishing waters became a tourist attraction; what had been a beach for relaxation or work became forbidden territory; what had been agricultural land became a national park; what had been their village became a tourist spectacle. In presenting these consequences of the imposition of tourism on Bayahibe, Macleod provides a useful illustration of the ways that people's surroundings are both construed and shaped by the imposition of powerful orientations and expectations.

Although Macleod describes far-reaching changes in the surroundings brought about by the arrival of tourism, he shows that this process, by which powerful interests sought to define their surroundings, was not a novel one. Rather, throughout its history, the meaning of Bayahibe had been a matter of contention. An important local family claimed to have founded the village around 1800 and to hold title to village land, and it pursued that claim in the face of opposition from others, both state agencies that claimed the land for themselves based on earlier transactions and villagers who claimed that their continued occupation of parcels of land gave them effective title. The histories of land disputes within Bayahibe are important, for they warn us against the tendency to see the tourist invasion as encroaching on a unified local people. Certainly, compared to the companies that run the tourist hotels, the people of Bayahibe look like an undifferentiated local group; indeed, compared to multinational corporations in the tourist industry, the Dominican Republic may look like an undifferentiated tropical country. Even so, with the historical background that Macleod provides, we can see that there are long-running social and political cleavages in the village and in the country. In this, Macleod's case illustrates a point that I made earlier: although the people of Bayahibe look distinctly indigenous, perhaps even tribal, their cleavages and conflicts show the dangers that inhere in treating as uniformly indigenous or tribal what is in fact a diversity of interests and orientations.

The second chapter in this opening pair looks at another set of coastal people who confront novel interpretations of their surroundings. That is Dimitrios Theodossopoulos's "'Working in Nature,' 'Caring for Nature': Diverse Views of the Environment in the Context of an Environmental Dispute." The site Theodossopoulos describes is far from Bayahibe: a village on Zakynthos, an island in the southwest of Greece. Villagers conventionally have been farmers, relying on both agriculture and animal husbandry. Recently, however, the island has begun to attract tourists, and villagers now commonly supplement their agricultural income with small-scale tourist enterprises, some of them centered on a beach not far from the village. However, that beach is a place where sea turtles lay their eggs, and this has attracted the interest of conservationists, largely middle class, from Athens, from the capital of Zakynthos, and from foreign countries. These conservationists have sought to protect turtles by restricting activities on and close to the village's beach, which means restricting villagers' tourist business activities. This confrontation between villagers and conservationists illustrates some of the important themes of this collection.

To begin with, like residents of Bayahibe, villagers confront powerful outside institutions that define their surroundings in particular ways. As Theodossopoulos describes them, these conservationists espouse an idea of the environment that is Modern, holding that the natural world is distinct from human action and, moreover, needs to be protected from that action. Thus, these activists see value in the marine environment and local woodlands, but ignore the cultivated areas of the village as not worthy of attention because not pristine. This, however, puts them at odds with the majority of villagers, for whom the surroundings are very different. For them, the natural world needs human intervention: human life entails a continual struggle with the natural surroundings, in which people work to protect and manage those surroundings, and hence care for them. Consequently, the very parts of the world that conservationists see and value when they look around them, villagers generally ignore as insignificant; the very actions that conservationists condemn as intervention in nature, villagers see as fundamental.

This chapter illustrates two other points that are important in this collection. First, these competing views of the natural surroundings are discourses of power.

Like Macleod's Bayahibe villagers, Theodossopoulos's villagers confront a set of people and institutions able to impose the terms of debate, and it seems likely that those villagers will be able to protect themselves only if they can overcome the problem of translation, can present themselves and their interests in terms that are recognized as legitimate in public discourse. The second theme this chapter illustrates is that it is risky to assume that particular sets of people have relatively uniform views of the natural surroundings. While most villagers hold the nonmodern view of the surroundings that I have described, not all do so. Rather, the economic power of tourist interest has led some to see virtue in a degree of environmental protection. In addition, the conservationists are not uniform in their views. While many may value a pristine nature, many of them also seek an intimate personal engagement with it, and this is, paradoxically, the sort of engagement that villagers routinely have.

The two opening chapters describe cases that illustrate what people's views of and relationships with their surroundings can mean. They do so by describing sets of people who confront intrusive outside agencies with different views and relationships. The next three chapters attend more closely to the ways that people negotiate their way between different views, a negotiation that points to the problem of translation. The first of these is Kenneth MacDonald's "Developing 'Nature': Global Ecology and the Politics of Conservation in Northern Pakistan." While Hushe, the village he describes, is very different from Bayahibe and Zakynthos, many of the processes at work in the three places are similar. Hushe is in Baltistan, a mountainous region that is home to many sorts of animals, particularly the ibex; it is because of the ibex that international environmentalist organizations, especially IUCN–The World Conservation Union, are interested in Hushe. These organizations are concerned that local hunting is threatening the survival of the ibex, and together with Pakistan's government have sought to persuade local people to stop their hunting. While this looks like straightforward environmental conservation, MacDonald shows that the situation is more complex, and even bizarre, than it might seem at first glance.

To begin with, MacDonald says that these environmental organizations have never accumulated the sort of data that would tell them if ibex numbers are in fact declining, and they have never conducted the sort of research that would tell how local hunters operate and how that hunting is related to other practices and beliefs. Rather, MacDonald says that these organizations simply assume that local people are ignorant and irresponsible and need to be controlled. In this they are heirs to older national and British colonial policies, which took the same view of local people and sought to constrain them by force, to preserve game for British and other foreign hunters. The conservation organizations MacDonald describes concluded that force, in the form of state policing, would not work. So, instead of seeking to coerce compliance, they sought to induce it. They persuaded local villagers to forgo hunting, in return for a portion of the proceeds of fees paid by outside tourists to enjoy local fauna, especially the ibex. Bizarrely, the enjoyment consists of a license to hunt ibex, which are highly valued by hunters in Europe and North America. In short, British colonial goals were resurrected by these international conservation organizations.

For people in Hushe, then, their surroundings underwent the same sort of transformation that occurred in Bayahibe and, to a lesser degree, in Zakynthos. What had been an environment exploited for subsistence and petty exchange became a tourist destination. What had been an animal sought for flesh to be consumed locally became a trophy for alien hunters. What had been an activity that brought food and honor to the hunter and that sustained the relations that bound him to others became an act of theft. However, and again like Bayahibe and Zakynthos, we should not assume that these interventions disrupted some uniform and timeless way of life. At the simplest level, villagers were not all equally persuaded of the new regime. Those with links to the tourist economy, hitherto largely hikers, were the leading proponents of the new regime and the concomitant stress on the virtue of conservation and biodiversity; others were less convinced. Equally, MacDonald shows that local relations with and understandings of the surroundings had been in flux for well over a thousand years, as varieties of Islam were laid over preexisting animism, and colonial and state systems were added to the mix. Hushe villagers, like others in Baltistan, may have confronted new practices and beliefs imposed from the outside, but this was only the latest in a history of imposition and accommodation.

In pointing to the history of accommodation to outside influences and the ways that this has led to repeated changes in people's understandings of their surroundings, MacDonald points to the ways that people shift from one rendering of their surroundings to another, which is the basis of translation. The next two chapters are concerned explicitly with the nature of translation, though the mechanisms of and motivations for translation that are involved are as different from Hushe as are the sites and people described. The first of these two chapters is Peter Kirby's "Getting Engaged: Pollution, Toxic Illness, and Discursive Shift in a Tokyo Community." It describes how, starting in 1996, people in the Izawa area of western Tokyo found themselves confronted with a change in their surroundings that threatened them, how people organized themselves, and how they agitated to challenge that threat.

Behind this archetypal narrative of community action is the process in which people's personal experiences were rendered in abstract terms like "environmental threat." From the perspective of Izawa's people, the story began when some of them felt ill, with digestive, respiratory, and skin complaints. Initially these were experienced as individual afflictions; after all, we all get sick from time to time. Further, a relatively small proportion of Izawa residents, as it turned out, had these complaints. Initially, then, people experienced individual malaise, which had meaning for them in terms of their individual lives, hopes, and relationships. Gradually, however, people in the area came to define their individual suffering in more abstract and naturalistic terms, as a material consequence of environmental pollution caused by a new waste-handling installation in the area. Their ability to define their situation in these impersonal terms did not guarantee that the waste facility would be dealt with. However, if they were to attract official notice, Izawa people had to strip their concern of its initial contextualization in their lives, and present it in terms of the abstraction of environmental science. Hopes for establishing one's own local business, or concerns about one's children, were replaced by statements about wind patterns and the toxicity of dioxin. Further, for some protestors the translation of their personal experiences into more broad-ranging terms was matched by their growing involvement in more broad-ranging environmentalist organizations and rhetorics. In other words, the shift from personal to general understandings of their experiences was matched and reinforced by a shift from personal to general institutions.

Kirby's chapter also bears on something that the preceding chapters addressed: the ways that people's surroundings are endowed with meaning, and the ways that those meanings can change. Kirby notes that the common Japanese understanding of nature differs from that found in environmentalist discourse; indeed, to a degree it resembles the Zakynthos farmers' view of the natural environs as requiring attention and managing. That Japanese understanding is of a tamed and domesticated nature, manifest in the well-tended nature of a park and perhaps exemplified in the bonsai tree. This positive valuation of a managed nature makes sense in terms of the tendency of urban Japanese to see "the inside" as a domain that is clean and "the outside" as a domain of dirt and illness. As Kirby notes, these constructions are marked by the washing of hands, the changing of shoes, and other practices undertaken when one moves from outside to inside. In their agitation against the waste facility in their area, however, some Izawa residents appear to have begun to modify their construction of their natural surroundings. The threat that they perceived came from the outside, to be sure. However, it did not come from "nature," but from human activity. Apparently as a consequence, some people began to adopt a view of the natural surroundings that is closer to the environmentalist construction of nature as something that is positively valued, at least compared to what they saw as the "unnatural" effects of the human activity that was the waste facility. For some, then, nature began to be transformed. Decreasingly was it seen as dirty, the source of disease and contamination, polluting. Increasingly, it came to be seen as both valuable and fragile, something worth protecting from the threat posed by human activity.

The final chapter in this set of three is my "Environmental Conservation and Institutional Environments in Jamaica." Like Theodossopoulos's and Macleod's cases, the setting is one in which tourism is important; like Kirby's, it looks at the ways that people translate their personal orientation to their surroundings into more abstract frames. However, the people who are my main focus are not the sort of local residents described in these other chapters, confronting a change in their relationship with their surroundings. Rather, I am concerned with environmental activists, some of the people who were important in the agitation and organizations that led to the establishment of marine parks in Montego Bay and Negril, the first two national parks in Jamaica that protected coastal waters. While my chapter is concerned with how these people confront circumstances that lead them to adopt particular understandings of their surroundings, it also shows how these people do not replace one set of understandings with another, but acquire new ones while maintaining the old.

As I show, these activists' personal histories were bound up with their marine surroundings, and this linkage of life and surroundings appears to have been important in motivating them to become environmental activists. The first step in this process was their acquisition of an objectivist, scientific orientation to the coastal waters. In this, they echo Kirby's Izawa residents, who translated their personal afflictions into the result of environmental threat. As a consequence, these activists held two sets of understandings of their marine surroundings, one that reflected their personal engagement and one that reflected a scientific environmentalism. However, this was only one step in their translation of their understandings of the marine surroundings. As these activists and their conservation organizations became more successful, they became engaged with the overseas and Jamaican governments and institutions that have been important for providing financial and other forms of support. Those institutions required these activists to present the pertinent areas of their surroundings, the waters of Negril and Montego Bay, in yet another set of terms. These were terms that reflected the political-economic pressures that those institutions embodied.

The institutions these activists confronted reflected the prevailing neoliberal political-economic ideology of the time. Consequently, the Jamaican government was under severe fiscal constraint, and while it could establish these national parks, it could provide almost no money to cover their costs. So, these parks were obliged to seek other sources of money. One source they pursued was overseas funding agencies. Those agencies, also reflecting neoliberalism, put their own pressure on these parks to be self-financing, for this was a condition of their financial support. As a result, these parks had to present themselves as commercial (if not necessarily profit-making) enterprises, and treat their coastal waters as commercial resources to be exploited. These activists, then, appeared to be operating in terms of three different orientations to their surroundings, the personal, the scientific, and the commercial.

The need to be self-financing also led these parks to embrace the tourist industry, for they sought to generate revenue by attracting ecotourists and charging them access fees to park waters. At this point, my tale in this chapter intersects with Macleod's tale of Bayahibe. Their desire to attract ecotourists increased the distance between these parks and the local fishing people whose exploitation of coastal waters they sought to restrict. These fishers, like Bayahibe people, found themselves confronting an effort to redefine their surroundings, turning fishing waters into tourist attractions, a redefinition that, as they saw it, would dispossess them, subordinating them to powerful commercial tourist interests.

The two sets of chapters that I have described thus far focus on sets of people whose changed situations have meant that they confront novel understandings of their surroundings. In these cases, there is a fairly clear conflict between a set of people oriented toward local and personal interests and values, and a set of people oriented toward more impersonal and global ones, whether they be ecological, commercial, or bureaucratic. The presentation of these cases implies that the more local and more global orientations can be distinguished relatively easily, at least at an analytical level (at the practical level, of course, the distinction between these two levels is more difficult to sustain). The nature of this distinction is central to the final pair of cases presented in this collection. They differ from the preceding chapters by raising questions about the ubiquity and utility of the contrast between the more local and personal and the more global. Perhaps appropriately, they differ as well in their approach. While the preceding chapters are based primarily on fieldwork with specific sets of people, these final two chapters are concerned with much larger sets of people and the debates that go on within them.

The first of this pair is Eeva Berglund's "A Situated Global Imperative: Debating (the Nation's) Forests in Finland." Important in Finnish debates about forestry policy is the concept of the national interest. This concept is important in Macleod's description of the Dominican Republic and my description of Jamaica, where an expansion of tourism served the nation's economic interest. In these two cases, that national interest was shown to end up standing opposed to some important local interests. However, Berglund makes it clear that it may not always be correct to make this easy assumption that the national is opposed to the local.

She makes this point by considering the ways that the concept of the nation is used in these Finnish debates. The debates themselves reflect the distinctive place of forests in Finland. For a very long time, the country has relied on its forests economically, in the form of the timber industry, and for just as long the country has defined itself in large part by those forests, making Finland a kind of ForestLand. Further, the forests commonly have not been vast, capitalist tracts owned by large corporations. Rather, the bulk of the country's timberland is in relatively small holdings, the property of households, either individually or in small groups. However, in the 1990s the declining economic importance of timber (as ForestLand became NokiaLand), entry into the European Union, and the global spread of environmentalism meant that the nature and future of the country's forests became a public issue.

Forests, then, have long been central to Finland, materially, socially, and conceptually, and it is understandable that in the debate around forest policy, the nation would be a powerful symbol. However, as Berglund shows, it is a symbol that has many resonances. On the one hand, in some of its invocations it is used in a way that invokes the more global and impersonal. This appears in arguments in which the national effectively is a surrogate for global economic or environmental policies or practices, which are themselves contrasted with the local interests of forest-owning households and forest-dependent regions. This resembles the construction of the nation that would benefit from tourism in the Dominican Republic and Jamaica. However, in other invocations, it means something rather different. There, the national is defined in a way that makes it more local and personal, and hence clearly distinguishes it from the global, whether the global economy or global environmentalism, both dominated by American-based experiences, values, and institutions. In these invocations the national is taken as an expression of local conditions and experiences, and of the aspects of personal identity that spring from those things.

Berglund is not arguing that those involved in these debates hold opposing views of the nation. Rather, it seems to be the case that this concept is so powerful and complex that people do not register the slippage or ambiguity in its different resonances. However, even if those involved do not articulate it, it is clear from her description that in these debates there is a tension between the more immediate and personal on the one hand, and on the other hand the more distant and abstract. It is also clear, though, that the ambiguity of the use of "the nation" in these debates shows that the nature of levels intermediate between the purely local and the purely global is more problematic than it may appear at first glance.

In her chapter, then, Berglund raises questions about the easy continuum drawn in this introduction between the purely personal and private on the one hand, and on the other hand the purely global and public. Her case shows that, while this continuum may have its uses, it also has its risks: what may seem on its face to be fiercely global and public may turn out to be more personal and private, or at least local, than we think. This continuum is also made more problematic by the second chapter in this pair, the final substantive one in this collection, Kay

Milton's "A Changing Sense of Place: Direct Action and Environmental Protest in the U.K."

Milton is concerned with a change in the nature of British environmentalism in the 1990s. Prior to then, debates about the environmental impact of this or that quarry or road were conducted primarily in local terms and attracted primarily local interest. This does not mean that the terms of debate were not relatively abstract; rather, the fora and the audiences for those debates were relatively circumscribed. However, beginning in the 1970s and culminating in the 1990s, this local orientation became supplemented, and even to some degree displaced, by fora and audiences that were national and even global. Part of the reason for this was a change in government regulations, procedures, and practices touching on planning permission. However, it is also the case that some of the basic assumptions about political and environmental legitimacy changed, changes that may have been roughly contemporaneous with administrative changes but which do not seem to have been causally linked to them in any straightforward way.

As Milton describes it, before this shift political legitimacy went primarily to people in the locality of the proposed development. After all, it was their area that was going to be affected. However, gradually local interest lost legitimacy, under the challenge that, for instance, a bigger airport was needed *somewhere* in southern England, so why not here? Enter the NIMBY: in this circumstance, local issues and concerns came to look distinctly parochial in the face of what were presented as overriding regional or national needs for facilities to handle air traffic, for quarries to produce aggregate for construction, and the like. As Milton notes, this expansion of the frame for justifying a particular project was met by an expansion of the locus of political opposition, as national and even international organizations entered the fray: national media, Friends of the Earth, and the like.

There is, however, an intriguing twist to this tale, which seems at first glance to be one of the straightforward expansion of the frame of debate and abstraction of its content. The twist is that many environmental disputes in the 1990s revolved around very local direct action, and a growing theme in that action was a stress on the unique nature of the specific area under threat. If England was a green and pleasant land, then every corner of it was special and deserved protection. For many of the more energetic protestors, this took the form of strong emotional attachment to the locality (a similar phenomenon is reported in Durman 2000). In a sense, then, these activities are the reverse of those of the Jamaican environmental activists and managers described in my chapter. While their increasing concern for and involvement with their local environment led them to adopt a more abstract and global perspective, for Milton's activists a general concern with the environment, which led them to get involved in direct action, led to a more concrete attachment to the specific local landscape under threat.

In varying degrees, the substantive chapters in this collection are concerned with the question of scale, from the personal and private at one extreme to the global at the other. In his concluding chapter, Josiah Heyman considers the importance of scale, but while the chapters that I have described approach it primarily in terms of the understandings of people and their situations, he does so in terms of environmental exploitation and conservation. Drawing on the substantive chapters and his own interest in political ecology, he notes that different environmental processes and problems exist at different levels. Some exist at a level that is truly global: atmospheric mixing means that CO_2 emissions, wherever they occur, affect us all. Some exist at a more regional level: acid rain downwind of a coal-fired power plant illustrates this. Yet others are more purely local: whatever the rhetorical force of the idea of biodiversity, the disappearance of a particular species of grass or crab that is unique to a particular place is primarily a local event with local consequences.

If we are to understand people's responses to conservation projects, he argues, we need to match the project to the environmental scale at issue. Failure to do so is to risk interventions that cannot be justified in terms of their effects on people's lives and livelihoods. To speak of global warming and the attendant death of coral as a justification for excluding Montego Bay fishers from their accustomed waters is to invite the rejoinder that stopping their fishing will not change the warming, and that there are other, more local causes of the degradation of coastal waters that can be addressed, if there is the political will to do so. In the face of these rejoinders, such projects are likely to fail. We would do better, Heyman says, to use our abstract and global frames to address the global environmental issues. Doing so, however, would oblige us to confront global interests much harder to challenge than Montego Bay fishers, Bayahibe villagers, and Hushe hunters.

Conclusion

I want to close with the set of issues that permeates this introduction: abstraction, translation, the specific vs. the general, the personal vs. the public. The chapters in the first parts of this collection point to the ways that concern with the surroundings often leads to a stress on abstract, general, public frames of meaning. This stress is understandable, for alterations in one's local surroundings or one's relationship with them often enough are the result of public, general forces and processes, frequently justified in abstract terms. Bayahibe villagers confronted a tourist industry responding to distant economic opportunities in a country that needed to improve its position in the global tourism market; Hushe villagers confronted the global environmentalist industry, one which seems to seek oversight of all that it defines as valuable; people living in Izawa confronted a new waste facility necessitated by regional and national pressures on waste disposal; Montego Bay and Negril park managers confronted the constraints of global political-economic ideology and the dictates of distant funding agencies and markets; Zakynthos villagers had to deal with tourism and environmentalist opportunities and pressures of national and even international scope.

However, the last two chapters in this collection raise questions about what looks like a process of relentless pressure to be abstract, public, global. In the Finnish forestry debates, the nation and its interests, which look so distant from the perspective of Hushe hunters, Tokyo suburbanites, Bayahibe villagers, or Jamaican park managers, can look distinctly local and personal when the nation confronts EU forestry policy or global environmental initiatives. In U.K. environmental protests supported by national and international environmentalist organizations, local attachment and distinctiveness turns out to be an important motivating force. What are we to make of the questions that these two chapters raise?

Two points seem worth keeping in mind. First, the personal and the abstract, like the local and the global, can have a range of meanings. It is true that, on their face, they seem to have absolute meanings. After all, the global is defined by the world as a whole; the personal is defined by the life of one individual. However, as I described in my discussion of abstraction in this introduction, the terms are also relative, and this is especially so when they define an opposition, as in the local versus the global. This relativity is apparent in Berglund's presentation of Finnish forestry debates. From one perspective, that of a household that owns a small stand of timber, the nation looks distant and distinct from themselves. However, from another perspective, that of Finns contemplating biodiversity or changes in the price and flow of timber, the nation can look fairly local and familiar. This point should not be particularly surprising; it is simply the old anthropological model of segmentary opposition put to a new use.

The other point we need to keep in mind is somewhat different, and leads back to Errington and Gewertz's generification, and to Wilk's structure of common difference. The point is a simple one. The locality that becomes a focus of attachment for an environmental protestor in Britain may be different in important ways from the locality that is woven into the lives of Zakynthos villagers or Bayahibe householders supplementing their diet by catching a few fish. The protestor may well be sincerely and strongly attached to the locality at issue, but we need to consider the possibility that what is at issue is the locality as a manifestation of a more abstract concept like "the local" or "the particular." And if this is the case, then we can expect that some localities or aspects of localities will be the focus of concern and attachment more than others. As Theodossopoulos argues, the Greek activists who wanted to protect the environment granted differing significance to different parts of it. I do not mean by this to argue that abstraction is all. Rather, I mean simply to emphasize what is implicit in many of the chapters in this collection: that the abstract, the global, the concrete, the personal, the particular, are not clear-cut entities or labels. Instead, they can be intertwined in different ways and have different referents in different situations.

Notes

I thank Josiah Heyman and Kevin Yelvington, as well as the contributors to this collection, for their helpful comments on this.

1. Describing lowland Scottish shepherds, John Gray (1999, 442), drawing on the work of de Certeau (1984), says that the distinction made here between the universal or generic and the particular is analogous to the distinction between *langue* and *parole*.

2. Of course Western thought contains constructions of people that put them firmly in "nature." Evolution is the most obvious of these; in academic thought over the past few decades there have been cultural materialism (Harris 1980), sociobiology (Wilson 1975), and the concern with "memes" (Dawkins 1976; e.g., Runciman 1998), which naturalize people in different ways. The denaturalization of people in environmental discourse is an intriguing issue, but one that is beyond the scope of this introduction.

3. The problem of translation should not be confused with what might be called the problem of articulation. This latter problem is concerned with the relationship between tacit knowledge based on practical experience on the one hand, and on the other hand verbal representation of that knowledge. The nature of this relationship has been a matter of concern for some time (e.g., Polanyi 1967) and has recently attracted the attention of anthropologists and geographers (Gray 1999, already mentioned, is a good illustration). While they differ in important ways, the problems of translation and of articulation both are concerned with the problem of rendering the personal in public terms (the sort of issue addressed by Bernstein, e.g., 1971).

References

Abramson, A., and D. Theodossopoulos, eds. 2000. *Land, law and environment*. London: Pluto.

Basso, K. 1996. Wisdom sits in places: Notes on a Western Apache language. In *Senses of place*, ed. S. Feld and K. Basso, 53–90. Santa Fe: School of American Research Press.

Beck, U. 1992. *Risk society: Towards a new modernity*. London: Sage.

Bender, B. 1995a. Stonehenge: Contested landscapes (Medieval to modern day). In *Landscape: Politics and perspectives*, ed. B. Bender, 245–79. Oxford: Berg.

———, ed. 1995b. *Landscape: Politics and perspectives*. Oxford: Berg.

Berglund, E. 1998. *Knowing nature, knowing science: An ethnography of environmental activism*. Cambridge: White Horse Press.

Bernstein, B. 1971. A sociolinguistic approach to socialization. In *Class, codes and control*. Vol. 1, 143–69. London: Routledge and Kegan Paul.

Brosius, J. P. 1999. Analyses and interventions: Anthropological engagements with environmentalism. *Current Anthropology* 40: 277–309.

Bryant, R. L., and S. Bailey. 1997. *Third World political ecology*. London: Routledge.

Burke, K. [1935] 1965. *Permanence and change*. Indianapolis: Bobbs-Merrill.

Burnham, P. 2000. Whose forest? Whose myth? Conceptualisations of community forests in Cameroon. In *Land, law and environment*, ed. A. Abramson and D. Theodosssopoulos, 31–58. London: Pluto.

Carrier, J. G. 1997. Introduction to *Meanings of the market: The free market in Western culture*, ed. J. Carrier, 1–67. Oxford: Berg.

———. 2001*a*. Diplomacy and indirection, constraint and authority. In *An anthropology of indirect communication*, ed. J. Hendry and B. Watson, 290–301. London: Routledge.

———. 2001*b*. Social aspects of abstraction. *Social Analysis* 9: 239–52.

De Certeau, M. 1984. *The practice of everyday life*. Berkeley: University of California Press.

Clifford, J. 1988. *The predicament of culture*. Cambridge, Mass: Harvard University Press.

Croll, E., and D. Parkin, eds. 1992. *Bush base: Forest farm: Culture, environment and development*. London: Routledge.

Cronon, W. 1995. The trouble with wilderness; or, getting back to the wrong nature. In *Uncommon ground: Toward reinventing nature*, ed. W. Cronon, 69–90. New York: W. W. Norton.

Dawkins, R. 1976. *The selfish gene*. Oxford: Oxford University Press.

Dominy, M. 2000. *Calling the station home: Place and identity in New Zealand's High Country*. Lanham, Md.: Rowman & Littlefield.

Douglas, M., and A. Wildavsky. 1982. *Risk and culture*. Berkeley: University of California Press.

Duany, J. 2000. Nation on the move: The construction of cultural identities in Puerto Rico and the diaspora. *American Ethnologist* 27: 5–30.

Durman, P. 2000. Tract: Locke, Heidegger and scruffy hippies in trees. In *Land, law and environment*, ed. A. Abramson and D. Theodossopoulos, 78–82. London: Pluto.

Edholm, F. 1995. The view from below: Paris in the 1880s. In *Landscape: Politics and perspectives*, ed. B. Bender, 139–68. Oxford: Berg.

Ellen, R., and K. Fukui, eds. 1996. *Redefining nature: Ecology, culture and domestication*. Oxford: Berg.

Errington, F., and D. Gewertz. 2001. On the generification of culture: From blow fish to Melanesian. *Journal of the Royal Anthropological Institute* (N.S.) 7: 509–25.

Escobar, A. 1996. Constructing nature: Elements for a poststructural political ecology. In *Liberation ecologies: Environment, development, social movements*, ed. R. Peet and M. Watts, 46–68. London: Routledge.

———. 1998. Whose knowledge? Whose nature? Biodiversity, conservation, and the political ecology of social movements. *Journal of Political Ecology* 5: 53–82.

———. 1999. After nature: Steps to an antiessentialist political ecology. *Current Anthropology* 40: 1–30.

Fairhead, J., and M. Leach. 1996. *Misreading the African landscape*. Cambridge: Cambridge University Press.

Forte, M. C. 2000. The contemporary context of Carib "revival" in Trinidad and Tobago: Creolization, developmentalism and the state. *Kacike* I: 18–33.

Geertz, C. 1973. *The interpretation of cultures.* New York: Basic Books.

Gewertz, D., and F. Errington. 1995. Duelling currencies in East New Britain: The construction of shell money as national cultural property. In *Occidentalism: Images of the West,* ed. J. G. Carrier, 161–91. Oxford: Oxford University Press.

Gray, J. 1999. Open spaces and dwelling places: Being at home on hill farms in the Scottish borders. *American Ethnologist* 26: 440–60.

Greenberg, J. Forthcoming. Territorialization, globalization, and dependent capitalism in the political ecology of fisheries in the upper Gulf of California. In *Imagining political ecology,* ed. A. Biersack and J. Greenberg. Durham, N.C.: Duke University Press.

Guha, R., and J. Martinez-Alier. 1997. *Varieties of environmentalism: Essays north and south.* London: Earthscan.

Gupta, A., and J. Ferguson, eds. 1997. *Culture, power, place.* Durham, N.C.: Duke University Press.

Harris, M. 1980. *Cultural materialism: The struggle for a science of culture.* New York: Vintage Books.

Hirsch, E., and M. O'Hanlon, eds. 1995. *The anthropology of landscape.* Oxford: Clarendon Press.

Ingold, T. 1993. Globes and spheres: The topology of environmentalism. In *Environmentalism: The view from anthropology,* ed. K. Milton, 31–42. London: Routledge.

Jameson, F. 1991. *Postmodernism, or, the cultural logic of late capitalism.* Durham, N.C.: Duke University Press.

Kirsch, S. 2001. Lost worlds: Environmental disaster, "cultural loss," and the law. *Current Anthropology* 42: 167–98.

Kottak, C. P. 1999. The new ecological anthropology. *American Anthropologist* 101: 23–35.

Little, P. E. 1999. Environments and environmentalism in anthropological research: Facing a new millennium. *Annual Review of Anthropology* 28: 253–84.

Lukes, S. 1974. *Power: A radical view.* London: Macmillan.

Luloff, A. E., S. L. Albrecht, and L. Bourne. 1998. NIMBY and the hazardous and toxic waste siting dilemma: The need for conceptual clarification. *Society and Natural Resources* 11: 81–89.

Macnaghten, P., and J. Urry. 1998. *Contested natures.* London: Sage.

Maffesoli, M. 1996. *The time of the tribes: The decline of individualism in mass society.* London: Sage.

Milton, K. 1996. *Environmentalism and cultural theory: Exploring the role of anthropology in environmental discourse.* London: Routledge.

———, ed. 1993. *Environmentalism: The view from anthropology.* London: Routledge.

Polanyi, M. 1967. *The tacit dimension.* New York: Anchor Books.

Read, P. 1996. *Returning to nothing: The meaning of lost places.* Cambridge: Cambridge University Press.

Runciman, W. G. 1998. Greek hoplites, warrior culture and indirect bias. *Journal of the Royal Anthropological Institute* (N.S.) 4: 731–51.

Scoones, I. 1999. New ecology and the social sciences: What prospects for a fruitful engagement? *Annual Review of Anthropology* 28: 479–507.

Scott, J. 1998. *Seeing like a state: How certain schemes to improve the human condition have failed.* New Haven, Conn.: Yale University Press.

Strang, V. 1996. Sustaining tourism in Far North Queensland. In *People and tourism in fragile environments*, ed. M. F. Price, 51–57. Chichester: John Wiley and Son.

———. 1997. *Uncommon ground.* Oxford: Berg.

———. 2000. Not so black and white: The effects of Aboriginal law on Australian legislation. In *Land, law and environment*, ed. A. Abramson and D. Theodossopoulos, 93–115. London: Pluto.

Theodossopoulos, D. 2000. The land people work and the land the ecologists want: Indigenous land valorisation in a Greek island community threatened by conservation law. In *Land, law and environment*, ed. A. Abramson and D. Theodossopoulos, 59–77. London: Pluto.

Tilley, C., and W. Bennett. 2001. An archaeology of super-natural places: The case of West Penwith. *Journal of the Royal Anthropological Institute* (N.S.) 7: 335–62.

Weiner, J. F. 1999. Culture in a sealed envelope: The concealment of Australian Aboriginal heritage and tradition in the Hindmarsh Island Bridge affair. *Journal of the Royal Anthropological Institute* (N.S.) 5: 193–210.

Wilk, R. 1995. Learning to be local in Belize: Global systems of common difference. In *Worlds apart: Modernity through the prism of the local*, ed. D. Miller, 110–33. London: Routledge.

Williams, R. 1976. *Keywords.* London: Fontana.

Wilson, E. O. 1975. *Sociobiology: The new synthesis.* Cambridge, Mass.: Harvard University Press.

Selling Space: Power and Resource Allocation in a Caribbean Coastal Community

I

DONALD MACLEOD

THIS CHAPTER IS BASED ON RESEARCH IN BAYAHIBE, a village in the Dominican Republic that has experienced a growth in tourism in nearby hotels and a rapid change in primary work patterns from fishing to tourist-oriented services. Patterns of resource use have changed dramatically on land, at sea, and even in the air. In 1973 a hotel company bought the land on which the village resided and moved the population half a mile along the coast; later, following the construction of the hotel, the company tried to ban the villagers from using the beach. Every day, tourists on horseback or driving beach buggies race through the narrow rocky paths in the village, while a tour helicopter buzzes overhead. And yet the hotel tourists are warned against venturing alone into the village and encouraged to remain within the protected perimeter of the hotel.

Bayahibe provides an excellent example of the way that the use and meaning of people's surroundings can be shaped by powerful interests. Somehow every bit of space in and surrounding the village is inscribed with a social relationship, underscored by power. The houses, the beach, and the coastal waters all speak of a struggle for resources and a current victor. There is a huge dispute over land ownership in the region, with the village's founding family claiming it has been cheated out of its land inheritance by a corrupt regional council, which in turn sold the land to a U.S. multinational: the stakes are high. Two miles away a thousand people squat in a satellite community, dependent on one water tap while living next to a pumping station that supplies the hotels on the coast. At the same time that tourists pay U.S. $200 a day to stay in a hotel, a national's monthly salary, young local people steal wooden boats to cross the treacherous sea channel to Puerto Rico. However, this struggle over control of people's surroundings is not just between local people and powerful outside interests, for also in Bayahibe one old fisherman, his two young sons, and Haitian neighbors have their homes demolished by police because the local landlord claims they did not buy the land that they had lived on for seven years.

Natural resources, and the surroundings more generally, are interpreted and used in different ways, influenced by cultural particulars and allocated along patterns of power. For example, the beach, once a place for mooring fishing boats and building homes, has become the domain of tourists, salesmen, and beach boys, its expanse demarcated according to hotel "ownership" and economic pursuits. The bay it overlooks is crowded by tour boats, and the waters that once teemed with fish are empty because of the constant traffic. A neighboring national park, the gift of an American businessman, occupies 110 square kilometers where local people once grazed cattle, hunted animals, and collected wood. The whole area has been transformed from a natural resource producing goods for food and shelter for local people, to a resource for aesthetic appreciation and recreation consumed by tourists and dominated by hotel chains. The state of local and global power relations in the area determines the socioeconomic lives of indigenous inhabitants, prescribing the range of possibilities in their lives.

Bayahibe, then, is useful for illustrating the importance of people's understandings of and relationships with their surroundings. This is because the introduction of tourism has meant the appearance of a set of understandings and relationships that appear to have been alien to the local population, and the contrast between the alien and the local makes each more visible. However, as will be clear, Bayahibe also shows the dangers in assuming that local populations are some uniform group. Rather, there have long been important tensions and cleavages in the local population, expressed in how people think about and deal with their surroundings. My particular concern in this chapter is to pursue a point made in the introduction to this collection, that these understandings and relationships are expressions of power that are themselves powerful. Appropriately, this chapter will refer to work by Foucault (1977) and Adams (1977) examining power, and build on a model of power and its material manifestations introduced in Macleod (1998). It will also use the ideas of other social scientists to help us understand human relationships with the environment and the relevance of tourism for these relationships. This will enable us to better appreciate the cultural interpretation and play of power that informs human interactions with the surroundings (embracing the natural environment, the built environment and the landscape), especially the relationship between abstract frameworks and particular, local perspectives. Put more simply, this chapter will seek to answer the question, How does power influence our surroundings?

Power and Our Surroundings

Many of those who consider the approach of tourists toward the objects of their desire make use of the concept of the "tourist gaze," introduced by Urry (1990), himself building on Foucault's notion of the "professional gaze." Urry indirectly encourages us to wonder whether there is anything that cannot be gazed upon through the lens of a tourist. He encourages us to be open toward the possibilities and pitfalls of a tourism-oriented environment. His essay on the Lake District (Urry 1995) illustrates his approach, for it shows the way a place can be reinvented as a fashionable commodity suited to the interests of a new generation, specifically those influenced by the Romantic movement of the nineteenth century.

The thrust of my chapter echoes Urry's discussion of the Lake District, for it is concerned to see how power, in the guise of the ideas and culturally influenced desires of contemporary tourists, eventually becomes imprinted on the surroundings. Here we can use Foucault again, with his meditation on Bentham's panopticon: "All that is needed, then, is to place a supervisor in a central tower and to shut up in each cell a madman, a patient, a condemned man, a worker or a schoolboy" (Foucault 1977, 200). I could add that a tourist might be placed in a cell, or perhaps in the central tower itself, and for a short period this would suffice for a pleasurable tourist experience. The example of the panopticon illustrates another important point, for it shows how an idea can become physically manifest, its manifestation not only symbolizing power but actually materializing it. And so the hotel guests, albeit more benign than the prison wardens, materialize and symbolize power. Their ostentatious habitat of the hotel and its grounds, their charmed, unhindered wanderings over land, sea, and air, demonstrate a kind of power, manifestly economic, by motivation cultural, at root ideological.

Adams (1977, 388) defines power as the "ability of a person or social unit to influence the conduct and decision-making of another through the control over energetic forms in the latter's environment (in the broadest sensed of that term)." I will argue that the hotel guests, through the beneficence of the hotel owners, are exercising control over energetic forms in the environment of another social group, the villagers. Tourists have power over people from Bayahibe. But at the same time, Bayahibe locals are not a unitary set of indigenous people. Rather, they too are differentiated, some of them having power over others.

This chapter approaches the play of power in Bayahibe in terms of a model (in Macleod 1998) that identifies three aspects of power. The primary aspect is the fundamental relationship linking the dominant and subordinate parties, dependent on one party's mutually recognized superiority in the physical, political, economic, or other realm. This is expressed through a contract or an acknowledged understanding between both parties. In the case of Bayahibe this aspect includes the state's relationship to its citizens through the rule of law, as well as the relationship between the state and other countries, based largely on economic status. In addition, this aspect includes the influence upon the Dominican Republic by other bodies, such as transnational corporations and international organizations including the IMF (International Monetary Fund), the World Bank, and the European Union.

The secondary aspect is the local, practical manifestation of the primary relationship, for example, the distribution of rights of access to resources or of the ability to relocate others in space. This is the most apparent consequence of the primary aspect because of its physicality, and in the case addressed in this chapter it is illustrated by the enforced transfer of Bayahibe village from one place to another. In this sense the tourists, with their freedom of movement around the village and protected hotel surroundings, are symbolic of the relationship between the villagers on the one hand, and on the other a state that supports the hotel industry. And of course tourism is also a manifestation of the relationship between the Dominican Republic and the wealthier countries that supply the tourists and own the hotels.

The tertiary aspect of power is the intellectual element reflecting the primary relationship and is apparent where ideas and communication are controlled to some degree. This aspect is apparent in the acceptance of the leisure industry and its underlying values; in the assumption that macroeconomic needs can determine microlevel resource allocation; and, in the case of the Caribbean, in a growing acceptance of neoliberal thought (cf. Klak 1997). This is the aspect of power that is described in this collection's introduction as imposing the terms of debate (Lukes 1974), as well as the abstractions used for political and economic purposes and the legal language used to enforce decisions.

This chapter will look at the historic development of Bayahibe and at recent events, exploring the transformation of the village and seeing where the different aspects of power have become manifest. In this manner the chapter will show how relationships of power can be interpreted by viewing the space within which human relationships operate. In some circumstances, power may be most apparent in the use of physical resources, and in those circumstances looking at the behavior of people and the appropriation of space and resources can help us make inferences about the pattern of power and type of society we are viewing. As this suggests, my basic premise is that power is inscribed on people's surroundings, and that through an examination and analysis of the surroundings we can learn much about the society.

Power over Space in Time: A Village History

A casual visitor might see the contrast between Bayahibe people and the tourist industry as the important contest over control of the surroundings, and such a visitor might be tempted to see Bayahibe people as a unified indigenous group, perhaps analogous to what was termed a "tribe" in the introduction to this collection. Such a view would, however, obscure the history of and conflicts within Bayahibe.

According to a villager, Eduardo Brito, his great-great-grandfather, Juan P. Brito, was the man who first settled the area. Juan P. Brito came over from Puerto Rico in 1798 and established himself as a fisherman and small farmer in the region. However, it is the youngest son of Juan P. who is considered the founder of Bayahibe. The two men have become occasionally conflated in the telling of the story, but Juan (son of Juan P.) was the man who purchased the land from the government to pass on to his nine children, an act of brilliant foresight in the opinion of Eduardo. And so began a struggle for possession of the land that continues to this day.

The central problem for Eduardo Brito and his 200 fellow descendants of Juan Brito is that the regional Council of Yuma claims Juan Brito donated the land to it back in the nineteenth century. The Brito family fiercely disputes the Council's claim and has gone to law, involving a struggle for more than a decade, to establish their ownership. Furthermore, the Council of Yuma actually sold some of the land to the Gulf and Western Corporation for development purposes in the 1970s (the Council since say it only rented the land out). This sale led to the village being moved from its attractive beach site to a rocky harbor half a mile down the coast: the deal was overseen by President Balaguer, who sought to encourage the business economy and also welcomed American interests.

It seems that the courts are now favoring the Britos' claim, but there remain two parcels of land in bitter dispute. One of these includes the hotel that Gulf and Western built, and the amount of 250 million pesos (U.S.$16.7 million) is mentioned in conversation by local people when they discuss the problem of the land and its rental value. In 1997 the owners of the hotel, the "Casa del Mar," decided to block off an access road to the adjoining beach, the one which had served the original village. Furthermore, the hotel intended to annex the entire beach for the use of its customers only. The people of Bayahibe were furious and arranged an early morning blockade of the main east-west highway in protest. This proved successful and currently only half of the beach is roped off, guarded by men with guns, thereby allowing villagers and others to enjoy the remaining portion of soft sand and sea.

One road, the Calle Juan Brito, forms the original backbone of the new village. It branches off the highway south to the coast and hugs the rocky shore for a quarter mile. Houses sprang up along this route, a ribbon development of wood and zinc-roofed huts, *bohios*, each one typically a large rectangular space divided lengthwise into two rooms, themselves sometimes divided by a curtain to create bedrooms: kitchens and washrooms are usually separate outbuildings. The Britos are the predominant family occupying these dwellings, as befits their historical origin and economic livelihood as fishermen. Some thirty houses, together with a wooden Catholic Church and a school building, formed the village in the mid-1970s. An increase in economic activity led to a very gradual growth in population, with migrants joining the core village and building their own houses on land donated for free; the properties were constructed farther inland and away from the sea shore.

Since the increase in employment opportunities in the middle of the 1980s, the population has grown rapidly, with the result that some 1,800 people inhabited Bayahibe in 2001. There has been an informal naming of different neighborhoods so that at least four areas are recognized: the original Bayahibe, Villa Espana, Villa Verde, and Aridente. These neighborhoods, *barrios*, have also established certain reputations within the village, with local loyalties to shops and bars, and the poorer ones of hastily built homes possess few if any facilities. So, within a period of less than thirty years, the village has grown into a heterogeneous community in which distinct zones have emerged. One woman, when telling a friend she had been to one end of the village, a peripheral neighborhood, got a shocked reply: "What on earth were you doing in *that* neighborhood?" This illustrates the highly particular way in which the villagers view Bayahibe, drawing on their local and individual experiences.

The Britos, who believe themselves to be the original owners of the village and surrounding land, have occasionally achieved wealth out of the location of their properties that overlook the sea (excellent for restaurants), as well as their establishment of tour boat businesses. They might be seen as the village aristocracy, occupying prime real estate in the most valuable part of Bayahibe. Indeed, Eduardo Brito proposed that it would be likely that the Britos would begin to charge rent for the occupancy of their land in the Bayahibe area, when the courts finally decide in their favor. This family is now able to exercise power through economic strength. They oversee land sales in the village and have come to occupy the positions of local political office.

Property and Ownership

Proof of ownership of land through legal title is not straightforward in Bayahibe, and seemingly throughout the country; the main problem is that there are sometimes many claimants with deeds of title for one parcel of land. Additionally, many of the earliest householders in Bayahibe do not have any title deeds to their land, which was simply given to them by the council and accepted as legal (although recognition of the Britos as landlords has been acknowledged in recent times). Besides this, many people have squatted on land throughout the country and been granted ownership by politicians eager to win favor. It is generally thought that the law is corrupt and payment to the right person will ensure the desired result; hence the proliferation of title deeds. Nevertheless, some settlers have purchased houses from the original owners and have documents of sale that they believe give them a legal right to the land as well.

On the periphery of the village are dwellings whose makeshift nature generally denotes the relative poverty of the occupants, which in turn indicates the social distance of the occupants from the village centers of power. This was certainly true of Luis, originally from Samana in the north of the island. He is a sixty-two-year-old man descended from U.S. slaves transported to the safety of the Dominican Republic in the nineteenth century. He could still speak his mother tongue, English, which he gave up in favor of Spanish from his earliest years. Luis was an excellent boat builder and was responsible for many of the gaff-rigged fishing yachts of which Bayahibe is so proud and which often represent the village in marketing images. He had also built many of the smaller fishing boats or *yolas*, mostly propelled by motor nowadays. He built his home over the past seven years on land bordering the village next to the forest. In addition, he built two wooden houses that he rented out to Haitian families.

It is generally reported that the relationship between the Dominican Republic and Haiti has been confrontational, and for the authorities in the Dominican Republic, Haitians represent cheap labor and often are a scapegoat for economic problems. In addition, people in the Dominican Republic tend to be prejudiced against Haitians because of the history of struggle between the two countries, as well as because of the Dominican Republic's tendency to exaggerate its Spanish origins and diminish its African roots, in stark contrast to Haiti's proud assertion of its African heritage. This situation is inflamed every time a presidential election occurs. The year 2000 witnessed a roundup of illegal Haitians, abundant news coverage of the Haitian economic disaster and the AIDS situation there, Haitian mothers giving birth in Dominican hospitals, and the contentious issue of the national identity of their offspring.

With this backdrop of anti-Haitian sentiment we might view the following incident involving the boat builder Luis as an example of a nationwide pattern, the imposition of an abstract set of values held by a power elite (cf. Howard 1999; Vega 1997). Luis has been in dispute with the man on whose land he had built his houses. The landlord claimed that Luis had not actually bought the land. Luis strongly disputed this in court, but lost his fight. One day in November 1999, about twenty policemen arrived at midday and demolished his house and those of his neighbors, scattering their belongings over half an acre of ground. Luis, homeless with his two young sons, survived in the woods for a few days and later in rented accommodation. He continued to protest his innocence, and his close neighbors and friends defended him. One, himself of Haitian origin, claimed that journalists and a television crew would investigate the case. However, the owner of the land, a Brito, was last seen brandishing his title deeds, in the process of selling the land to the local Protestant evangelist church. Power over dwelling space, as well as the fragmented nature of the local community, is explicitly and strongly demonstrated in this example. The state's policies and sense of history create international friction that fuels local prejudices. Through the power of its legal system and police, the state stamps its authority on land ownership, resulting in heavy-handed physical control over people and their domestic environment.

Padre Nuestro: A Satellite Community

The two Haitian families who had been dispossessed by the police fled for a nearby settlement known as Padre Nuestro. It is a mile inland of Bayahibe and is a poor sister to its increasingly active sibling. In the 1980s it was a tiny hamlet next to a river, supporting twenty-five people who worked the land. Within fifteen years it has grown to a village of almost 1,000 inhabitants, who share one water tap. The river, which reportedly flows from a subterranean lake, has been captured to supply the nearby hotels on the coast flanking Bayahibe. The huge pumping station sited in the village depletes the river and can be heard from half a mile away. However, Bayahibe does not receive any of this water. A project to supply Bayahibe began in the 1970s, but due to a lack of funds or will, the government did not complete it. Meanwhile, private enterprise takes the resource.

Land ownership is even more insecure in Padre Nuestro than in Bayahibe, and the place is dotted with half-built houses bordered with barbed wire. People will erect a building to certify their claim to land, believing that this strengthens their claim to ownership in the eyes of the general public, apparently a belief that has grown in the face of an obscure legal system. In 1998 a man from the capital city, Santo Domingo, visited the settlement to inform them of his (doubtful) ownership of the land. He was strongly challenged by the villagers, whose physical presence and determination seem to have deterred him. His visit, however, was a sign of future difficulties. The power of the state, manifest through legal activities, finds itself at odds with the problems of poverty and homelessness, of people migrating to find work and trying to build their own settlements, create their own private space, organize their surroundings. These poor and uneducated people, armed only with their local knowledge and beliefs, have problems defending themselves against the abstract and general laws of the state.

By August 2001 the water pipeline had finally been completed, with an aqueduct supplying Bayahibe with water from the underground source in Padre Nuestro. People could now use this water in place of the brackish supply from garden wells, although most would not drink the new supply and continued to buy bottled water. The completion of the aqueduct was a result of the initiatives of the government headed by President Hipolito, which took office in May 2000. The completion was celebrated by the president's visit to the village in order to turn on the water tap, and this was the first such visit to Bayahibe in seventy-two years. It was a huge public relations coup, with the president arriving by helicopter, escorted by numerous military personnel, and delivering a televised speech to a specially gathered audience.

Meanwhile, plans for the transfer of Padre Nuestro's inhabitants to another site are under way. Eduardo Brito says that a consortium, including the government, American business interests, and hotel groups, hope to turn the area by the river pumping station into a botanical garden and center for craft workers. It is intended to provide alternative accommodation for the current inhabitants in a nearby village, Benerito. Some commentators in the region suggest the hotels on the coast are orchestrating this move to safeguard their source of water.

These incidents illustrate the secondary aspect of power in the control over and manipulation of physical resources. As my brief look at its history shows, the recent experience of Bayahibe has been dominated by the issue of control over resources, with the state and business interests gaining the upper hand, occasionally excessively so, as was the case during the Balaguer era. At times local people have been able to wrest control over aspects of their surroundings through direct confrontation, as in the beach road protest and notably in the Britos' legal claim to ownership within the village area. However, Bayahibe is not an undifferentiated entity, and the poorest sections of the population remain on the periphery of the village, without access to water or electricity. Moreover, their right to land is fundamentally insecure, as is demonstrated by the removal of Luis from his home at the behest of the local landlord and by the probable enforced relocation of the inhabitants of Padre Nuestro.

Organizing Space in the Village

We might say that the spatial organization of Bayahibe is a weak reflection of a commonplace urban layout, in which the central zone contains the institutions of the state as well as the church, school, shops, and public transport. This central zone is then surrounded by residential quarters that become poorer the farther away they are. The plan reflects a template based on a generalized and abstract view of how a Dominican Republic village should be organized, and is the layout found elsewhere in the Caribbean. For instance, Horowitz (1967, 18–19) describes Morne-Paysan, a peasant village in Martinique, this way:

> The simple white plaster church rises up above the street on the right, approached by wide steps. This is the centre of town. The road widens in front of the church, and it is here that the two buses load and unload. Across from the church is a small, square yellow wooden structure, labelled PTT (post, telephone, and telegraph). All the accoutrements of the modern state are strung out along the road.

In Bayahibe the buses drive into the central square of the village, where the biggest shop presides and the taxi stand operates, and it is the site of the building that functions as the home of the recently created Foundation for the Development of Bayahibe. The foundation was created by villagers and forms a central institution representing their interests. For example, it dealt with the arrival of electricity to the village, acting as a forum for discussion and dissemination; it operates a rubbish collection service and coordinates events such as environmental cleanups. The foundation is headed by an elected and unpaid president supported by a vice president. However, the official who currently does most of the work—the planning, organizing, writing, and typing—is the secretary, Eduardo Brito. Eduardo has written letters to the national government complaining about the lack of facilities in the village, and he also coordinated the Brito land claim from his office.

The central square is also host to commemorative media celebrating village heroes, which enhance the sense of community and identity. An oil portrait of Juan Brito has been nailed onto a tree, with "Village Founder" painted underneath. Similarly, a full-length picture of Alberto Giraldi has been nailed onto an adjoining tree, together with the words "Father of the Liberation of Bayahibe." Giraldi was the senator for the nearby large town of La Romana, and he defended the Britos' land claim, giving them invaluable support in an antagonistic political climate during the 1980s. Outside the foundation building itself a notice is nailed onto a tree: "A village united is a village strengthened." These symbols and slogans, as well as the appropriation of space, are representations of a particular interpretation of the locale, peculiar to Bayahibe and a section of its population. They were put up by villagers and form a focal point and a reminder of the village's history, during which time the people of Bayahibe have actually opposed the state's representatives in their contestation of ownership and control of the land.

This initiative is clearly a representation of local history as interpreted by some local people. It exists as a spontaneous showing of political identity, and is a reminder that there is a degree of freedom of speech in the country. However, it is very informal, the handmade productions nailed onto trees indicating the haphazard status and lack of serious force that the local population represents within the broader national political environment.

There is a palpable variation between the more formal buildings of this central zone and the informal creation of the local political statements displayed within it. These can be usefully described in terms of Lefebvre's (1991; see also Meethen 2001) distinction between "representations of space" and "representational spaces." Representations of space relate to the space of planners and social engineers, people who conceptualize in terms of policies in an abstract bureaucratic and managerial way, illustrated by the main metalled road with its linear housing and purposeful buildings. In contrast, representational spaces are those concerned with inhabitants and users, and they can provide a focus for identity. They are created through lived experience, and are apparent in the use of the central zone to announce village interests and to display identity and political history; they are also seen in the locally specific delineations of village zones. In this model we see the two power blocs, that of the state and that of the main faction in the locality, expressing themselves through the tangible processes of organizing and utilizing village space.

With the painting and slogans, people of the village, specifically foundation members and the Brito family, are publicly celebrating their past and creating a visible sense of history, continuity, and struggle. This local, particular perspective also contrasts with another abstract, general image, the one being projected onto Bayahibe by the tourist industry, for Bayahibe is becoming known internationally through tourist literature. It is portrayed in tour guides, those representations of space from a tourist perspective, as a beautiful fishing village with beaches and a charmed, relaxing atmosphere.

> The town of Bayahibe, founded by Puerto Ricans, was once a quiet fishing village. Today it's a meeting place for independent travellers, attracted by the great beach, cafes and restaurants run by both locals and foreigners and a good choice of private accommodation. Bayahibe is the starting-point for the highly recommended excursion to the Isla Saona. (Insight Guides 1998, 69)

What is not mentioned in the tourist literature is that Bayahibe has been a neglected village, its inhabitants going without electricity, piped drinking water, or paved roads, as well as going without a bank, post office, or public telephone. In fact it has been a small fishing village, surviving by its own efforts through much of the twentieth century, treated as a minor consideration by politicians and big business. This has been apparent by the priority given to the tourism industry in this part of the country.

Tourism and the Material Manifestation of Power in the Region

As I noted earlier, in 1973 the entire village of Bayahibe was moved from its site on a large beach to a spot a half mile along the coast. This followed the (supposedly legal) purchase of land by the Gulf and Western Corporation, which intended to build a hotel. Gulf and Western built new housing for the villagers along a road constructed by the American troops during the occupation of the 1920s. A letter written in 1998 to the president of the Dominican Republic from the foundation recalls how the villagers were "treated like animals" during this transfer, when few facilities were available. This act is a clear example of a group of individuals exercising power through the spatial relocation of others for economic reasons based on cultural values. And the dominance of economic power, in the guise of the hotel and tourism industry, continues to manifest itself through the utilization and possession of spatial and other resources within Bayahibe and throughout the region.

Casa del Mar, the hotel in question, sits snugly next to Bayahibe, with its side of the beach cordoned off by rope. The sand at this border changes abruptly from a natural collection of golden grains blown about into tiny dunes, to a regimented, flat, well-raked plain. The two sections are also divided by recently planted, neatly arranged palm trees, and the hotel beach is host to an array of leisure objects, including paddle boats, a massive inflatable banana, small dinghies, subaqua gear, and a microlight aircraft. All these are silently guarded by armed men, their eyes peeled for intruders who do not wear the brightly colored plastic bracelet that is the uniform of the hotel guest. And intruders are certainly dealt with promptly. One such person, an American Peace Corps volunteer, with her visiting mother and sister, was shown the way out at a different hotel, having invaded the beach area. When protesting that she had a legal right to walk on the beach (national law deems the nine meters of shoreline to be owned by the state), the guard cocked his gun in readiness. Shocked and scared, she reported this to the management, who gave her a day's free use of hotel facilities in compensation.

Nevertheless, casual stragglers are normally shown off the cordoned space with gusto and the hotel's boundary is crossed at the intruder's peril. A reciprocal, respectful attitude toward village space is not, however, forthcoming from the hotel management. Hotel guests are encouraged to enter and indeed enjoy the village arena during planned leisure activities. Tours on quad-bikes race at all times through the small roads of Bayahibe, and while they stick to the main route, a convoy of a dozen bikes still blasts all others out of the way. These would-be rally drivers race along the more deserted pathways, skidding about, creating miniature dust storms and generally scaring human and animal life. Even bolder in their exploration are the horse tours, with up to ten riders wandering through the smallest of pathways, horses stepping over discarded toys, their riders ducking under low boughs. The villagers might get a sensation of being residents on display. To cap this sense of being observed, or perhaps rudely ignored, by fun-seeking foreigners, a helicopter regularly swoops over the village and its small harbor, waking up the siesta-seekers and giving the helicopter's passengers a clear view of the whites of the villagers' eyes. There are no parts of the village that are off-limits to the hotel guests when on tour. Ironically, though, they very rarely venture into it alone, as they are warned of its dangers by the hotel management. The village becomes an extension of the entertainment pursuits offered by the hotel, a resource to be appropriated, a Caribbean living museum.

Farther along the coast, between Bayahibe and the National Park Del Este (described at greater length below), are to be found five more big hotels. They are currently enjoying water from the river at Padre Nuestro. Cable electricity has been connected to the hotels and was later introduced into Bayahibe in 2000: the electric lines supplying the hotels passed by the village and a deal was struck allowing villagers access to the main supply for the first time. Again the villagers' interests were subordinate to those of the hotels. These developments are the secondary, physical manifestations of the primary aspects of power: the relationship between the local people and the state, and in turn the state's relationship with international political and economic power blocs.

In a paper entitled "How states sell their countries and their people," looking at the situation in the Caribbean, Klak and Myers (1998, 108) write in their conclusion:

> A collapse in traditional export markets and an overexposure to foreign indebtedness brought economic decline and swelling poverty to the Caribbean in the 1980s. Caribbean governments responded to these events with some prodding from the IMF, the World Bank, and Western governments, with a rapid economic opening and incentives to attract foreign capital to produce for export. They aimed to emulate East Asia's industrialization trajectory. Indeed, there has been a remarkably rapid global unification of policy around a neoliberal development model.

This describes the situation in which the Dominican Republic finds itself, with a need to attract investment and impose restrictive conditions on its population. The tourism industry is particularly subject to international capital movement and marketing trends. It is, however, a very successful industry, the largest source of foreign exchange in the Dominican Republic, earning U.S.$1.86 billion in 1997 (Howard 1999), and it is given strong encouragement by the government.

The power of the large corporations that own the hotels is most apparent in the construction and utilization of physical resources. This is often initiated in a process that seems to be haphazard. Pattullo (1996, 35) draws attention to this fact in her observation of the construction of hotels throughout the Caribbean:

> The overall lack of planning results in spasmodic and unco-ordinated infrastructural development with governments accepting whatever help and funding is on offer at any one time: an airport from the Canadians here, a road project from the

Americans there, a hotel from the British somewhere else. . . . What development plans do exist are often drawn up by overseas consultants who are unaccountable, who are paid large sums of money to make recommendations and then leave without ensuring any effective follow up.

The hotels dominate the area of Bayahibe in a number of ways. Physically, they take up a large space, up to a quarter of a mile of coastline each, transforming the landscape; in addition to the beachfront, they also use up other local resources, specifically water and the sea. Preexisting environments of wetlands and woods are turned into concrete and grass lawns, and effluent production increases dramatically. However, it is in the economic sphere that the hotels are having the greatest social impact: they bring foreign exchange into the country and supply employment to many locals and migrants. For the actual construction work, teams of Haitians are employed, many living in squatter settlements at the site or sleeping within the empty shells of buildings. The service workers—the hotel guards, gardeners, receptionists, maids, waiters, chefs, and so on—are usually nationals, while the "animators" employed to motivate the tourists are often Europeans speaking the guests' languages. In Padre Nuestro people say that almost every household is supported by hotel labor.

In addition to hotel employment, people can work in the associated service industries, one example being the popular boat ride to the island of Saona with its pristine beaches, part of the National Park Del Este. The men of Bayahibe have cornered this labor market, with about one hundred working as boat captains, ferrying the tourists, up to 1,000 each day, on the thirty-minute journey. Some villagers own their own boats, although the majority of younger men are employed as drivers or crew. This specialist work has grown over the past twelve years, and has replaced the fishing that had supported Bayahibe households. So, by August 2001 there were only fifteen full-time fishermen in the village, though many other men fish in their spare time or while they are on duty with their boats anchored at sea. The economic power that the hotels exercise keeps the politicians favorable to their demands and the local population acquiescent to the regular infringement of their everyday activities.

The National Park Del Este

Another example of the secondary aspect of power, the physical, was the creation of the National Park Del Este. The park covers some 110 square kilometers; it includes the island of Saona and has Bayahibe on its border. As I have already said, after the Gulf and Western Corporation purchased a large block of land from the Puerto Rican Sugar Company, the corporation donated land to the government with the proviso that it should be a national park. The government accepted this gift and added additional land taken from local owners. Today, after twenty-five years, many local people say that they have not yet been fully compensated for their land. People in Bayahibe are especially bitter over the loss of beach, which they realize is very valuable now. Few, if any, villagers visit the park (see Guerrero and Rose 1998; Macleod 2001).[1]

Within the national park the ecologically significant area, home to rare species, attracts few visitors. Instead, tourists take boats to the island of Saona to sunbathe on the beach, generating a huge sum of money for the national park system in user fees. These sunbathers are a mark of how the economic power of the tourist industry overrides the ecological interests of the region, for the boat traffic catering to these tourists has important negative effects. Its water pollution and noise drive fish away from the coastline, obliging fishermen to go farther afield, and some appear to fish illegally in the channel between Saona and the mainland, which is a nursery for marine life on the south coast that needs to be protected. Moreover, in August 2001 a section of this ecologically important channel was opened up for access by divers and tour boats.

The Cultural Interpretation of the Surroundings

I have described the transformation of Bayahibe: its use as a staging post and tour feature, the creation of the national park, the construction of hotels. This transformation illustrates changes in the utilization of the surroundings in Bayahibe: the natural environment, the built environment, the landscape.

These changes reflect transforming cultural constructions, perceptions and values, as well as the exercise of power by specific groups of people. In her book on Australian Aboriginal and Western land practices, Strang (1997, 134) writes:

> Spatial order is an active medium through which society is reproduced. Visible methods of land use, and the spatial ordering of people and landscape, are only outward manifestations of a dynamic interaction with the land, in which underlying social structures and cultural concepts are as crucial as economic and environmental pressures.

The utilization and interpretation of these physical resources are at heart culturally constructed. In this sense, they can be seen as the tertiary aspect of power in its broadest sense, for specific power groups are able to exert control over ideas and actions. Thus, my orientation departs somewhat from what Strang puts forward. Her reference to "underlying social structures and cultural concepts" implies a relatively uniform, homogeneous sociocultural system, one which would make it easy to see Bayahibe people, for instance, as a unified social group, or easy to see Bayahibe people, the state, and other pertinent actors as part of a unified overarching system.

Rather, a focus on power of the sort I use in this chapter fractures this unit, showing how stronger and more influential groups can impose their values onto the surroundings of weaker groups in a field of contested ideas and values in constant transition.

Tourism and its associated effects provides an excellent example of the cultural construction of the surroundings and the consequent imposition of values (with its emphasis on leisure activities), again culturally determined by a dominant group. The built environment of the hotel complex is organized and clean, full of entertainment facilities that focus on beach activities (seacraft, volleyball, bars, deck chairs) and the control of the natural environment (subdued plants, groomed sand, sea enclosure). This all adds up to what many people consider the ideal holiday experience. Similarly, the surrounding natural environment is viewed as a resource for exploitation and an aesthetic commodity. This abstract perspective translates into the particular when embodied by individual tourists, the hedonistic consumption that they undertake at these hotels, and the environmentally damaging quad-bike and boat rides and other activities that the hotels provide for them. It expresses a pleasure-oriented ethos that is inherently unsustainable.

In contrast to the tourism economy, the earlier local economy was driven by the need to exploit the natural environment for food and energy at a subsistence level. Aesthetic sensitivities were rarely entertained, whereas survival was uppermost in the inhabitants' minds. And while many from Bayahibe work in the tourist sector, this older concern with survival continues. One young Bayahibe boat captain said: "When I'm at work I sit in the boat for hours getting baked by the sun. For you it's a sort of paradise, for me it's the same boring shit every day." This brings home the particularity of experience in such a place.

Thus it is that the rise of tourism means that the natural environment of Bayahibe and the region are being interpreted and exploited in a way very different from what went before. Western concepts of leisure opposed to work, and of the ludic and the liminoid state of the tourist, the enjoyment of sunshine in a carefree state, and guiltless consumption, all come together to help create and promote the package-tour hotel experience that so dominates this region. Behind this phenomenon is the contemporary economic power of Western metropolitan centers, centers from which the tourists arrive, together with their work ethic and its counterpointed leisure entitlement, centers that are home to the tourist industry that facilitates all of this (cf. Graburn 1989; Nash 1989). Similarly, Western attitudes toward the natural environment, manifest in the conservation movement, influenced the creation of the National Park Del Este.

Concluding Comments

In short, the primary aspect of power, the political and economic relationship between the Dominican Republic and wealthier countries, has profoundly influenced the secondary aspect of power, its physical manifestation in hotels and associated tourism activities. I have noted how power has influenced the surroundings of the people of Bayahibe. This influence appears in the planned design and subsequent spread of the village; in the control over land and resources, including water and the national park; in the limitations on access to fishing grounds. And most spectacular is the power exhibited by hotels and associated businesses in their use of resources—of beaches, sea, land, and water—and in the freedom of movement of the tourists through the village, in contrast with villagers' exclusion from hotel premises and beaches.

The tripartite model of power that I presented at the beginning of this chapter has enabled us to analyze the problem of power and its manifestations in Bayahibe, and it has drawn attention to the groups exercising control over the surroundings. Lefebvre's distinction between representations of space and representational spaces illustrates the various arenas of power: the state's abstracting planners making their "representations of space" as opposed to the villagers and their particularistic interpretation of history expressed in their "representational space." These divisions relate to the tertiary, intellectual aspect of the model of power, with its emphasis on ideas and values.

These ideas and values are important in Bayahibe, and they range from the growing influence and acceptance of free-market economics to Western ideas concerning leisure, environmental aesthetics, and individualism. In an exercise of power, these ideas and values have been imposed on and embodied in the region, so that the organization and interpretation of the surroundings have begun to reflect the power relationship at work in the area. That is a power relationship in which abstract knowledge and approaches in the hands of powerful groups (the state and the tourism business) dominate the particular knowledge and approaches of villagers in terms of everyday practices and access to resources.

Notes

This chapter is based on fieldwork between July 1999 and March 2000, and in August 2001. Thanks are given to members of the Foundation for the Development of Bayahibe, the National Park Directorate, the Peace Corps volunteers, and those people of Bayahibe who have been most supportive during my time in the Dominican Republic.

1. This situation parallels Laurence Rockefeller's gift to the U.S. government of a number of cattle estates on St. John, in the U.S. Virgin Islands, for a park. As with people from Bayahibe, local people in St. John are finding that they have restricted access to resources within the park (see Olwig 1985).

References

Adams, R. N. 1977. Power in human societies: A synthesis. In *The anthropology of power: Ethnographic studies from Asia, Oceania, and the New World*, ed. R. N. Adams and R. D. Fogelson, 387–410. New York: Academic Press.

Foucault, M. 1977. *Discipline and punish: The birth of the prison*. London: Penguin.

Graburn, N. 1989. Tourism: The sacred journey. In *Hosts and guests: The anthropology of tourism*, ed. V. Smith, 21–36. Philadelphia: University of Pennsylvania Press.

Guerrero, K., and D. Rose. 1998. Dominican Republic: Del Este National Park. In *Parks in peril: People, politics and protected areas*, ed. K. Brandon, K. Redford, and S. Sanderson, 193–216. Washington, D.C.: Island Press.

Horowitz, M. 1967. *Morne-Paysan: Peasant village in Martinique*. New York: Holt, Rhinehart and Winston.

Howard, D. 1999. *Dominican Republic: A guide to the people, politics and culture*. New York: Latin American Bureau.

Insight Guides. 1998. *Insight compact guides: Dominican Republic*. London: APA Publications.

Klak, T., ed. 1997. *Globalization and neoliberalism: The Caribbean context*. Lanham, Md.: Rowman & Littlefield.

Klak, T., and G. Myers. 1998. How states sell their countries and their people. In *Globalization and neoliberalism: The Caribbean context*, ed. T. Klak, 87–110. Lanham, Md.: Rowman & Littlefield.

Lefebvre, H. 1991. *The production of space*. Oxford: Blackwell.

Lukes, S. 1974. *Power: A radical view*. London: Macmillan.

Macleod, D. 1998. Office politics: Power in the London salesroom. *Journal of the Anthropological Society of Oxford* 28: 213–29.

———. 2001. Parks or people? National parks and the case of Del Este. *Progress in Development Studies* 1: 221–35.

Meethen, K. 2001. *Tourism in global society: Place, culture, consumption*. Basingstoke: Palgrave.

Nash, D. 1989. Tourism as a form of imperialism. In *Hosts and guests: The anthropology of tourism*, ed. V. Smith, 37–54. Philadelphia: University of Pennsylvania Press.

Olwig, K. 1985. *Cultural adaptation and resistance on St. John: Three centuries of Afro-Caribbean life*. Gainesville: University of Florida Press.

Pattullo, K. 1996. *Last resorts: The cost of tourism in the Caribbean*. London: Cassell.

Strang, V. 1997. *Uncommon ground: Cultural landscapes and environmental values*. Oxford: Berg.

Urry, J. 1990. *The tourist gaze: Leisure and travel in contemporary societies*. London: Sage.

———. 1995. *Consuming places*. London: Routledge.

Vega, B., ed. 1997. *Ensayos sobre Cultura Dominicana*. Santo Domingo: Museo del Hombre Dominicano.

"Working in Nature," "Caring for Nature": Diverse Views of the Environment in the Context of an Environmental Dispute

2

DIMITRIOS THEODOSSOPOULOS

ON THE ISLAND OF ZAKYNTHOS, in southwest Greece, groups of environmentalists and some of the islanders have engaged in a twenty-year-long dispute. The dispute in question concerns access to and rights over particular parts of the local environment, which comprise the breeding ground of sea turtles threatened with extinction and a development area for tourism. The environmentalists are trying to establish a marine park on Zakynthos that includes sections of the coastal environment and inhibits tourism development on adjacent land. The local landowners affected by those measures vigorously protest against conservation, creatively bringing together arguments that stress the labor or "struggle" that they have invested in "taking care" of their land and their animals. Similarly, the conservationists justify their own involvement in local environmental politics by highlighting the work that they have invested in "protecting" and "taking care of" the local environment and its fauna.

The confrontation of the two groups has provided me with an ideal setting for studying the human-environmental relationship as this reveals itself within particular social contexts, a task in which I have been engaged as an anthropologist since the early 1990s. In this chapter I explore how the environmentalists and the protesting landowners understand the local environment and their relationship with it. I compare the environmental attitudes of both groups,[1] paying special attention to Tim Ingold's work and, in particular, his concern with more or less "engaged" or "detached" perspectives of the environment (1993, 1995). I argue that the environmental attitudes of the two groups—the conservationists and their indigenous opponents—are representative, although to different extents, of both the engaged and the detached approach to the environment.

This observation and the ethnography that supports it bear witness to the complexity of environmental attitudes as these reveal themselves in local contexts and within particular debates. The environmental attitudes of the two groups I studied in Zakynthos do not neatly fit within all-inclusive descriptive categories. On the contrary, diverse attitudes toward the environment coexist within the arguments put forward by the same individuals and the same social groups. The environmentalists, for example, systematically criticize their local opponents for their anthropocentric priorities, while at the same time they claim the power to intervene in "nature's affairs" in order to protect "nature" itself, an interventionist perspective that entails elements of anthropocentrism. Similarly, the local Zakynthians' involved engagement with the local ecosystem manifests itself side by side with a more detached attitude toward the environment that encompasses the notions of control and order.

The first of the three sections that constitute the main body of this chapter is devoted to the environmentalists and provides a brief sketch of their goals, ideals, and social background. Then, in the second section, I examine the relationship of the local landowners with their immediate environment as this reveals itself in different fields of action, such as their involvement with farming and tourism. In the third section, I compare the environmental values of both groups and highlight some of the similarities and fundamental differences in their approaches toward the natural world. I also stress the discrepancies between environmental values and actual engagements with particular aspects of the environment. I conclude by arguing in favor of an approach that acknowledges the complex character of ideas about the environment and their interrelationship with considerations that expand beyond given engagements with particular environments. The protagonists of the ethnography that follows dwell not merely in a physical environment, but also in a social world that encompasses social inequalities, differential access to power structures, and, more importantly, other groups of people who maintain different ideas and priorities.

"Caring for Nature"

The familiarity of the contemporary Greek public with environmentalist ideals is a rather recent phenomenon. The idea that the protection of endangered wildlife should be every citizen's concern is nowadays taken as axiomatic in the discourse of journalists, politicians, and primary and secondary school teachers. As recently as twenty years ago, however, environmental conservation in Greece was not a concern for the general public, but the preoccupation of the specialist few. The first group of environmentalists who attempted to introduce the protection of sea turtles in Zakynthos in the early 1980s felt like pioneers covering unfamiliar ground. They had to introduce practices and ideas that were well established in Western Europe and North America but were, so far, untested on Greek soil. In this respect, their involvement with turtle conservation in Zakynthos was from the very start a challenge. It was also an opportunity for those interested seriously in conservation to obtain first-hand experience with wildlife management projects in a Greek context.

In 1984 the first nucleus of Greek environmentalists, who were seriously concerned with the fate of the Loggerhead turtles (*Caretta caretta*) in Zakynthos, founded an NGO (nongovernmental organization) entitled the Sea Turtle Protection Society of Greece (STPS). The majority of the first generation of the society's members were students or graduates of biology. University students from other subjects, primarily but not exclusively the hard sciences, were also recruited. For most, their experiences in the Greek national university, a highly politicized context, were instrumental in shaping the ideological impetus of their involvement in conservation. Environmental activism was perceived by most of them as not completely disengaged from politics, but at the same time, as untouched by the dark side of politics. From this perspective, investing time and energy in the protection of natural ecosystems was understood as pure and unselfish action, divorced from the materialist calculations of everyday life in the capitalist world. Not surprisingly, environmental ideals appeared particularly attractive to disillusioned Marxists and other leftists who had previously demystified the motives and objectives of leftist organizations and were looking for new inspiration elsewhere. In addition, the success of Green parties in other EU countries in the late 1980s further enhanced the popularity of environmentalism as a new, fashionable, politically correct—but political enough—ideological perspective.

The university-related background of the majority of STPS members added a middle-class flavor to the makeup of the society, which, like most other environmental NGOs subsequently involved with turtle conservation in Zakynthos, was dependent upon the support and participation of urbanites. The urban middle-class constitution of environmental groups has been reported by social scientists before (cf. Argyrou 1997, 160–64; Berglund 1998, 37; Cotgrove 1982, 19, 34, 52, 93; Harries-Jones 1993, 46; Lowe and Goyder 1983, 10–11). For the social dynamics of the environmental dispute in Zakynthos, this bourgeois bias meant that most defenders of the turtle were not Zakynthians, but were outsiders, the inhabitants of large urban centers such as Athens and Thessalonika. It also meant that they were equipped with the necessary education to engage in effective advocacy for the cause of the turtle and that they were more intimately aware of decision-making institutions and the centers of power.

The STPS organized particular programs for the protection of the Loggerhead turtles in Zakynthos and elsewhere in Greece.[2] These programs enrolled existing and more experienced members of the society and additional Greek and foreign volunteers. The latter were individuals, mostly in their early twenties, seeking working experience in conservation, an opportunity to contribute to the welfare of a species threatened with extinction, or simply an excuse to partake in a fascinating adventure in the natural world. In all cases, their motivations projected noble intentions, permeated by unconditional love for the natural world, a sentiment sharply distinguished in their discourse from the pursuit of material gains. The emphasis on the uncalculating, nonmaterial aspect of their contribution was implicitly and explicitly contrasted with the attitudes of all those who were perceived as not aspiring to the same environmental ideals. The young protectors of the turtles favorably compared themselves to business-oriented capitalists indifferent to the fate of the planet, ordinary lower-middle-class citizens preoccupied with their daily routines, or Zakynthian tourist entrepreneurs who attempted to develop tourism in the turtle nesting sites. The latter were soon to become their most bitter adversaries.

As the environmentalists soon realized, the beautiful sandy beaches of Zakynthos were visited by both tourists and turtles alike, both choosing the summer period for their annual visit. By the 1980s, two out of the six turtle nesting sites on the island had been irreparably affected by uncontrolled building and tourism development. The nesting activity of the turtles was seriously compromised by the noise, light, and environmental pollution generated by numerous tourist resorts, restaurants, clubs, and other amenities. According to the environmentalists' careful and systematic measurements, the turtles prefer much quieter and unobtrusive conditions (Arapis 1992; Margaritoulis, Dimopoulos, and Kornaraki 1991), such as the relative tranquillity of the remaining nesting beaches, most of which are located in the community of Vassilikos. The protectors of the turtles set as their goal the protection of the remaining turtle beaches by inhibiting further development on the contiguous land. They proposed the establishment of a national park, imposing restrictions on building and regulating the access of tourists to the area.

As I will explain in the following section, the inhabitants of Vassilikos, like their fellow islanders in other communities, could not afford to loose the opportunity to join the prosperous economy of tourism. They openly protested against the foundation of a national park and opposed the environmentalists' plans by trying to stop their activities and presence on their land. On the other hand, the environmentalists responded to this opposition with marked determination, steadily and systematically increasing their efforts to safeguard the future of the turtle. They organized public education programs on the island, disseminated information to foreign and Greek tourists and collected systematic measurements of the turtle nesting frequency and behavior. In addition, they extended their activities in urban centers, lobbying persistently for the creation of the national park or delivering persuasive figures about the turtles and their conservation to the media.[3] In all these respects their advocacy has been resolute and remarkably effective.

Even more outstanding has been the resilience of the environmentalists to the threats encountered at the site of conservation and, in particular, in their confrontations with agitated Zakynthians who attempted to deter their activities. In the late 1980s and early 1990s, local crowds of protesting Zakynthian landowners attempted on several occasions to evict the protectors of the turtles from their summer camps in Vassilikos and stopped them from completing their measurements on the various nesting beaches around the island. At times like these, the STPS volunteers would escape from their local adversaries and return a few days later to continue their work with enhanced enthusiasm. In fact, the harder the local opposition encountered, the greater was the environmentalists' determination. A couple of STPS volunteers remember:

> The locals were coming down the turtle beach in great numbers. Old men with sticks and women screaming: "Get off of our land, get off of our land." An old man started knocking down our equipment and our tent. Another broke a sand thermometer. They pushed us towards the sea and our only way out was escaping with our boats. It was a windy day and the waves were hitting our boat, which was packed with our belongings and all the scientific equipment we could rescue. The local crowd on the beach was hailing a victory. If they only knew how soon we would return. . . .
>
> They've tried to block the main road to the beach several times. But in vain. Tired from their daily work they would lie in wait for us until late at night. They were fighting a battle they couldn't win. Early at dusk we would reappear, arriving on the same beach by sea, in boats. We would take our measurements and leave, well before we were discovered by the angry locals. As you clearly see, they can't stop us with violence and threats.

Stories like these were narrated at the environmentalists' camps to raise the morale of the younger and less experienced volunteers and further inspire the devotion of the older members. In this respect, the defenders of the turtle were gradually developing their own myth about their contribution to the particular conservation project, the local ecosystem, and the world in general. These levels—the local and the global—were linked in their discourse, which emphasized the interconnectedness of natural elements and beings in the cosmic order. The turtle and its fate was not merely the focus of their efforts, the emblem of their crusade, and the totem of their particular environmental group; the scope of their "neo-totemistic" philosophy was much greater (Willis 1990, 6). "We care for the future of the turtles," the young environmentalists persistently repeated, "we care for nature." In the interconnected threads of the greater ecosystem, and in the environmentalists' syllogisms, the turtle was as significant as every other living creature, and "nature" would have been incomplete without it. As one of the defenders of the turtle once told me:

> The turtle has every right to exist, as much as we do. We are all parts of nature and we cannot exist without each other. We will not sacrifice the turtle—or any other species for that matter—for the sake of a few greedy tourist entrepreneurs. The value of any given tourist resort or taverna can not substitute the worth of a single turtle hatchling. Nature is priceless.

In the context of conservation advocacy, arguments like these appear to be particularly powerful. Filled with concrete natural metaphors, the call of the environmentalists for the protection of the sea turtles became particularly successful in urban centers and beyond. In 1981, a presidential decree officially declared the Loggerhead sea turtle as a species under protection, and a series of subsequent laws (1982, 1984, 1990) introduced a number of restrictions on tourism development and other human activities in the lands and waters surrounding the remaining turtle-hatching beaches in Vassilikos. The pioneer conservationists of the STPS found more powerful allies in well-known environmental NGOs, such as the World Wildlife Fund (WWF) and Greenpeace. Veteran members of the STPS found employment in the newly founded offices of these two organizations in Athens (WWF-Greece and Greenpeace-Greece), and their acquaintance with each other, as well as their commitment to turtle conservation, resulted in unusually close cooperation between the two international NGOs in Zakynthos.

In Zakynthos itself, a group of Zakynthian environmentalists, mostly representatives of the island's educated and professional elite (cf. Argyrou 1997, 164), founded the Ecological Movement of Zakynthos (ZOK). They offered much-needed help and advice to successive generations of environmentalists working for the NGOs mentioned above. They also made the argument that environmental conservation was not purely the concern of outsiders or a premeditated scheme imposed on the local society from above. Finally, a fifth NGO, the Athens-based Mediterranean Association to Save the Sea Turtles (MEDASET), lobbied for the conservation of the sea turtles, disseminating information and raising additional publicity for the cause of the turtles. MEDASET was less well coordinated with STPS, and there has been some competition for recognition and access to resources between those two NGOs (Botetzagias 2001). Despite this contention, however, and occasional ideological disagreements between individual environmentalists, the environmental groups involved in the protection of the sea turtles in Zakynthos have demonstrated remarkable cooperation at the level of action and practice, putting theoretical and other disagreements aside for the sake of the common goal (Milton 1996, 78; Norton 1991).

In this respect, the dispute about the sea turtles, as this developed in the late 1980s and early 1990s in Zakynthos, was not merely a debate about the conservation of a particular species. It was instrumental in the growth of an environmentalist culture in Greece. The efforts of the first generation of turtle conservationists in Zakynthos to implement environmental policies for the protection of the local ecosystem inspired other groups of environmentalists interested in the conservation of other species and other ecosystems. More importantly, the early achievements and errors of the defenders of the turtle served as an experience reservoir in the attempts of subsequent environmentalists to pave the way toward greater institutionalization and professionalism. Some of the young volunteers, who had accumulated valuable experiences in the projects of the STPS, completed postgraduate degrees in the UK, while others improved their skill in practical environmental advocacy. In time, the NGOs concerned with turtle conservation in Zakynthos became increasingly institutionalized (Princen and Finger 1994, 8; for the Greek context, see Botetzagias 2001) and their discourse reflected adherence to a more systematically presented ideological paradigm, "which was undeveloped and unarticulated in the 1970s," but became "a coherent and well-defined ideology" later (Milton 1996, 77).

"Working in Nature"

The increasingly professional attitude of the environmentalists in Zakynthos was reached too late in the day to compensate for their negative profile among the local population. Their success with environmental advocacy was not matched with popularity on the island itself, and although the defenders of the turtles realized with time that good relations with the local people were necessary, they failed to transcend the suspicion and resentment generated in earlier periods of the turtle dispute. From the point of view of those Zakynthians affected by the restrictions of conservation, the environmentalists—locally referred to with the generalizing term the "ecologists" (*oi oikologoi*)—had been firmly classified as enemies, untrustworthy outsiders whose action would only impair the aspirations of the local community for a better life. "The ecologists have done harm (*kanan zimia*) to this island," some would say with disapproval, "they did a lot of damage to the people living on this land."

In Vassilikos, more than any other community in Zakynthos, the antienvironmentalist spirit was particularly conspicuous. In this particular community, the intensity of local resistance to conservation is rooted in painful memories of landlessness and feudal exploitation in the past (Theodossopoulos 2000). The landowners affected by conservation in Vassilikos, like the majority of Vassilikiots, are the descendants of tenant laborers, landless people who had been working on the estates of landlords. As recently as two generations ago, the Vassilikiot tenants were victims of highly exploitative arrangements by their landlords (whom they called "masters": *afentades*), following a system of rules and rights regulating cultivation and animal husbandry with roots in the feudal past of the island from the times of the Venetian occupation (1485–1797).[4] Trapped in perpetual poverty, most Vassilikiots remained landless until the years following the Second World War. After this, they started buying small plots of land and, slowly but gradually, escaped from what they call "the fate of the landless tenant" (*I moira tou ftohou sembrou*).

The booming tourist economy of the 1980s offered new possibilities to the underprivileged population of the Zakynthian countryside: the emigration of younger men declined and most local families heavily invested in dreams about a future career in tourism. Much to the Vassilikiots' dismay, however, the aspiration of several local individuals to develop tourism was constrained by the restrictions of turtle conservation. There was passionate resistance to the establishment of the national park and to the environmentalists' model of conservation on the part of those local landowners who were prevented from engaging in tourism-related enterprises on the three turtle-hatching beaches of Vassilikos, and they were supported by their immediate and more distant relatives and the greater local community.[5] These landowners found themselves in legal possession of land that they could not develop, while at the same time their neighbors in other Zakynthian communities were making significant profits out of tourism. Unable to enter the advantageous economy of tourism and follow the new social standards of wealth and prosperity associated with it, they understood the constraints of conservation as the appropriation of their right to control their landed property and its future (Theodossopoulos 2000).

Not all Vassilikiots, however, had the means to invest in tourism immediately. Most continued cultivating their land and retained their farms, while at the same time starting small enterprises such as room rentals, small family tavernas, minimarkets, umbrella- and canoe-hiring at the beach—often the same beach claimed by the turtles in their reproductive season. Success, in most of the above-mentioned fields of action, was dependent upon the strategic sharing of labor and responsibilities between household members and a collective family-based definition of "self-interest" (Theodossopoulos 1999). In all cases, the united endeavors of the Vassilikiot men and women had as a common denominator the prosperity of every given household, and especially the enhancement of living standards—and eventually the social mobility—of the younger generations (cf. Just 2000). In most cases the constant parameter in the Vassilikiots' endeavor was investment in hard daily work, a process Vassilikiots describe as constant "struggle."

The term "struggle" (agonas, pali), as this is used in the Greek ethnographic context, has not escaped the attention of anthropologists (cf. Argyrou 1997, 163; du Boulay 1974, 56; 1986, 154; Dubisch 1995, 215; Friedl 1962, 75; Hart 1992, 65–66; Kenna 1990, 149–50). It is frequently employed in rural Greece to refer, in the literal sense, to the physical fatigue embodied in the context of daily work—the labor exerted for the sake of one's family subsistence—and, metaphorically, to the more general effort required to meet the social criteria of success and prosperity (Theodossopoulos 2003). As such, the notion of "struggle" relates to a more general combative attitude toward life, which becomes more explicit and straightforward in the context of human interaction with the natural world. The struggle of the human protagonists bears connotations of the effort or contest that demarcates, in turn, the immediate environment, or even the limits of one's stamina, in terms defined by an endless, continual confrontation. As Argyrou (1997, 163) further explains, "out of this confrontation—akin to physical combat—the world emerges as a formidable adversary and the Self emerges as a physically and mentally strong individual who, far from being deterred by the challenge, welcomes and even provokes it."

Successfully accomplished acts of struggle could reinforce new and more confident endeavors in the future and, in this respect, the Vassilikiots' struggle against environmental conservation is part and parcel of their general effort to safeguard the future of their households. Far beyond the performative level, however, the Vassilikiots' struggle—in all fields of action—is purposeful conduct; it constitutes "sensible practices," meaningful undertakings (Bourdieu 1977, 1990) that tell a lot about what it means to be a sociable and successful human being. In fact, it is the exact meaningfulness of the Vassilikiots' struggle—their general project of furthering the future success and prosperity of their households—that renders their daily battles worth fighting. In the fields of farming and tourism, but also in their confrontation with the environmentalists, Vassilikiots devote their energies to the service of their families and dependents. In the context of efforts of this kind, as I have argued before (Theodossopoulos 1999, 2002, 2003), the labor invested in agriculture and in tourism cannot be radically separated. Extending the same argument here, I see the struggle of the Vassilikiots against the defenders of the turtles as a similar manifestation of the same attitude, a further expression of the same "agonistic quality in human relations" (Friedl 1970, 216).

Vassilikiots perceive themselves as engaging in an everyday battle with the environment that surrounds them. They fight with weeds and unwanted vegetation in cultivated fields, on their farms, around the tourist apartments built in their olive groves and next to their own dwellings. They complain about the power of the wild to constantly regenerate itself and say, while wiping away their sweat, "this struggle will never end." They also combat the weather, the winds and the rain, the unpredictable elements of physical nature. They similarly protest about the damaging effect of either drought or heavy rain and worry about the future of their olives or the quality of their produce. As du Boulay (1974, 56) reports from her own fieldwork in a Greek rural community:

> [T]he winning of bread from the rocky fields is, as the villagers say, "an agonising struggle" (αγωνια). For the greater part of the year nature, if not actually hostile to man, is at least relatively intractable. Day after day the farmer wears himself out in clearing, burning, ploughing, double-ploughing, sowing, hoeing, weeding; all through the year there are risks from hail, floods, drought, locusts, diseases.

Wild animals, such as martens, hedgehogs, and large rats, prey upon the Vassilikiots' domestic animals, particularly poultry and rabbits. The farmers insist that they "care a lot" for "their own" animals and do not hide their anger and frustration when they "lose them" *(ta hanoun)* to wild predators. Vassilikiots express their disappointment at these unpredictable circumstances with words that resemble those used to relate natural calamities. They maintain that wild predators "do damage" *(kanoun zimia)* and waste the care and struggle invested in the caring of "their" animals. Domestic animals are locally perceived as participating in a reciprocal relationship with their owners, one that entails both rights and duties: the animals are entitled to receive the farmers' care and protection and are expected, in turn, to offer their own lives for the benefit and well-being of the farm (Theodossopoulos forthcoming).

Wild animals, however, exist independently of the reciprocal relationship of care and duties established on the farm, and are treated by the local farmers with indifference or hostility. In particular, wild intruders that are considered harmful, such as wild predators, are hunted down persistently, a further manifestation of "struggle" that Vassilikiots carry out as an obligation to their households, but also as a public duty and a service to their community (cf. Knight 2000, 7). Those wild creatures that do not pose a threat to human protagonists do not usually attract their attention and rarely figure in their conversation. In the past, the sea turtle was part of this neutral category of animals Vassilikiots treat with indifference. "We never paid special attention to the turtle," the older villagers remember, "the turtle was not harmful or useful to anyone, it didn't bother anyone!" The recent introduction of environmental conservation in Zakynthos, however, has urged some Vassilikiots to reconsider their previous opinion about these ancient reptiles. They are now willing to blame the turtles, along with their protectors, for the restrictions imposed on their lives. The turtles and "the ecologists," they argue, "did damage" to the local community and "harmed" the efforts of two successive generations of Vassilikiots, who have been struggling to bring prosperity to Vassilikos.

As I have highlighted so far, the Vassilikiots' commitment toward most aspects of their daily struggle has been remarkably consistent. Since the time they acquired land of their own, they have been engaged in an effort to take advantage and put to good use the productive resources of that land. The potential to develop tourism, like farming and cultivation, has been understood as a further resource of that kind. Approached from this perspective, the Vassilikiots' relationship with their immediate environment is primarily a working relationship: they engage with it in the context of their endeavors to make the most of what life has to offer. The restrictions of conservation and the advocacy of the environmentalists disrupted their committed and meaningful struggle. Like a wild predator or a natural calamity, conservation "did damage" to their lives; it interrupted their energetic practice-oriented relationship with their environment. The Vassilikiots resent this fact and complain: "We are the ones who live and work on this land. We work the land and take care of it. We are the ones who know about this land. What do the ecologists know? They only care for turtles."

Engaging with the Natural World

The two opposing groups in the turtle dispute in Zakynthos, the defenders of the turtle and the indigenous community, persistently assert that they care for nature (*gia tin physi*). The ancient Greek term *physis* is used in modern Greek, like its English equivalent "nature," to relate to a broad spectrum of concepts. It is in fact this vague and unspecified character of the term that renders it responsible for all sorts of use and abuse in everyday rhetoric and argument. Socially or culturally or historically constructed truths and concepts often become legitimized by association with "natural" facts or metaphors, a process anthropologists call "naturalization" (Yanagisako and Delaney 1995; for the Greek context, Herzfeld 1997). Situational considerations related to particular arguments or conversations inspire divergent references to the term "nature." These might indicate defined spaces, parts of the physical environment, or human dispositions, the attributes of human actors, such as the protagonists of the turtle dispute in Zakynthos.

The defenders of the turtle openly advocate their love for nature. As nature lovers they feel compelled to protect the natural environment and devote part of their lives and energy to activities that contribute to nature's well-being. Environmental conservation is such a noble exercise, they maintain; it is about the preservation of nature from "all those who threaten nature" or attempt to further their personal interests at "nature's expense." The kind of nature the environmentalists claim to protect is a passive one. It is perceived as in need of protection and care, a fragile ecosystem that depends upon their care and protection. Like the environmentalists, the Vassilikiots threatened by the restrictions of conservation also claim that they care for nature. Although they do not see nature as being in need of protection, they do conceptualize a nature that is passively subdued by human agency and control. They argue that "nature needs care" and they think of themselves as the most appropriate and legitimate caretakers. This is why they struggle with remarkable consistency to manage the natural environment in their immediate vicinity and invest great effort in the process. Drawing upon their experience, they feel justified to claim that since they work in nature, "they know," better than anybody else, how to care for it.

There is one further similarity in the discourse of the environmentalists and the Vassilikiots. Both groups are seriously concerned with the future, or what they call "a better future." The former declare that their work contributes to the future of the planet, "a better world," to be eventually inherited by the generations to come. The latter claim that they carry out their daily "struggle" for the sake of their families, and especially their children, the next generation of Vassilikiots who will not have to leave their village in search for work elsewhere, and will not suffer from poverty or dependency upon landlords. From this perspective, the environmentalists and the Vassilikiot landowners appear to have at heart a greater objective, a desire to endow to a larger project: the fate of the planet or the benefit of the local community. In a rather similar way, both groups severely criticize the ephemeral and overtly monetary character of tourist transactions. From the point of view of the environmentalists, the pursuit of profit in the domain of tourism is responsible for the degradation of the island's ecosystem, while, from the point of view of some Vassilikiots, the commercialization of services in tourism contradicts the local standards of hospitality and interpersonal relationships at the village level (Theodossopoulos 2003).

In several societies, Parry and Bloch (1989) argue, prolonged preoccupation with the short-term profit-oriented sphere of exchange could be considered as a threat to the long-term well-being of the greater community. It is not surprising, therefore, that those who work for conservation and those who resist it consistently emphasize the long-term constitution of their objectives and dissociate themselves from the short-lived interests of their respective endeavors. This is a process of transforming or upgrading their short-term motivations to objectives associated with a long-term transactional sphere. In the context of this particular environmental dispute, this process is paired with an equally enthusiastic attempt to downplay the motives of one's opponent. The Vassilikiots frequently make postulations about the presumed "dark interests of the ecologists," their ruthless careerism, and "those grants and moneys they appropriate from the EU" and other international funding bodies. The conservationists, in turn, condemn the Vassilikiots' desire to develop tourism, which they portray as part of the Vassilikiots' exclusive and inconsiderate obsession with the maximization of personal profit at the cost of the natural environment. As I have already underlined, aphorisms of this kind are always followed with praises of one's own noble and selfless motives.

Last among the similarities between those who attempt to establish turtle conservation in Zakynthos and those who vigorously oppose it, is one that highlights a discrepancy between discourse and action. Although both groups—each in its own way—claim that they do care for nature, neither of the two is concerned with all aspects of the Zakynthian environment as a whole. In fact, both the Vassilikiots and the environmentalists neglect significant sections of the local environment. To put it in another way, the conservationists on the one hand, and the local farmers and tourist entrepreneurs on the other hand, consistently engage with selected aspects or parts of the Zakynthian environment, which do not, if at all, coincide. To this disparity, which lies at the heart of the turtle dispute, is related a great number of dissimilarities in the views of the two groups toward the environment. In fact, it is not surprising that when the local Zakynthians and the conservationists discuss the protection of the environment, they talk about different environments.

The turtle conservationists in Zakynthos are concerned with the marine biosphere and primarily with the parts of the marine environment frequented by the turtles. They are also interested in the seashore and the land proximate to it. It is not only the sandy beaches of Lagana Bay, the nesting grounds of the turtles, that are the focus of the conservationists' attention. Environmentally sound management of the areas surrounding the beaches, they argue, is crucial for maintaining the conditions that will facilitate turtle reproduction. By advocating the establishment of a national park, the environmentalists hope to restrict human presence and activity in all these areas, and they direct a great part of their energy and resources toward this goal. Despite their effort to prohibit or restrict human presence on particular beaches, they do claim for themselves the right of accessing those beaches for the sake of scientific measurements and research. These studies, they argue, will provide humans with valuable information to further safeguard the future of the turtles.

Busy with advocacy in urban centers and scientific studies of the turtle-hatching beaches, they spend little time in the remaining parts of the Zakynthian environment. Unintentionally, they ignore the cultivated fields, the vast olive groves, the local farms, and the inhabited, but sparsely developed, tourist spaces of rural communities such as Vassilikos. They rarely refer to those inhabited, cultivated, or developed parts of the environment as "nature" and, in their informal comments and arguments, do not present areas like these as in need of any immediate protection. This attitude is founded upon the romantic belief in a "pristine nature," a kind of nature that is uncontaminated by human presence and that does not include the social world (cf. Burnham 2000; Strang 1997; Carrier's introduction in this volume). This "'naturalness' in the sense of freedom from human interference" (Milton 2000, 240–41) is often conceived by the environmentalists as an essential characteristic of "pure nature" or "nature proper," an unspoiled domain that is fragile, threatened by human activities and requiring protection.

Yet, at the same time, often in the context of the same conversations, the defenders of the turtle put forward a different conceptualization of nature. They describe the environment in holistic terms that stress the interconnection among organisms and the interdependency of the elements of the planetary ecosystem as a whole. According to this discourse, human beings, like turtle hatchlings, participate in a mutually dependent chain of events, and have an equal right to exist and an equally important role. This worldview, compared to the ideal of an untouched and pristine nature, highlights a major conceptual contradiction between the turtle conservationists' holistic understanding of the natural world and their tendency, in certain conversations or policies, to exclude humans and the spaces inhabited by them from "nature." The paradox I have just described becomes more perplexing if we consider that the conservationists I studied, like many other environmentalists, reserve for themselves the right to intervene for the benefit of "nature." Here, their faith in their own intervention contrasts sharply with their understanding of nature, which is conceived either as a pristine natural world with exclusion of all human beings (including the environmentalists themselves) or an egalitarian ecosystem that deprives humans (including the environmentalists themselves) of the agency of intervention. This observation has led Kay Milton to argue that "the very project of nature conservation is contradictory, since it seeks to conserve what is natural through unnatural means (human agency)" (Milton 2000, 243).

Having said that, I should underline that the ideas and contradictions I have just described do not accurately represent all environmentalists in Zakynthos. For example, those supporters of environmentalism who are permanent residents of the island maintain a much less disengaged perception of the local environment. They usually have relatives or property in the Zakynthian countryside and are well acquainted with cultivated, inhabited, and closely managed parts of the local environment. They are also interested in traditional architecture and do not separate the protection of nature from their more general efforts to make their island "a more beautiful place to live." Similar perceptions are shared by a small minority of non-Zakynthian environmentalists, in particular those who have spent time on the island during the winter season, the period when other urbanites, tourists, and turtles depart for other destinations. Their winter experiences have helped them obtain a better grasp of the complexity of the local human-environmental relationship. In cases like the ones I have just outlined, a more intense and involved engagement with the environment has contributed to the development of more pragmatic and less contradictory attitudes toward it.

Much more engaged and involved with the local environment are the indigenous inhabitants of the Zakynthian countryside. As I described in the previous section, those landowners of Vassilikos who are threatened by environmental conservation are farmers and tourist entrepreneurs, who devote their yearly labor to the maintenance of small farms and small-scale tourist enterprises. The physical and moral foundation of most of their activity is their landed property, which they acquired with hard work over the last four decades and which they look after with remarkable devotion. Vassilikiots' "own land" is made up of highly inhabited, managed, and controlled spaces that include cultivated lands, animal shelters, tourist apartments, tavernas, and other private or commercial establishments. The community follows a dispersed pattern of residence, and all "green spaces" located between the human dwellings are accounted for by the Vassilikiots as "nature" (*physis*). It is to this "nature" that Vassilikiots refer when they claim that they "care for nature" and argue that they invest "a lot of struggle" in its safe-keeping.

In this respect, the Vassilikiot conception of nature, which includes cultivated lands and closely managed and controlled spaces, sharply contrasts with the environmentalists' notion of a pristine nature. The Vassilikiots do not completely exclude wild and uncontrolled environments from their understanding of what constitutes "nature." They are, however, less directly concerned with the wilderness and do not feel directly accountable for it. Their primary responsibility lies with their "own" land, which they work, not only in order to fulfil its productive potential—its ability to bear fruit in the fields of farming and tourism—but also in order to prevent it from becoming, or transforming itself into, wilderness. For Vassilikiots, "well-cared nature" is a well-managed and orderly environment, which in turn requires their care and constant vigilance, exactly because it has the inherent quality of converting itself back to wilderness if unattended.

Cultivation, domestic animals, and tourist apartments all need constant attention and are all destined, according to Vassilikiots' point of view, to fall in disorder or decay if left unattended. This pragmatic consideration guides Vassilikiots' engagement with the productive resources of their immediate environment and their working—or struggling—relationship with it. A strong hardworking ethos or "struggle" pertains to their labor investments in tourism and farming, since both modes of economic activity require the close management of their immediate surroundings. This ethos of struggle, engendered by persistent practices of struggle in the local environment, informs their more general confrontational attitude toward the natural world. Caught in an everyday struggle against the limitations of one's own body, the climate, wild vegetation, or predators, they have little, if any, opportunity to think of the environment as being fragile or in need of protection. In fact, it is their effort to keep their immediate environment in order that creates the impression that the environment resists human control and is, therefore, a persistent adversary.

Far from being fragile or threatened by human activity, Vassilikiots' "nature" is enduring and constantly regenerating, keeping its human protagonists busy with the task of controlling it. In this sense, nature needs human care and Vassilikiots see themselves as its caretakers—the caring, but controlling agents in the local environment. Unlike the environmentalists, they do not experience any profound ambivalence about their intervention in "nature's" affairs. On the contrary, they\feel confident in making decisions about their immediate environment and proceeding, without any hesitation, with the clearing, cultivation, and transformation (which might or might not include tourist development) of their land. Their attitude accords with, and is further reinforced by, a well-established Christian cosmology, which, as many scholars argue (Davies 1994; Ingold 1988, 1994; Morris 1981; Ritvo 1987; Serpell 1986; Tapper 1988; Thomas 1983; White 1968; Willis 1990; Worster 1977), upholds a rather anthropocentric orientation toward the natural world. According to this perspective, the human protagonists have a legitimate right, but also a duty, to manage and take care of the land, safeguarding domestic creatures, cultivated areas, and themselves from the harassment of wild nature. As Ingold argues, "traditional cosmology places the person at the centre of an ordered universe of meaningful relations . . . and enjoys an understanding of these relations as a foundation for proper conduct towards the environment" (1993, 41).

The Vassilikiots, who have assumed the role of the caretakers of their land and who have identified with its moral undertones, have a serious difficulty with coming to terms with the priorities of the environmentalists, whom they perceive as favoring "useless" animals like turtles, seals, or other wild creatures. From their point of view, environmental conservation, with its measures and restrictions, imposes a regime of external control on their land that, according to the local moral code, is illegitimate. It invalidates their role as caretakers of their own environment and disqualifies their right to safeguard order in it. Furthermore, it deprives them of their long-awaited opportunity to realize the full productive potential of their land by developing tourism and, thus, escape from the discomforts and financial disadvantages of a life in the countryside. What makes Vassilikiots even more frustrated is the realization that environmental conservation is imposed by individuals who do not share the disadvantages of a life in the countryside and who wish to protect the environment on other people's property.

There are, of course, a few individuals in the local community who disagree with the mainstream Vassilikiot antienvironmental discourse, and who have adopted environmentally friendly positions. Their working experience in tourism has taught them that tourists are interested in the protection of rare species of animals and the environment. In an effort to turn the turtle scenario to an advantage, they envisage a future that combines tourist development with a certain form of environmental protection. Having adopted the discourse of ecotourism, they maintain a greater respect for traditional architecture and a vision of tourism development that is carried out on a human scale, prioritizing or enhancing the interaction of the tourists with the local culture. Their views have not been met with enthusiasm by the majority of their fellow villagers, who maintain a profound distrust toward environmentalism and also the most radical among the conservationists, who use hard scientific data and measurements to argue that the reproduction of the turtles is totally incompatible with human activity.

Conclusion

The two cases examined in this chapter testify to the complex character of environmental attitudes as they reveal themselves in particular debates and in particular groups. In Zakynthos, the environmentalists and the inhabitants of Vassilikos articulate different views of the natural world, but as I have shown in the previous section, they also share some general dispositions. Most striking among them is that both groups reserve for themselves the agency to care for "nature" and shape "nature's" destiny. At the abstract level of environmental values, the anthropocentric priorities of the indigenous Zakynthians are consistently challenged by the ecocentric holistic worldviews of the conservationists. But at the most pragmatic level of conservation policy, or in the context of the environmental dispute itself, the environmentalists unequivocally assert the self-acclaimed right to intervene and set the priorities for the benefit of "nature." Paradoxically, the Zakynthian farmers and tourist entrepreneurs who "work in nature" and the conservationists who "care for nature's future" both pursue the rather anthropocentric, and paternalistic (Pálsson 1996),[6] role of becoming nature's caretakers.

When the conservationists in Zakynthos are called upon to make decisions about the environment, their ambivalence toward "the separation of nature from humanity" (Milton 2000, 243) becomes apparent. Similar contradictions highlight the uncertainty of several environmentalists about the exact place of humanity, and in particular their own selves, in the greater cosmic order. Their contemplation of a kind of nature untouched by humans presupposes some degree of detachment from the world, a standpoint that separates the self from the organic and inorganic environment. On the other hand, their insistence that human intervention for the sake of nature is necessary, and their confidence in their own judgment, puts them in an unequal relationship of power with respect to the nonhuman elements of the environment.

Ingold (1993) has used the metaphors of the globe and the sphere to refer to these two different points of view. The global perspective places human protagonists outside the physical world and equips them with a degree of power and control over the environment. The spherical perspective locates human actors at the very center of the natural creation and emanates from a more involved relationship with the immediate environment. I see the views of the environmentalists, at least those I encountered in Zakynthos, as oscillating between the perspective of the globe and the perspective of the sphere. As Ingold (1993, 41–42) puts it, "both perspectives are caught up in the dialectical interplay between engagement and detachment, between human beings' involvement in the world and their separation from it." Similarly, the local Zakynthians' approach to the environment, and in particular that of the Vassilikiots, although primarily spherical and deeply immersed in action, contains some traces of the more disengaged and controlling perspective of the globe.

At the end of a hard day's work the Vassilikiot laborers look at their well-cared farmland, and the renovated tourist apartments within it, and praise themselves for the orderly appearance of objects and domestic creatures in this environment. They also contemplate the future of their land—their own land—and the changes that have to be made on it. Although much smaller than the globe, the immediate environment of the Vassilikiot farmer and tourist entrepreneur is conceptualized, at certain times, from a more distant point of view. At other times, most of the time, the Vassilikiot laborers are seriously involved with their immediate surroundings, thoroughly engaged with the concrete manifestations of what is locally understood as "nature": a physical terrain that includes cultivated land and a landscape heavily managed by human activity. This is Vassilikiot laborers' immediate sphere of activity, the center of the local environment, from which emanates a more "spherical" point of view that appoints the Self as the center of natural creation.

Compared with the environmentalists' more "global" perspective, the Vassilikiots' local point of view fosters a more direct version of anthropocentrism. In the limited world of the local environment the human actor assumes proportionally a greater magnitude. In the environmentalists' global reflections, on the other hand, the human self looks much smaller when compared to the magnitude and significance of the greater ecosystem. This is partly how the worldview of the environmentalists acquires its ecocentric holistic overtones, which are so appealing to urban conservationists such as those involved in the environmental dispute in Zakynthos. The practice of conservation, however, presupposes a direct—and in certain cases more confrontational—engagement with the environment, one that brings the conservationists much closer to the "spherical" and anthropocentric orientation of the indigenous Zakynthians. In practice, environmental conservation requires the ability to make decisions, decisions made by human actors who are forced to intervene in "nature" "on behalf of nature."

As I have highlighted in this chapter, both the environmentalists and the indigenous farmers and tourist entrepreneurs engage with limited parts of the local environment. Their dwelling experiences, as Ingold (1995) persuasively argues, can explain some of their views of that environment. Vassilikiots' working relationship with the productive resources of their land directly informs their confrontational attitudes toward the natural world. Their culture of the environment reflects this close interrelationship as this has developed and continues to develop in time (Theodossopoulos 2003). Vassilikiots "act in the world" and their knowledge of it is the result of "a continual interweaving or folding of both cultural and physical experiences" with it (Green 1997, 639). On the environmentalists' side, an absence of direct lived experience with the Zakynthian environment can be related to their "abstract" and "idealized" views of this particular environment. But at the same time, the environmentalists' growing experience with selected parts of the Zakynthian ecosystem has also affected their views toward particular animals or aspects of this environment.

At this point, however, I would like to stress that a direct relationship with an environment, although instrumental, is not the only available explanatory tool for deciphering the development and maintenance of particular environmental attitudes. Social engagements with particular groups of people (outsiders, environmentalists, bureaucrats, indigenous actors) and power structures (state bureaucracy, local politics, environmental legislation or restrictions) also relate to the choices by certain protagonists to adopt and articulate certain views about the natural world. Thus, dwelling in a given "nature," working in it and caring for it, is not enough to explain its inhabitants' relationship with it. Particular environmental perceptions are often overshadowed and mediated by social relationships that expand far beyond one's own dwelling experiences. This is why the analysis of particular engagements with the environment should be conceived in terms that acknowledge social interaction.

Diverse attitudes toward the environment, although dependent upon particular engagements with it, often coexist within the arguments put forward by the same individuals and the same social groups. Thus, anthropological interpretation would benefit from carefully avoiding all-inclusive generalizations that abruptly classify environmental attitudes in broad social categories. The human-environmental relationship of the two groups examined in this chapter, the Vassilikiots and the conservationists in Zakynthos, do not neatly fit into ideal types of environmental values (e.g., farming traditions, environmental perspectives, hunter-gatherer lifestyles). Dissimilar ideas about the environment are negotiated in everyday life through direct engagement with specific parts of particular environments, but also through direct confrontation with individuals or groups who maintain similar or conflicting views and occupy equal or unequal positions in hierarchical social relations. Furthermore, ideological contradictions, such as the anthropocentric/ecocentric opposition, however important those might be in theory, often lose their significance in the domain of practice.

In the environmental politics of Zakynthos, social actors, whatever their loyalties might be, have to make pragmatic decisions that presuppose asserting control over particular environmental resources. They might temporarily adopt a more or less engaged relationship with the environment, only to articulate, at a later stage, a less or more disengaged understanding of it, and vice versa. The inhabitants of Vassilikos relate to this observation when they argue: "The ecologists talk theory, we talk action." The environmentalists make a similar point when they say: "At the end of the day, we should never forget that we are here to save the turtles."

Notes

1. In my previous work I have primarily focused on the human-environmental relationship of the indigenous Zakynthian community (Theodossopoulos 1997, 1999, 2002, 2003). In this chapter I pay equal attention to both local Zakynthians and environmentalists for the first time.

2. Zakynthos is the most important reproductive site of the Mediterranean Loggerhead sea turtle in Greece. Apart from Zakynthos, however, there exist a number of egg-laying beaches of secondary importance in other parts of Greece, such as west and south Peloponnese and Crete.

3. They also invested considerable energy in organizing children's awareness projects in primary schools throughout Greece, initiating a new generation of Greek children to the ideals of popular ecology and the protection of the environment.

4. The landless peasants were entrusted by their landlords with parcels of land to cultivate, and were entitled in return to a small portion—usually approximately one fourth (*quarto*)—of the agricultural produce (for more details, see Theodossopoulos 2002).

5. Ties of kinship connect most local families in Vassilikos.

6. Gisli Pálsson (1996: 66–67, 76) has used the terms "orientalism," "paternalism," and "communalism" to distinguish (respectively) between negative, balanced, and generalized reciprocity in the human-environmental relations. Although both orientalism and paternalism favor human intervention and control over the environment, the former fosters exploitative attitudes, while the latter embodies a protective and caring spirit. In turn, communalism is indicative of a less controlling and more dialogical relationship with the natural world, challenging the dichotomy between nature and society.

References

Arapis, T., ed. 1992. Θαλάσσιο Πάρκο Ζακύνθου. Προυποθέσεις και προτάσεις για το σχεδιασμό, την ίδρυση και λειτουργεία του. Independent study, supported by WWF-Greece, Greenpeace-Greece, Sea Turtle Protection Society of Greece.

Argyrou, V. 1997. "Keep Cyprus Clean": Littering, pollution, and otherness. *Cultural Anthropology* 12: 159–78.

Berglund, E. K. 1998. *Knowing nature, knowing science: An ethnography of environmental activism.* Cambridge: White Horse Press.

Botetzagias, I. 2001. "Nobody does it better": Intra-movement conflict concerning species conservation in Greece. Paper presented in the ECPR twenty-ninth joint sessions of workshops: Environmental politics at the local level, Grenoble, France.

Bourdieu, P. 1977. *Outline of a theory of practice.* Cambridge: Cambridge University Press.

———. 1990. *The logic of practice.* Stanford, Calif.: Stanford University Press.

Burnham, P. 2000. Whose forest? Whose myth? Conceptualisations of community forests in Cameroon. In *Land, law and environment: Mythical lands, legal boundaries,* ed. A. Abramson and D. Theodossopoulos, 31–58. London: Pluto Press.

Cotgrove, S. 1982. *Catastrophe or cornucopia.* Chichester: John Wiley and Sons.

Davies, D. 1994. Christianity. In *Attitudes to nature*, ed. J. Holm, 28–52. London: Pinter Publishers.

Dubisch, J. 1995. *In a different place: Pilgrimage, gender, and politics of a Greek island shrine*. Princeton, N.J.: Princeton University Press.

Du Boulay, J. 1974. *Portrait of a Greek mountain village*. Oxford: Clarendon Press.

———. 1986. Women—images of their nature and destiny in rural Greece. In *Gender and power in rural Greece*, ed. J. Dubisch, 139–68. Princeton, N.J.: Princeton University Press.

Friedl, E. 1962. *Vassilika: A village in modern Greece*. New York: Holt, Rinehart and Winston.

———. 1970. Field work in a Greek village. In *Women in the field: Anthropological experiences*, ed. P. Golde, 195–217. Berkeley: University of California Press.

Green, S. 1997. Interweaving landscapes: The relevance of ethnographic data on rural groups in Epirus for Palaeolithic research. In *Klithi: Palaeolithic settlement and quaternary landscapes in northwest Greece*. Vol. 2, *Klithi in its local and regional setting*, ed. G. Bailey, 637–52. Cambridge: McDonald Institute Monographs.

Harries-Jones, P. 1993. Between science and shamanism: The advocacy of environmentalism in Toronto. In *Environmentalism: The view from anthropology*, ed. K. Milton, 43–58. London: Routledge.

Hart, L. K. 1992. *Time, religion, and social experience in rural Greece*. Lanham, Md.: Rowman & Littlefield.

Herzfeld, M. 1997. *Cultural intimacy: Social poetics in the nation-state*. New York: Routledge.

Ingold, T. 1988. Introduction to *What is an animal?*, ed. T. Ingold, 1–16. London: Unwin Hyman (republished by Routledge, 1994, with a new preface).

———. 1993. Globes and spheres: The topology of environmentalism. In *Environmentalism: The view from anthropology*, ed. K. Milton, 31–42. London: Routledge.

———. 1994. From trust to domination: An alternative history of human-animal relations. In *Animals and human society*, ed. A. Manning and J. Serpell, 1–22. London: Routledge.

———. 1995. Building, dwelling, living. In *Shifting contexts*, ed. M. Strathern, 57–80. London: Routledge.

Just, R. 2000. *A Greek island cosmos: Kinship and community on Meganisi*. Oxford: James Currey.

Kenna, M. E. 1990. Family, economy and community on a Greek island. In *Family, economy and community*, ed. C. C. Harris, 143–63. Cardiff: University of Wales Press.

Knight, J. 2000. Introduction. In *Natural enemies: People-wildlife conflict in anthropological perspective*, ed. J. Knight, 1–35. London: Routledge.

Lowe, P., and J. Goyder 1983. *Environmental groups in politics*. London: Allen and Unwin.

Margaritoulis, D., D. Dimopoulos, and E. Kornaraki. 1991. Monitoring and conservation of *Caretta caretta* on Zakynthos. Report submitted to the EEC (Medspa-90-1/GR/28/GR/05) and WWF (project 3825).

Milton, K. 1996. *Environmentalism and cultural theory: Exploring the role of anthropology in environmental discourse*. London: Routledge.

———. 2000. Ducks out of water: Nature conservation as boundary maintenance. In *Natural enemies: People-wildlife conflict in anthropological perspective*, ed. J. Knight, 229–48. London: Routledge.

Morris, B. 1981. Changing views of nature. *The Ecologist* 2: 130–37.

Norton, B. G. 1991. *Toward unity among environmentalists.* Oxford: Oxford University Press.

Pálsson, G. 1996. Constructing natures: Symbolic ecology and social practice. In *Nature and society: Anthropological perspectives,* ed. P. Descola and G. Pálsson, 63–81. London: Routledge.

Parry. J., and M. Bloch. 1989. Introduction: Money and the morality of exchange. In *Money and the morality of exchange,* ed. J. Parry and M. Bloch, 1–32. Cambridge: Cambridge University Press.

Princen, T., and M. Finger, eds. 1994. *Environmental NGOs in world politics: Linking the local and the global.* London: Routledge.

Ritvo, H. 1987. *The animal estate.* Cambridge, Mass: Harvard University Press.

Serpell, J. 1986. *In the company of animals.* Oxford: Blackwell.

Strang, V. 1997. *Uncommon ground: Cultural landscapes and environmental values.* Oxford: Berg.

Tapper, R. L. 1988. Animality, humanity, morality, society. In *What is an animal?,* ed. T. Ingold, 47–62. London: Unwin Hyman.

Theodossopoulos, D. 1997. Turtles, farmers and "ecologists": The cultural reason behind a community's resistance to environmental conservation. *Journal of Mediterranean Studies* 7: 250–67.

———. 1999. The pace of the work and the logic of the harvest: Women, labour and the olive harvest in a Greek island community. *Journal of the Royal Anthropological Institute* (N.S.) 5: 611–26.

———. 2000. The land people work and the land the "ecologists" want: Indigenous land valorisation in a rural Greek community threatened by conservation law. In *Land, law and environment: Mythical lands, legal boundaries,* ed. A. Abramson and D. Theodossopoulos, 59–77. London: Pluto Press.

———. 2002. Environmental conservation and indigenous culture in a Greek island community: The dispute over the sea turtles. In *Conservation and mobile indigenous peoples: Displacement, forced settlement and sustainable development,* ed. D. Chatty and M. Colchester, 244–60. Oxford: Berghahn.

———. 2003. *Troubles with turtles: Cultural understandings of the environment in a Greek island.* Oxford: Berghahn.

———. Forthcoming. Care, order and usefulness: The context of the human-animal relationship in a Greek island community. In *Animals in person: Cultural perspectives on human-animal intimacies,* ed. J. Knight. Oxford: Berg.

Thomas, K. 1983. *Man and the natural world: Changing attitudes in England 1500–1800.* Harmondsworth: Penguin.

White, L. 1968. *Machina ex deo: Essays on the dynamism of Western culture.* Cambridge, Mass.: MIT Press.

Willis, R. 1990. Introduction. In *Signifying animals,* ed. R. Willis, 1–24. London: Unwin Hyman.

Worster, D. 1977. *Nature's economy: A history of ecological ideas.* Cambridge: Cambridge University Press.

Yanagisako, S., and C. Delaney. 1995. Naturalizing power. In *Naturalizing power: Essays in feminist cultural analysis,* ed. S. Yanagisako and C. Delaney, 1–22. New York: Routledge.

Developing "Nature": Global Ecology and the Politics of Conservation in Northern Pakistan 3

KENNETH IAIN MACDONALD

WHEN I WAS IN BALTISTAN, a mountainous region of northern Pakistan, I went hunting with three village men. We left early one morning and traveled up the valley for a day, sheltering in a cave for the night. The following morning found us scrambling up a scree slope to a high mountain spur where my companions thought they might have some luck. Late in the afternoon we reached a small stone shelter, had a smoke and a cup of tea, made dinner, and went to sleep. The next morning, I was awoken by Ali (names are changed) poking my shoulder. He asked me to look at my watch and tell him what day it was (the others had digital watches just like mine). I looked, and looked again. My watch was telling me that three days had passed since we had left the village. The other watches said the same thing. All of us had slept through a night, the next day and the next night. Confused, but lacking an explanation, we continued to hunt. Faizal shot an ibex (*capra* ibex), a mountain goat native to the region, and we returned home five days after leaving. When we reached the village, we explained to a few old men what had happened, but they did not seem surprised. They had a ready explanation. "Rgyelpo Gesar" they said, "wanted to go hunting, and put you to sleep so that you wouldn't disturb his hunt."

Rgyelpo, or King, Gesar, is a culture hero among Tibetan-speaking groups and has a variety of powers, including transformation, transmutation, and invisibility (cf. David-Neel and Yongden 1933). In the short versions of the epic that I heard, Gesar is said to have been born of an ibex, and marks, at least locally, a link between nature and humanity. Not only is Gesar seen as a product of nature, whose role is to conquer the evil of humanity, but his life is embodied in local landscapes, features of which are drawn from events in the epic. For example, *Lacha Khar* (wax palace), a name for a set of hot springs and the sulfur terraces that surround them, is taken from an episode in which Gesar's archrival, the King of Hor-yul, raids Gesar's wax palace, steals his wife, *Langa Blongo*, and puts the palace to the torch. Another is *Chogo-ri Cho* (great peak of the King), a sharp spire that rises ramplike from a lush mountain spur, said to be the pathway to Gesar's celestial palace. Notably, the lush spur beneath *Chogo-ri Cho* has not been used as livestock pasture but has been conserved as a space in which ibex can graze, and villagers can hunt.

This story of the hunt and its association with Gesar are relevant for understanding how nature can be seen differently from the way it is seen by the international conservation organizations that have recently set out to alter local human-environment relations in the region. For villagers, ibex have long been both an instrumental and a symbolic resource. In addition to being a source of protein and raw materials, ibex are also a symbol of fertility, vitality, and strength in the animist belief system that continues to lay under the surface of this seemingly Islamic community. Accordingly, when one is killed, its essential organs—the heart, liver, and kidney—are distributed to people significant to the hunter as a means of wishing them good health and commenting on the continued significance of their authority and its importance to the social reproduction of the community. Ibex meat is also distributed amongst filial and fictive kin as a means of expressing a social commitment to their well-being and of fostering strategic allegiances. "Nature," embodied in the ibex, is thus inseparable from its use value and its symbolic and material connection to the reproduction of community, including an integral environment, the physical site of the village, and the continued legitimacy of traditional institutions of authority. This form of consumption and redistribution indicates one way in which cultural meanings and the social relations that derive from them are first ascribed to nature and then derived from it. Here, ibex are defined by the positive virtues of strength, virility, and fertility, qualities subsequently taken from nature and entered into human social relations through acts of consumption.

The significance of this story, and of ibex in general, did not strike me until a few years later when I returned to the Karakoram to find that a project implemented in one of the villages, called Hushe, was being held up as a shining example of the power of market-oriented conservation practices, practices that rely upon the capitalization of nature. Villagers in Hushe had been asked to stop subsistence hunting, and in return IUCN–The World Conservation Union (hereinafter IUCN), a large international conservation nongovernmental organization (NGO), would arrange for wealthy foreign hunters to pay for the privilege of hunting on village lands. Villagers would then have access to some of the money generated through hunting. This use of international sport trophy hunting as a "conservation-as-development" initiative has become a key part of conservation planning around the world (Corn and Fletcher 1997; Gibson 1999). But it has also brought the community within the sway of a new ideology of "nature" and conservation promoted by large international conservation organizations. When I looked more closely at the terms of the project, read project documents, talked to representatives of international conservation organizations, and observed the workings of the project in the village, it became clear that this intervention was having specific, if unintended, effects that can be traced to the emergence of a discourse of global ecology. The effects include a repositioning of community resources within a new system of meaning, alterations in social relations within the community, modifications in human-environment interactions, and the creation of a new form of governmentality that attempts to position authority for environmental decision making within the institutional arrangements of these same international organizations. While a consideration of these is useful in itself in helping to understand the unintended and often controversial effects of conservation-as-development projects, the point of juxtaposing the story of the hunt with that of a conservation intervention is to elucidate two markedly different understandings of "nature" or "the environment."

In this chapter, I use the case of Hushe to examine how market-oriented conservation interventions, put in place by NGOs like IUCN, rely on an understanding of nature, defined through an emerging discourse of global ecology, to incorporate local human-environment relations within the material organizational sphere of such institutions. What is happening in Hushe, I argue, is the implementation of an ideology of nature that relies rhetorically on a discourse of global ecology, and of local people as incapable environmental managers, to legitimate an allegedly scientifically and ethically superior force able to respond to that assumed degradation. In focusing on this project, I hope to show how meanings of environment, formed within and through social networks of "global" environmental institutions, are used to justify the modification of particularized human-environment relations and, in the process, change the meaning of "environment." This perspective reveals conservation projects as useful vehicles for analyzing the cultural politics of nature, and for identifying the specific sources and mechanisms of new forms of ideological domination.

Two Stories of Nature

In the case that I deal with in this chapter, I tend to delineate two groups, villagers and conservation agents. This divide, however, is too neat, and is better framed in terms of the social relations produced within what Pratt has termed a contact zone. Pratt (1992, 6) defines this as "the space in which peoples geographically and historically separated come into contact with each other and establish ongoing relations, usually involving conditions of coercion, radical inequality, and intractable conflict." A contact perspective "emphasises how subjects are constituted in and by their relations to each other . . . in terms of co-presence, interaction, interlocking understandings and practices, often within radically asymmetrical relations of power" (1992, 7). While this concept has been used mostly to refer to relations of colonialism, it is apposite to an understanding of the social relations involved in conservation interventions, and here I treat the interactions generated through the implementation of a conservation project as a "contact zone." These interactions are structured by different concerns on the part of the participants in the project but they occur, inescapably, within radically asymmetrical relations of power that lead to the introduction of a new narrative of "the environment" meant to reorient the way in which villagers make sense of their surroundings.

The Place

The village of Hushe sits at the top of a valley of the same name in the central Karakoram mountains of northern Pakistan. Part of the district of Baltistan, territory now disputed by India and Pakistan, villagers belong to an ethnic group known as Baltis and speak a proto-Tibetan language of the same name, left behind when the Tibetan empire scaled back its hold on the Himalaya in the eighth century. Long-standing connections between valley-based villages have contributed to a strong valley-based identity in Baltistan, but colonial rulers took advantage of the physical divides in the mountains to generate distrust between villages in neighboring valleys, contributing to an extremely strong village-based identity. Hushe is an upper-valley village, the last and highest one in the valley. Subsistence and settlement patterns in upper-valley villages are different from those at lower elevations. Villages are organized as nucleated settlements surrounded by a zone of cultivated land. People grow wheat, buckwheat, peas, and turnips for consumption and for barter, though over the past few years, barter has declined as a cash economy has penetrated the village. Subsistence in these upper villages is also dependent on irrigation water taken from high glaciers or snow accumulation basins. People also rely on livestock (sheep, goats, cattle, yak, and *dzo*, a cattle-yak hybrid) for dairy products, wool, and draft labor. Livestock are moved farther and higher from the village as the summer progresses and, except for yak, return to the village to be stall-fed through the winter. People live in both nuclear and extended family households. Marriage partners are always taken from outside of the clan grouping and usually from outside of the village. Land is held in common within a household and, until recently, it was expected that any individual income would be contributed to the household. Fields, rooftops, laneways—public spaces in general—are the places where people interact and develop the social relationships necessary to an ethos of reciprocity that is integral to the agricultural production system here (again, though, this ethos is changing of late). Although purdah is not practiced, there is a marked gendering of space, and the home is really the only space where men and women interact on a regular basis. Men also socialize through their participation in activities closed to women. Hunting is one of these. In the past, men would leave the village for four or five days when their labor could be spared to hunt ibex, but both the meaning and practice of hunting are changing. Working as porters for mountaineering or trekking expeditions also allows men to earn cash and brings them into contact with men from other villages. Adventure tourism has increased markedly over the past ten years and is now a heavily capitalized business run by firms, rather than the small-scale ad hoc operation that it was just fifteen years ago (MacDonald and Butz 1998). This has been accompanied by an increase in the number of international conservation organizations working in the region. Since 1989, the World Wide Fund for Nature (WWF) and IUCN have been operating locally, focusing mostly on biodiversity protection through the establishment of protected areas, and more recently attempts to put in place market-oriented conservation programs.

This fairly dry description of Hushe is the kind that generates an image of a place in one's head. It is the kind that we might read in the pamphlets and reports of conservation organizations if they bothered to do enough research to collect it. But it is devoid of the elements of community that give meaning to surroundings, devoid of the understanding that can make people's practice seem rational in light of those meanings. It is to a different sort of description that I turn now, one in which I came to an understanding of the surroundings of others.

The story of King Gesar is important to local understandings of environment, but it is problematic to reduce those understandings to one in which a culture hero links built and natural space in his origin, his abilities, and the way that he is inscribed on the landscape. While the Gesar epic represents this connection in Hushe and in other outpost villages in Baltistan, it simplifies what is a complex and contested relationship among ideological practices involved in assigning meaning to nature. It is difficult to discern a singular ideological force that produces a singular "nature" in a community like Hushe. This outpost village lacks the basic amenities and services that are available in Khapalu and Skardu, the main regional market towns, even though both can be reached in a matter of hours by jeep. Though a small hydroelectric generator, installed with the assistance of a U.K. trekking firm that operates in the area, provides an irregular supply of power, agriculture is not mechanized. People are, as it were, closer to the land. Residents of Skardu and Khapalu characterize themselves as more urbane and point to villages like Hushe as representative of a more "traditional" way of life. Through the pejorative vernacular of development and modernization, townspeople refer to high valley villagers as *"jungli"* (of the jungle), wild, as people low on the ladder of development and, consequently, as "closer to nature." There is no doubt that *Hushepong* (people of Hushe), more than townsfolk, rely on their surrounding environment and depend on the "forces of nature" for their sustenance. And it is examining attitudes to these "forces of nature" and the forces that shape them, and give rise to practice, that helps us to appreciate the contradictory meanings of nature in a place like Hushe. Yet to homogenize this group of villagers would itself be a mistake, for positionality and subjectivity, the personal biographies to which Carrier refers in the introduction to this volume, are important in tracking both the evolution of "nature" as a concept and the alterations in practice that accompany that evolution (Gupta 1999).

The day I first heard mention of the Gesar epic, I was sitting in a small village shop talking to a group of men. For days I had been trying to locate any evidence of a fort that was identified on a map of the area. I decided to ask the men if they knew of it. They went into a huddle and began talking among themselves. I caught mention of this fantastical character called Gesar, and proceeded to probe the story. The men, however, were reluctant to talk in public. I managed to reconcile my reading of the fort's location with their assertion that the only fort up the valley was Gesar's celestial palace reached from *Chogo-ri Cho,* but that was as much as they were willing to tell me in the public space of the shop. Over a space of days, I continued to ask about the story and convinced three young men to share with me what they knew of it. They told me to meet them in the *katsa* (basement) of one of their houses late one night and they would recite what they knew. I appeared at the appointed time and was hustled down into the *katsa* out of sight of the rest of the household, long since gone to bed.

As we sat around a small fire, the tale began. The telling of the epic entails an enthusiastic call and response (speaker: "Do you want to hear more?"; audience: "Yes, yes, tell us more"). As the story proceeded we all grew progressively louder, until a gentle woman's voice whispered down through the hole in the floor, "Be quiet, you know what will happen if your father hears you." This made it apparent that I was unknowingly participating in a somewhat illicit activity. The telling of the Gesar epic, it turned out, was frowned upon by most middle-aged men in the village. These men had been children around the time of partition, when a more conservative variety of Shia Islam made its way into the region. During the lifetime of this generation the singing of folk songs had been discouraged and many villagers had been persuaded to destroy their musical instruments. I found myself in the field at a time when young men were turning to their grandfathers to learn much of what their fathers had forsaken. This generational divide is also an ideological competition for the authority to frame how people make sense of their surroundings, a constant, dynamic process that results in a hybrid outcome that is evident in everyday practice.

As a consequence of this process, religious belief systems overlap in many higher villages in Baltistan. Traces of animist and shamanist traditions, prevalent around 2,000 years ago, have been overlaid by Buddhism (around the eighth century A.D.) and Islam (starting early in the sixteenth century). Yet practices that demonstrate lingering adherence to all of these persist (MacDonald 1995). Willow trees adjacent to springs are left untouched, a remnant of the fear of disturbing Lu, the water spirit who resides in the tree and oversees the flow of water, essential to production in these arid valleys. Talismans are placed in piles of threshed wheat in the hope of invoking nature's support to increase the abundance of the harvest. Men and women whistle to call the wind while winnowing wheat, recognizing the wind as an animate being and a willful agent. Statues in the shape of ibex, the animist embodiment of fertility, are built at pasture, the site where the material wealth of the household—livestock—is reproduced. The first ripe stalks of wheat are pulled from the field and tied around the *sgo* (central pillar of the house) marking the continuance between the household and the field. These and other practices are in conflict with the increasingly conservative interpretations of Islam that are penetrating to the village level,[1] and villagers do not talk about these practices openly or easily. Nonetheless, these practices persist, cohere with, and reproduce an understanding of their surroundings and the forces that shape them. In simple terms, people retain what they have no good reason to, or have not been forced to, dispose of. They have accommodated elements of new ideologies into an existing understanding of "nature" in ways that allow continued physical and social reproduction. This is a picture of a continuous adjustment in an understanding of the environment that is derived, in part, from the meshing of direct experience of the physical reality of nature with ideological narratives that assign meaning both to that reality and to that interaction in an effort to make sense of the world and direct practice in particular ways. As a result, local knowledge is never statically or boundedly "local," for the local is always a product of a broader political, social, and economic context (MacDonald 1998).

This description of a generalized understanding of "nature," subject to contested but reconciled ideological processes, points to a belief system in which nature is not necessarily understood as a coherent whole (Gupta 1999), and people differ in their degree of ideological subscription and practice. The practices that I describe for Hushe are unheard of in the market town of Skardu, where people no longer winnow wheat by hand and so have no need to call the wind, where they are subject to the scrutiny of a more conservative Islam, where people tend to have a higher level of formal education and tend to treat these high villages as anachronistic. Lines of division also exist between elements of nature. Whereas ibex receive a particular form of reverence, the Himalayan brown bear is another kind of being altogether, which can be killed simply for being a nuisance. Similarly, lines of division in the landscape are drawn differently between Hushe villagers and those who intervene in and visit that landscape. Visitors tend to invoke divisions between civilized and uncivilized, inhabited and uninhabited, but it is elevation that has become the subject of fascination for those who increasingly penetrate these valleys: climbers and trekkers are seduced by altitude; conservation agencies focus on species that inhabit high altitudes; development agencies even mark an altitudinal dividing line that represents as much an ideological division of space as a material one, speaking of "above and below the channel" (Velle 1998, 3). However, within local systems of meaning altitude is not a dividing line. Despite the difference between green villages and the more arid gray-browns of non-cultivated lands, villages are definitively not the mountain oases that have been portrayed in Western narratives since the late nineteenth century (World Bank 1990). Rather, flows of resources, goods, and people across space, from pasture to village, and the temporal fluxes in these flows, are seen as part of a larger, interlinked whole. This is not to say that specific places like the village or the pasture (*bloq*) are not marked, bounded, and signified as having their own distinct qualities or features, and as yielding their own distinct experiences or encounters. They are, but this does not lead to some strict dividing line that separates "nature" from "non-nature" or "humanity," or "wilderness" from "civilization." Rather, they are the sites of different experiences, all of which come together to form the coherent whole of one's surroundings.

Consider high pastures. Skills are learned and activities engaged in there that could not and would not occur in the village. However, there are continual sets of relations between pasture and village that connect these spaces into a coherent and fluid space. Travelling to the pasture for young men and boys is a mark of responsibility, and undertaking activities in high-altitude pastures is a mark of the transition from childhood to adulthood. It is, just like the village or the fields, a place where one learns what it is to be a man or a woman. For men, it is place to engage in the hunt, and enjoy all of the social benefits this conveys. For both, it is a place to escape the pervasiveness of Islam in the village and to participate in more animist practices. It is no great surprise that my companions and I experienced the unusual while we were hunting, for high places are the abode of the mysterious, the site of events that can only be explained through appeals to what Westerners might call supernatural, but what Hushe see as natural. But, for all of this distinction, it is not a place seen to be disconnected from the fields or the village. It is a place where fodder is cut to support livestock in the village through the winter. It is a place where dung is collected to heat the household. It is a place where butter, a particularly prized possession, is made. The skills and knowledge associated with pasture are not used to mark a disjuncture between these places, but rather to reveal the connections and continuity in one's surroundings, just as ibex represent the continuity between "nature" and "society."

But the contours are shifting yet again. As I indicated, the terms for framing an understanding of the surroundings in Hushe are being subject to a new ideology, a brand of conservation that derives from an alliance between market-based capitalism, science, nationalist concerns, and global environmental politics. I want to describe a project that represents a new broader context within which people are being forced to make sense of their surroundings.

The Project

In 1996 IUCN approached village leaders in Hushe with a plan. If the leaders would agree to prevent villagers from hunting ibex, IUCN would pursue an agreement with the government of Pakistan and the Convention on International Trade in Endangered Species (CITES) to allow the sale of permits to international hunters to stalk ibex on Hushe lands. Ibex are a valued trophy and the hope was that opening a limited hunt would bring in substantial funds. Eventually the government approved, and said that 75 percent of the proceeds from the permits would go to the village, the remainder going to the government, and CITES (1997) agreed to allow the transport of the carcasses to the hunter's country of origin. In Hushe, it was decided that during the first year the proceeds would be distributed equitably among households in an effort to convince all villagers of the project's value and to refrain from hunting ibex.

IUCN had multiple objectives in this project. One was to try to protect what they felt was a declining number of ibex in the area, but another was to use this project as a demonstration of the links between conservation and development. It served as a way to show villagers that "nature protection" could be used as a means to acquire the stuff of development. This project was part of a wider $6 million Global Environment Facility and United Nations Development Program (GEF/UNDP) initiative, "Maintaining biodiversity in Pakistan with rural community development" (Government of Pakistan n.d.). As the implementing agency, IUCN was responsible for helping villages to prepare "Village biodiversity management plans" that would link biodiversity protection with community development. The aim was to "demonstrate how conservation of Pakistan's biodiversity [could] be enhanced by providing rural villages with the technical skills to manage wild species and habitats for sustainable use and to assess the effectiveness of rural village management of natural resources" (Ahmed and Hussain 1998, 1). This objective falls within a wider GEF/UNDP interest, "to test and perfect a new approach in conserving biodiversity, replicable both nationally and internationally" (Government of Pakistan n.d., 2).

The project emerged in 1991 from an IUCN reconnaissance mission to "examine the feasibility of a community-based natural resource management project" (Ahmed and Hussain 1998, 1) to conserve the "fragile ecosystems" (Government of Pakistan n.d., 3) in northern Pakistan. A project proposal was submitted for GEF funding through UNDP and approved, and the pilot project began in 1995. The project documents show how representations of incompetent locals and a discourse of global ecology align to structure the aims of the project, which were to: "a) Demonstrate how conservation of biodiversity can be enhanced by providing rural people with technical skills; b) Demonstrate how local institutions can manage wild species and habitats for sustainable use; and, c) Assess the effectiveness of rural village management of natural resources" (Ahmed and Hussain 1998, 1). With these objectives in mind, the project framework claims to put

> local people in the "driving seat," transferring control and building their capacity to conserve and sustainably use natural resources. This conservation approach becomes the agenda of the local communities, the government institutions, and the local NGOs, while the donors assume a supporting and facilitating role. (Ahmed and Hussain 1998, 3)

Within the proposed plan, a Project Management Committee (PMC) oversees IUCN and government personnel who work together to implement the project. In practice, however, the PMC selected a set of sites, based on institutional criteria that were seen to influence their potential for success. Each selected village was approached in a process that culminated in the development of a village biodiversity management plan and the signing of a "terms of partnership agreement" between IUCN and the village for implementation and future cooperation. Management plans focus on a particular "management activity" selected by the village and "identify an important resource that they wish to conserve as an agenda for biodiversity conservation, and define a regime for its sustainable use" (Ahmed and Hussain 1998, 8). Yet, in this project we can identify a strategic environmental initiative in which development assumes the forefront, for "it is *expected* that they [villages] will develop biodiversity management plans for purposes like sport hunting, game bird hunting, management and use of medicinal plants and ecotourism" (emphasis added; Government of Pakistan n.d., 5). This indicates that "putting local people in the drivers seat," providing them "with the skills to appropriately manage their resources," and "demonstrating how local institutions can manage wild species and habitats for sustainable use" actually mean commodifying wild resources and inserting them into global circuits of exchange (see Goodwin 1998).

A number of project assumptions legitimate this goal. The first is a set of assumptions about biodiversity. This is never actually defined. Instead, it is expressed in terms of the fairly typical charismatic megafauna species that "merit enhanced protection" and plant species "that have potential economic value." These are said to be in decline because of hunting pressure, which is being exacerbated "because natural habitats are being converted to agricultural production at an ever increasing rate" (Government of Pakistan n.d., 1). This classic "blame the villager" trope[2] does not stand up under scrutiny, simply because there has been no pertinent research, and the Karakoram region has never been subject to a detailed floral or faunal survey, so there is no benchmark against which to judge current numbers of ibex or their status.

While this absence of data is remarkable, more important is a set of assumptions about the role of community institutions in resource management. None of the organizations associated with this project has conducted detailed social or biogeographical research in any of the communities involved, nor have they spent sufficient time in these communities to learn about local agroecological practice, conceptions of nature, or the role of local institutions in "managing wild resources." Consider, for example, the rationale for adopting a "community based approach to biodiversity protection" that "the earlier approach of conservation through legislation and keeping local communities out of resource management, have failed" (Government of Pakistan n.d., 2). This seriously overestimates the salience of government in the daily lives of rural villagers: the most government that people usually see are the police or the army, neither of whom show much regard for local resources. Indeed, far from being kept out of resource management, rural villagers have been the primary environmental managers in the central Karakoram for centuries. From the perspective of the project, however, this does not matter, for these people are seen to lack "appropriate" environmental knowledge or skills. This is apparent in the project justification statement: "[N]eed for the project: At present, there are few incentives for rural people to maintain or manage renewable natural resources sustainably" (Government of Pakistan n.d., 23). This ignores local people's sophisticated knowledge of environmental processes and the ways that they link "natural" processes to the social reproduction of their community. Rather, village management strategies and environmental knowledge are assumed to be ineffective, relieving project planners of the need to address their third stated objective, assessing the effectiveness of village management of natural resources. This assumption is grounded in a belief that:

> Government agencies have a very limited capacity to . . . control rural people's use of wild resources—especially when they need these resources to meet their subsistence requirements. The problem will become more acute with increasing human population if mechanisms are not provided for rural people to acquire the technical skills to manage wild resources. An alternative approach is needed that involves rural people in the solution rather than considering them the cause. (Government of Pakistan n.d., 23)

The irony here, of course, is that the project objectives *do* consider them the cause.

To some extent, however, this is not really relevant. The ultimate goal of the project is not to understand local human-environment relations, but to satisfy institutional objectives, to demonstrate the project's "relevance to and furtherance of GEF objectives."

> [I]n relation to the principal criteria under the Biodiversity sector of GEF, the project will conserve ecosystems and threatened species through development of village biodiversity management plans with sufficient incentives to sustain their management of resources. . . . The model evolved through this study for rural villages to integrate management of their environment with their economic development activities will be very useful. Enhancement of government and NGO capacities to advise and assist rural communities to manage wild resources sustainably will ensure replication to other regions of the country and abroad. . . . The project will screen plant material that has potential international economic value and ensure that rights to use those resources are retained in Pakistan. The commercial benefits of these indigenous materials will be demonstrated to villagers. (Government of Pakistan n.d., 23–24)

Such statements contain the implicit assumptions that underpin the entire project: "rural people" threaten biodiversity, and as government cannot coerce them, the means for people to discipline their own activities must be established. The project sets out to achieve this through the realization of the exchange value, as opposed to the use value, of local plants and animals, and through inculcating skills to manage resources in accordance with production goals determined by exchange value rather than use value.

It is in this equation of biodiversity with economic gain that the interests of the state, conservation organizations, and capital align to affect the daily lives of villagers (Knudsen 1995, 1999). The key, of course, is that to link biodiversity protection with development, "nature" must be seen as something with exchange value that exceeds use value. Trophy hunting is one way to do this, but it is also part of a cultural politics of conservation that has specific local effects (Flitner 1999; see Escobar 1997). I turn to these effects now, to show how conservation interventions in Hushe set in motion processes that both implicitly and explicitly seek to redefine social relations by asserting that biodiversity can be saved through an odd combination of villagers embracing selective ecological theory and realizing the exchange value of ibex: in essence, accepting the rationality of science and the market as the frames for making sense of nature.

The "Nature" of Development:
Trophy Hunting as Ecodevelopment

The logic of relying on trophy hunting as a means to protect biodiversity is not difficult to grasp (Gibson 1999). It is the subjugation of nature to capital and the use of that capital in the pursuit of development. This form of ecodevelopment has certain prerequisites, rooted in desire and in control of access to property.

Some international conservation organizations desire the protection of elements of biodiversity that they deem to be important. Just as important, however, is the desire of European and North American hunters to kill those very same elements of biodiversity, and their willingness to pay to do so. Third is the desire of at least some villagers to acquire the benefits of "development." Within this logic, all of these desires can be satisfied by two things: the acquisition and enclosure of "state property"—the species; and the willingness of village authorities to provide access to land on which that property resides (even though they do not see wildlife as state property).

Just as ibex have symbolic value for villagers, they also have symbolic value for international trophy hunters. This is fed by a particular reward structure among hunters. Organizations like Safari Club International or the Grand Slam Club, for example, offer awards to hunters who kill one representative of all the subspecies of a particular species (the "World Slam"), or who kill the largest individual of a particular species in any given year. The words of one American hunter who engaged in a trophy hunt in the Karakoram highlight the significance of the status of the hunt:

> This will probably be one of the highlights of your hunting career, in that this is a very important trophy and everything, that very few people can claim to have come to this country to hunt. Years ago it was pretty big on the international scene, with a lot of kings and people of wealth used to hunt here quite a bit. Now it's opening it up to the average hunter. (Galpin 1999)

The value of the hunt resides in its geographical exclusivity and its association with a particular class and race status (see Davis 1998; Gibson 1999)—the "average hunter" does not include local subsistence hunters. Equally, however, this hunt follows the logic of trophy collecting, the structured desire that creates ibex as a value-added species. International conservation organizations have been quick to appropriate that added value and use it to meet the ends of biodiversity protection. For the hunter, however, the relation between capital and biodiversity protection revolves around the question of "development." While the trope of the "rapacious native" has been used to justify conservationist intervention, it has been modified of late to accommodate a desired link between hunting and conservation. While earlier representations of local ignorance were framed in what would now be unacceptably racist terms, contemporary trophy hunting frames these representations in terms of "development." From the perspective of the hunter, local villages like Hushe lack the amenities of the hunter's home and thus are seen as undeveloped. Consequently, recognizing, and capitalizing on, the exchange value of wildlife is seen as one means to enhance local livelihoods. In effect, the capitalization of nature, mobilized through the rhetoric of development, demands that "natives" learn the "true" value and meaning of wildlife. And within this rhetoric, subsistence hunting is emblematic of underdevelopment, an unprofitable activity, while trophy hunting reflects a developed condition achieved through the conversion of natural biomass to exchangeable capital.

It is no surprise that village hunters, now relegated to the role of guide, identify easily with foreign hunters. They share an interest in the animals they hunt, the age of the animal, size of the horns, the social activity that is the hunt, the stories of tracking that can be told after the hunt.[3] These shared interests do not, however, explain the willingness of villagers to forsake the right to hunt, something with long-standing social, material, and symbolic importance. In explaining Hushe's participation in this project, the rhetoric of development again appears. Village leaders provided many reasons for participating in the project, but primary among these was the chance to acquire the cash through which they could realize the long-promised material benefits of development. Increased household income or the benefits of social or physical infrastructure are taken as a measure of increased development so that wildlife, as a commodity, becomes one basis of community development. Of course, this logic only works where there is a vast difference in the material conditions of those providing access to wildlife and those paying for the hunt. It is this association of wildlife with development, rooted as it is in inequality, and the acceptance of that association by all parties that provides the leverage to develop a new form of discipline in villages like Hushe. We might call this envirodiscipline, and it relies on the intersection of capital and a discourse of global ecology to achieve conservation ends. In the following section, I lay out the emergence of a discourse of global ecology that invests international institutions with the power to intervene in local ecologies, and that provides them with the grounds to legitimate these interventions and set about altering human-environment relations in ways that accord with institutional agendas.

Mobilizing a Global Ecology

The extension of international conservation interests in northern Pakistan is directly related to the production and circulation of a discourse of global ecology that has emerged over the past thirty years (Adger et al. 2001; Bramwell 1989; Taylor and Buttel 1992). This discourse emphasizes the protection of biodiversity, but it is grounded in the idea of a global environmental commons. The dominance of "global ecology" has come about in part through the power of transnational institutions to produce and circulate knowledge, and through their control over access to funding that governments can use to pursue development goals. Through this power and control, a rhetoric of global ecology wends its way into national institutions and emanates from them through regional and local nodes until it takes on a material reality in the form of specific projects in local environments.

The ability of international agencies to garner support for their activities stems, in part, from their history of mediating international environmental relations. International organizations such as IUCN point to their nongovernmental status to assert a nonpartisan position, but what allows them to transcend nationalist interests is the way in which they have rendered environmental problems as global problems (Goldman 1999). The idea of biodiversity has been central to this production (Takacs 1996), for it has collapsed a range of environmental concepts—localized terms like habitat or ecosystem, for example—into one essential subject, the protection of global biodiversity. Biodiversity has become the emblem that dominates perceptions of the ecological dilemma through its global image of an interconnected web of life and through the assertion that human survival relies upon the maintenance of biodiversity. This has led to the emergence of a global biopolitics, expressed through the rise of an institutional ecology manifest in global organizations such as IUCN, WWF, and GEF. These organizations have established themselves as effective watchdogs that use their authority to define global environmental problems and solutions, and to influence national politics and decision making. In many cases, such agencies act as mediators between national governments and supranational agencies, and influence the design of international scientific research programs that frame the official environmental agendas of many governments in developing countries.

Public support for this endeavor relies on "translating expert discourse into politics, and also recombining specialist expert knowledges into policy-oriented packages" (Jamison 1996, 224). This, Jamison says, has been accomplished through the marketing strategies of international conservation organizations, which have helped to create an institutional environmentalism of the global commons, in which global environmental processes have assumed priority over local ones. Through their globalization of environmental problems, transnational NGOs have assumed an enhanced political significance and have come to play a crucial role in "the transnational arenas where agreements are negotiated over the exploitation of the 'global commons'" (Jamison 1996, 219). Hence, agencies like IUCN and WWF, taking their cues from the science of ecology, spread the mantra of biodiversity, and trade in the techniques through which a normative and uniform management of biodiversity can be exercised around the world. In doing so, they create a new frame through which a species like the ibex becomes of global, rather than simply local, importance, endowing it with significance not just for those who have contact with it, but also for those who know little or nothing about it, have never come into contact with it, and never expect to do so.

These political, scientific, and institutional connections are important for understanding how institutions engage in the production of a global scale and use the authority attached to it to gain physical and ideological access to particular locales. If we accept Rosen's (1991) definition of organizations as devices for the attainment of goals and instruments of power, underlain and mediated by cultural and ideational factors, we can begin to appreciate how the idea of scale is both an instrument in that process and a basis for the formulation and attainment of institutional goals. Operating from a distance, for example, facilitates acts of abstraction that annihilate context and sacrifice the detail of community and its environmental context to a unifying gaze that allows comparability across space and facilitates the application of a normative standardized managerial logic to the human-environment relations captured by that gaze (Latour 1999). Under such a gaze, communities like Hushe find themselves and their ecological practices abstracted from their immediate contexts, and identified and classified in terms of their relevance to the projects of institutions that, in recent years, have found themselves under pressure to adopt a capitalist logic and managerial practices (see Hough 1994; Carrier this volume). But the universalized and decontextualized rationality of these organizations and the understanding of environment implicit within it also structure certain demands. Rosen (1991) describes organizations not simply as hierarchies, but as sites where selective knowledge is accumulated and action designed, which flow in turn to distant places. This flow, while not necessarily as unidirectional or dominating as some (e.g., Escobar 1994; Smith 1999) assert, demands a response from those distant places. We can imagine this response as taking different forms. Individuals or social groups may resist categorization; they may accommodate, but manipulate, assigned labels (Neumann 1995). But whatever the response, people confront the persistent demand to rationalize and modify local knowledge or practice within the ideological boundaries of understanding subscribed to by IUCN (consider, for example, the spread of "environmental education" programs developed and sponsored by international conservation organizations such as the IUCN Commission on Education and Communication). While the correspondence between demand and reply is uncertain, a reply there must be, and it occurs within and through a network of local power relations that is increasingly connected to these institutions operating at a distance.

The Social and Spatial Effects of Global Ecology

Rather than being simply objects of conservation actions in northern Pakistan, villages and villagers have become instrumental subjects in satisfying the multiple agendas of transnational conservation organizations. This is, to some extent, grounded in a realization that state regulatory efforts, such as legislation, have not achieved the ends they seek. People in Hushe and other Karakoram villages have not felt bound to an ideology of nationalism that underlies such legislation, or at least not to the point where they would willingly cede sovereignty over what they have historically thought of as community land (Cooper 1998; Knudsen 1995, 1999). In the eyes of conservation NGOs, these regulations do not fail because they are flawed in themselves, but because the government has no way of enforcing them in the "remote" territories inhabited by the species they are designed to protect. The NGOs' solution, then, is not to do away with the legislation, but to find a mechanism through which villages will act to satisfy institutional objectives. While the rhetoric of the global commons may generate public support and money and the acquiescence of states, it does little to mobilize villagers. It is in the search for village cooperation that we find the logic behind the rhetoric of market-oriented "sustainable use initiatives." In trophy hunting, the conversion of subsistence biomass to potential accumulative capital continues, at least superficially, to recognize village sovereignty while holding out the promise of the development that the state has not brought about. Cash is intended to exercise ecological discipline, to modify the behavior of villagers and make them conform to a set of practices prescribed by the demands of an external worldview of capitalized nature.

Whether or not it works, this regime is salient to the cultural politics of conservation in Hushe. In some ways, trophy hunting is unsettling the familiar by extracting local ecologies from entrenched networks of class, gender, cultural, and ethnic domination. Along with other interventions, it acts to situate local ecologies within new contexts of domination, and to reorient local exclusionary practices. International hunters and conservation NGOs proclaim an ethic of "true" conservation as they facilitate the means through which ibex is assigned a monetary value, effectively an attempt to remove ibex from local control and management and situate it within the domain of national and international institutions. This has much the same intent as the British Indian administration that established hunting preserves and dictated that villagers not own firearms (Neumann 1996), but it is now capital that makes the demand rather than colonial legislation and police. Capital, however, does require social and physical force to minimize resistance. It finds this force not only in the sanctioning power and policies of global and national institutions, but also in the social pressure exercised by those within the village who stand to benefit from the proceeds of hunting (shop owners, guides, etc.). The capitalization of wildlife as a mode of social control is able to take advantage of the fact that communities are not bodies of homogeneous or uniform interest but social groups with a web of common and contradictory interests (Agrawal and Gibson 1999; Breman 1989).

It is this recognition of divisions within the community that brings us back to a consideration of the ways in which the meaning of and practice regarding nature are changing in Hushe. Earlier I pointed to differences between market towns and outpost villages in Baltistan. Similar divisions exist within villages like Hushe, where some individuals readily adopt a modernist subjectivity and are positioned to act on the village in ways that others are not (MacDonald 2001). Notably, it is those who have already commandeered the social, economic, and political resources associated with adventure tourism that are able to do this. It is, for example, the village leaders who negotiated the project with IUCN who have begun to adopt and use the language of biodiversity protection. These same men are those with the most direct contact with and interest in the adventure tourism industry. Thus, the shift in environmental understanding is associated with an economic interest in adventure tourism, the desire to increase the attractiveness of the community to tourists, and the desire to present the village as an "environmentally responsible" community in terms that foreign tourists understand.

One manifestation of this is the establishment of a "community protected area." One of the first things that visitors to Hushe see is a sign decorated with images of local wildlife (predominant among these is the ibex), and IUCN, GEF, and UNDP logos, asking visitors to help protect the resources of Hushe, not for the sake of wild plant or animal life, but for the benefit of village children. The sign signifies the link between community and environmental well-being, and expresses it in terms that visitors, primarily North Americans and Europeans, can understand. It also links the village with major international environmental organizations. The "conservation area" exists in little more than name, but this does not matter so much as the proficiency of village leaders in talking the conservation talk. The direct benefit of this can be seen in the way that community conservation programs have become the site of adventure tourist destinations:

> The local wildlife of Hushe is Pakistan's richest—the Asiatic ibex, the snow leopard, the wolf, and the fox being some of them. Life in parts of the Hushe Valley hasn't changed in centuries and can still be seen set against the rugged snow cloaked peaks and cobalt blue skies. Its [sic] hard to imagine a more majestic setting. . . . You will . . . spend 4/5 days accompanying IUCN and local Village Wildlife Guides on their monitoring of wildlife in this conservation area. Local community awareness for conservation is constantly being raised—their rich environment is their biggest asset when managed locally and sustainably. Since the completion of an ecotourism survey report in 1996, IUCN has been working with the Hushe community to raise awareness, targeting both locals and visitors, about the environmental impacts associated with unregulated tourism. Your participation in this programme will practically and financially help to support the local environmental and community based efforts mentioned. (Discovery Initiatives n.d.)

Thus, a segment of the village that has used a long-standing engagement with tourist interests to acquire influence in the village has come to adopt the terms of the conservation debate and to "present themselves and their interests in terms that are recognized as legitimate" in a wider public discourse of the environment (Carrier, introduction to this volume), terms that have increasing ramifications for the fortunes of the village. Not all villagers share these views of the village's surroundings or its future, but they too have been forced to deal with the terms of debate imposed by external institutions like IUCN. They also have to contend with the mechanisms through which these terms are reproduced in new institutions within the village. The village school is a classic example of a site where values are transformed, and institutions that support particular environmental worldviews have not missed this opportunity to propagate a "new" understanding of environment. Backed by a broad institutional focus on environmental education by IUCN, regional education officials and village leaders have introduced a program of environmental education in the village school, which was itself financed by an American NGO using funds generated largely from travelers who had visited the area.

To some extent, this talking the conservation talk is strategic, an effort by those doing the talking to get the most that they can out of the project. It is, of course, difficult to know just how much this reflects strategic concerns, both financial gain and the status acquired by being able to converse effectively with political elites and NGO representatives in the main market towns. The talk of conservation and biodiversity is restricted to a very few people in Hushe. Indeed, it would be surprising if it were widespread, for the message delivered to Hushe, as opposed to that presented to funding agencies and published in project documents, is a simple one: ibex are worth money, and money can be used to acquire the stuff of development. Ironically, this reconceptualization of ibex as a route to development retains the significance of ibex to community well-being that I described earlier. But it is in the mediating role played by cash and the hope of development that a change in meaning, and a reaction, lies. Rather than its older significance in reinforcing social relations or bringing "natural" properties to institutions of authority in the village, ibex has become the route to individual gain. So, rather than strengthening community processes, capitalizing nature in Hushe has individualizing effects.

One example of this is a diminished symbolic value attached to being a good hunter, and in the right to hunt. Historically, village members recognized a free right to hunt within village lands. This was a part of what it was to be a village member and, as I have already described, important in a variety of symbolic ways. Wildlife on community commons was open to community members, subject to household need, the ability to acquire a weapon, and the ability to go hunting in the face of labor constraints or other communal responsibilities. Alternatively, the distribution of capital, as it flows from the proceeds of trophy hunting licenses, uses new conservationist values to curtail that right. It also makes resistance more difficult because of the modifications in the meaning of wildlife and the attendant alterations in village social relations. Indeed, it is in this way that state subjectivities penetrate the village. The subsistence hunter, for example, is no longer a criminal only in the eyes of the state, but also in the eyes of some of his neighbors, who most stand to gain from trophy hunting. As one village man said to me, "Now whenever I leave the village at an odd time or with a firearm, people suspect that I am going hunting." For those people, his hunting is now an act of theft against "the community" and, of course, against capital—the capital of the foreign hunter who will pay to kill the animal that has been "poached." This is one example of how the intervention of international conservation NGOs, in the act of redefining wildlife, redefines nature-society relations by redefining wildlife as property and increases the legitimacy of global trophy hunters. Although they are interested in little more than using money to purchase a right to hunt that they cannot gain through other means (such as village membership), when they buy the right to kill they are, within the terms of the discourse of global ecology, protecting global property. This is a local manifestation of the way that discourses of globalism deterritorialize local property and property rights, and reterritorialize them in global terms in the context of the neoliberal demand that achieving "development" requires enforcing the power of capital to gain access to property.

This process of de- and reterritorialization relies on mechanisms that allow the hunter access to wildlife in "remote" places of the world, while restricting local access to those same resources. And those mechanisms exist in the brokerage role that international conservation NGOs play in translating and transmitting the knowledge involved in the production of a discourse of global ecology. This brokerage role is facilitated by agreements with national governments and local communities, but it is also facilitated by the ontological foundation of "global ecology." It would be difficult, for example, to legitimate international sport trophy hunting *without* the existence of a "global commons" and the "biodiversity" that resides within it. Nor could it be maintained without the representation of an incapable local population, who lack the knowledge, skills, and inclination to manage that biodiversity (see Butz 1999). This is what allows foreign hunters to claim to be struggling against the rapacious tendencies of local villagers who are taking advantage of a common resource. Leaving the responsibility of "wildlife management" to locals, they claim, will lead to extinction. International environmental organizations concur. Local residents are exploiters who need to be curtailed in their killing of wildlife, and one way to achieve this goal and gain access to local hunting grounds is to reconfigure wildlife not as local property but as global property, as a resource that everyone in the world has a duty to protect. If wildlife can be identified as a global resource, the moral claim can be made that it should be cared for and protected in the interests of a global citizenry, and within this discourse the subsistence value of game for individual households, or its symbolic and instrumental value for "community," vanishes from view.

Conclusion

I have described two stories. One is of a community where practice is an expression of an understanding of "nature" developed through successive and competing ideologies over a period of 2,000 years. The lesson of this story, not a new one by any means, is that "nature" is emergent, always coming into being through processes of ideological and material domination. The outcome is a set of beliefs and practices in which people appear not to have completely forsaken earlier beliefs, but accommodated elements of introduced ideologies that can be seen to work to people's cognitive or material advantage. Accepting new ideologies entails an alteration of practice, as it reframes the context within that people understand their surroundings and subsequently act on them, surroundings that include "objective nature" (Serre 1990).

The other story is of an international conservation agency operating in northern Pakistan that has an understanding of nature that is also generated historically, but within different ideological contexts. This agency is actively seeking to change ecological practice in the area to achieve an outcome that accords with its understanding of "nature" and its surroundings. Here, however, the understandings are generated not through direct interaction with a specific environment, but through the agency's position as a center of accumulation, collecting information from a diversity of contexts around the world and shaping a new ideological context for itself, the context of "global ecology." To achieve its aims it needs to mobilize political, social, and economic support. It needs to appeal to, and be able to take advantage of, other ideological formations. In the case that I have described here, the mechanism for the alteration of practice in Hushe relies on a combination of ideologies of science and the market. It also relies heavily on, and perhaps cynically takes advantage of, the success of ideologies of development that have, over the past twenty years, framed the expression of desire and expectation of many within Hushe.

In telling these stories, my point has been to demonstrate the emergent properties of nature, created as they are through processes of domination. These processes have particular and historically contingent outcomes. In Hushe, for example, "nature" is coming into being through the ideological domination exercised by a particular variety of development grounded in the mechanisms of the market and its agents, which include not only development agency workers, but also villagers who have acquired the language of development and incorporated it as an element of their identity. This process has had specific results: villagers have been forbidden to hunt, foreigners have hunted in the village, and social relations within the village and between neighboring villages have become strained. This new "nature" will be years in the making, just as it has already been centuries in the making. But the message is clear. Just as Gesar, symbolic savior of humanity born of an ibex, marked a connection between nature and humanity, influenced practice, and was symbolically and materially inscribed on the landscape, so market-based development is now born of the ibex, is represented as the new savior of humanity, and is leaving its mark on the landscape by shaping how people understand their surroundings. This equation is, of course, too simple, but it does mark a contest that is now occurring within the contact zone of environmental politics in northern Pakistan, where new ideologies of nature are being accommodated and challenged. This is a zone where power takes advantage of inequality to achieve dominance. It is a zone where things are happening that we ought to attend to if we are to understand how people's understandings of their surroundings are shaped, how their practices derive from that understanding, how ideologies of nature are flowing from new centers of accumulation and relying on new practices of domination to achieve particular ends.

In the case that I have described, the authority of science vested in transnational institutions and the contemporary significance of ecology embody power. The combined operation of these interests is not simply a form of innocuous intervention. Rather, it can be seen as a new form of governance that has accompanied the rise of environmentalism. Luke (1999, 122) has referred to this as green governmentality, which arises when "the environment, particularly the goals of its protection, has become a key theme of many political operations, economic interventions and ideological campaigns to raise public standards of collective morality, and personal responsibility." This form of green governmentality, however, relies on a discourse that "tells us that today's allegedly unsustainable environments need to be disassembled, recombined and subjected to the disciplinary designs of expert management." The example I have presented is just one case among many where assertions of unsustainability and a discourse of global ecology are used as devices to enter a community in order to apply expert designs to a local environment. For this to occur, however, existing forms of environmental practice and understandings must be constructed as ineffective; old modes of domination must be replaced; new instrumental rationalities need to be put in place. In Hushe, trophy hunting serves as Max Weber's "booty," through which the realization of nature as capital acts as a means to extend the reach of a Western scientific rationale for environmental management into local spaces, resulting in the creation of translocal ecologies.

It is still too early to see what kinds of nature will emerge. As I pointed out previously, the application of new frames of meaning has been going on in Hushe for centuries, and the outcome of the exercise of power has always been conflicted and dynamic. What is certain is that the structuring terms of a discourse of global ecology and the transnational, governmental, and capitalist institutions that produce and deploy it are becoming more pervasive in their attempts to redefine nature, property, and space in ways that mediate and attempt to universalize understandings of nature.

Notes

1. While main market towns like Khapalu and Skardu have been under the influence of imported clerics for some time, villages have historically been served by mullahs from their own community. These men, raised in a situation where seemingly contradictory belief systems were accommodated, aided in that accommodation. However, as villages become increasingly linked to main market centers, and as religious NGOs from the Middle East build mosques in villages, accommodation seems to be in decline. Increasingly, village mullahs are not from the region, or are adjusting their practice to accord with the emergence of a nonlocal religious elite in the region.

2. This is the modern form of the ideological representations of people and place produced during the British control of Kashmir, when "nature" was also contested and when the trope of the "rapacious native" was used to legitimate the enclosure of space in the interest of conservation.

3. Letters from foreign hunters that I have seen in Hushe, and stories told by their Hushe guides, reveal these forms of identification. They also suggest that hunters tend to keep in touch with villagers more than the conservation agents responsible for implementing the project.

References

Adger, W. N., et al. 2001. Advancing a political ecology of global environmental discourses. *Development and Change* 32: 682–715.

Agrawal, A., and C. C. Gibson. 1999. Enchantment and disenchantment: The role of community in natural resource conservation. *World Development* 27: 629–49.

Ahmed, J., and S. Hussain. 1998. Community-based natural resource management in northern Pakistan. Presented at the International Workshop on Community-Based Natural Resource Management, Washington, D.C. www.worldbank.org/wbi/conatrem/Pakistan-Paper.htm.

Bell, B. G., ed. 1991. *Proceedings of the international workshop on the management planning of Khunjerab National Park June 7–16, 1989.* Washington, D.C.: U.S. National Park Service, Office of International Affairs.

Bramwell, A. 1989. *Ecology in the twentieth century: A history.* New Haven, Conn.: Yale University Press.

Breman, J. 1989. *The shattered image: Construction and deconstruction of the village in colonial Asia.* Dordrecht: Foris Publications.

Butz, D. 1999. Orientalist representations of resource use in Shimshal, Pakistan, and their extra-discursive effects. In *Karakoram-HinduKush-Himalaya: Dynamics of change,* ed. I. Stellrecht, 357–86. Cologne: Rudiger Koppe.

CITES (Convention on International Trade in Endangered Species of Wild Fauna and Flora). 1997. *Resolution of the conference of the parties.* Tenth meeting of the Conference of the Parties, Harare, Zimbabwe.

Cooper, D. 1998. *Governing out of order: Space, law and the politics of belonging.* London: Rivers Oram Press.

Corn, M. L., and S. R. Fletcher. 1997. *African elephant issues: CITES and CAMPFIRE.* (Congressional Research Service report for Congress.) Washington, D.C.: The Committee for the National Institute for the Environment.

David-Neel, A., and Lama Yongden. 1933. *The superhuman life of Gesar of Ling; the legendary Tibetan hero, as sung by the bards of his country.* London: Rider and Co.

Davis, M. 1998. *Ecology of fear: Los Angeles and the imagination of disaster.* New York: Vintage.

Discovery Initiatives. n.d. Pakistan-Northwest Frontier Province. (Ecotourism advertisement.) www.ecotour.org/destin/places/DISCOV3.HTM.

Escobar, A. 1994. *Encountering development: The making and unmaking of the Third World.* Princeton, N.J.: Princeton University Press.

———. 1997. Cultural politics and biological diversity: State, capital and social movements in the Pacific coast of Columbia. In *The politics of culture in the shadow of capital,* ed. D. Lloyd and L. Lowe, 201–26. New York: Routledge.

Flitner, M. 1999. Biodiversity: Of local commons and global commodities. In *Privatizing nature: Political struggles for the global commons,* ed. M. Goldman, 144–66. New Brunswick, N.J.: Rutgers University Press.

Galpin, R. 1999. Hunting the rare ibex. *Living on earth,* National Public Radio, 9 April. Transcript: www.loe.org/archives/000409.htm# feature2.

Gibson, C. C. 1999. *Politicians and poachers: The political economy of wildlife policy in Africa.* Cambridge: Cambridge University Press.

Goldman, M. 1999. Inventing the commons: Theories and practices of the "commons" professional. In *Privatizing nature: Political struggles for the global commons,* ed. M. Goldman, 20–53. New Brunswick, N.J.: Rutgers University Press.

Goodwin, P. 1998. "Hired hands" or "local voices": Understandings and experience of local participation in conservation. *Transactions of the Institute of British Geographers* 23: 481–99.

Government of Pakistan. n.d. *Maintaining biodiversity in Pakistan with rural community development: PCII.* Islamabad: Environment and Urban Affairs Division.

Government of Pakistan, and IUCN–The World Conservation Union. 1992. *The Pakistan national conservation strategy: Where we are, where we should be and how to get there.* Islamabad: Environment and Urban Affairs Division.

Gupta, A. 1999. *Postcolonial developments: Agriculture in the making of modern India.* Durham, N.C.: Duke University Press.

Hough, L. 1994. Institutional constraints to the integration of conservation and development: A case study from Madagascar. *Society and Natural Resources* 7: 119–24.

Jamison, A. 1996. The shaping of the global environmental agenda: The role of nongovernmental organisations. In *Risk, environment and modernity: Towards a new ecology,* ed. S. Lash, B. Szerszynski, and B. Wynne, 224–45. London: Sage.

Knudsen, J. A. 1995. State intervention and community protest: Nature conservation in Hunza, Northern Pakistan. In *Asian perceptions of nature: A critical approach*, ed. O. Bruun and A. Kalland, 103–25. Richmond, Surrey: Curzon Press.

———. 1999. Conservation and controversy in the Karakoram: Khunjerab National Park, Pakistan. *Journal of Political Ecology* 6: 1–30.

Latour, B. 1999. *Pandora's hope: Essays on the reality of science studies.* Cambridge, Mass.: Harvard University Press.

Luke, T. W. 1999. Environmentality as green governmentality. In *Discourses of the environment*, ed. E. Darier, 121–52. Oxford: Blackwell Publishers.

MacDonald, K. I. 1995. The mediation of risk: Ecology, society, and authority in a Karakoram mountain community. Ph.D. dissertation, Department of Geography, University of Waterloo.

———. 1998. Rationality, representation and the risk mediating characteristics of a Karakoram mountain farming system. *Human Ecology* 26: 287–322.

———. 2001. Where the wild things are: Capitalized nature and the cultural politics of "community" in northern Pakistan. Presented at the annual meeting of the American Anthropological Association, Washington, D.C. Available from the author.

———. In press. Of "coolies" and "sahibs": "Exploration", adventure travel and the place colonization of pre-partition Baltistan. In *North Pakistan: Karakoram conquered*, ed. N. J. R. Allan. New York: Oxford University Press.

MacDonald, K. I., and D. Butz. 1998. Investigating portering relations as a locus for transcultural interaction in the Karakoram region of northern Pakistan. *Mountain Research and Development* 18: 333–43.

Mock, J. 1995. Objects of desire in the Northern Areas. *Himal* 8: 8–10.

———. Forthcoming. Mountain protected areas in northern Pakistan: The case of the national parks. In *Proceedings of the third international Hindukush cultural conference*, ed. E. Bashir. Karachi: Oxford University Press.

Mock, J., and K. O'Neill. 1996. *Survey on ecotourism potential in the biodiversity project area.* Islamabad: The World Conservation Union (IUCN).

Neumann, R. P. 1995. Local challenges to global agendas: Conservation, economic liberalization and the pastoralists' rights movement in Tanzania. *Antipode* 27: 363–82.

———. 1996. Dukes, earls, and ersatz edens: Aristocratic nature preservationists in colonial Africa. *Environment and Planning D: Society and Space* 14: 79–98.

Pratt, M. L. 1992. *Imperial eyes: Travel writing and transculturation.* London: Routledge.

Rosen, M. 1991. Coming to terms with the field: Understanding and doing organizational ethnography. *Journal of Management Studies* 28: 1–24.

Schaller, G. 1979. *Stones of silence: Journeys in the Himalaya.* New York: Bantam Books.

Schroeder, R. A. 1999. Geographies of environmental intervention in Africa. *Progress in Human Geography* 23: 359–78.

Serre, M. 1990. *Vers un contrat naturel.* Paris: François Bourin.

Smith, D. E. 1999. *Writing the social: Critique, theory and investigations.* Toronto: University of Toronto Press.

Takacs, D. 1996. *The idea of biodiversity: Philosophies of paradise.* Baltimore: Johns Hopkins University Press.

Taylor, P. J., and F. H. Buttel. 1992. How do we know we have global environmental problems: Science and the globalization of environmental discourse. *Geoforum* 23: 404–16.

Velle, K. 1998. *High altitude integrated resource management.* Oslo: Aga Khan Rural Support Program; Agricultural University of Norway.

Wegge, P. 1989. Khunjerab National Park in Pakistan: A case study of constraints to proper conservation management. In *Proceedings of conservation of mammals in developing countries,* ed. P. Wegge and J. Thornback, 57–64 (Fifth Theriological Congress, Rome). Nor-Agric Occasional Papers, Series C, 11. Oslo: Agricultural University of Norway.

Whiteman, P. T. S. 1988. Mountain agronomy in Ethiopia, Nepal and Pakistan. In *Human impacts on mountains,* ed. N. J. R. Allan, G. W. Knapp, and C. Stadel, 57–82. Totowa, N.J.: Rowman & Littlefield.

World Bank. 1990. *The Aga Khan rural support program in Pakistan: A second interim evaluation.* Washington, D.C.: Operations Evaluation Department, World Bank.

Getting Engaged: Pollution, Toxic Illness, and Discursive Shift in a Tokyo Community

4

PETER WYNN KIRBY

ONTEMPORARY JAPAN resonates with interest for environmental anthropologists primarily due to tectonic friction between two massive elements there: on the one hand, Japan's fixation with "Japanese nature," perhaps best metonymically represented by bonsai trees and manicured traditional-style gardens; and on the other hand, the undeniable hyperurbanization, hyperdevelopment, and pollution of much of postwar Japanese society. While Japan, by and large, imagines itself as existing in harmony with "nature," this nation's postwar "economic miracle" has also brought environmental debacle to numerous Japanese communities, and pollutant architectures of consumption and production have given toxic waste a place of prominence in the lives of a not inconsiderable number of Japanese. It is hardly surprising, given these circumstances, that the threat and reality of toxic pollution began to transform the ways that Japanese construct and articulate environmental knowledge.

This chapter explores the tension between prevalent Japanese natural-cultural imaginings and this society's environmental perplexities by analyzing local reactions to extreme toxic illness and ecological defilement in one of my ethnographic field sites in western Tokyo. Specifically, it analyzes the transformation of environmental engagement there and scrutinizes how urbanites exposed to the ravages of toxic damage reinterpreted their surroundings, converting often traumatic personal experience into more generalized, abstract, even clinical terms in the course of community activism. Romanticized, nostalgic evocations of Japanese nature were an early casualty of the advent of toxic symptoms in the community; those afflicted with what came to be known as "Azuma disease" were less apt to embrace notions of Japanese nature and invocations of cozy traditional and inclusive community values of the sort familiar to Japanese urban and rural communities. Yet the appeal of Western-influenced global environmentalist discourse and the obvious need of protesters to "prove" the existence of toxins in their community led to a marked shift from embodied particularity to discursive abstraction in the way that protesters articulated their plight.

In this chapter, I explore some of the complexities of urban life in Japan by demonstrating how toxic illness transformed the enduring detachment of some urban denizens into intense, embodied engagement with their surroundings. Below, I first delve into some theoretical approaches to engagement. I then launch into detailed narratives of toxic suffering in the Tokyo field site, mapping residents' reactions to the scourge of toxic waste in their homes and families. In doing so, I in turn address the extent to which protesters' attachments to technoscience and global environmentalism filled something of a discursive void in the relative absence of the appeal of cultural constructions of nature among the victims of toxic illness.[1]

"Environments" and Engagement

The world presents few, if any, unambiguous facts to anthropologists, and our material surroundings are hardly an exception. Human environs consist of interpenetrating domains whose blurred boundaries and contested historical and political topographies consistently defy easy definitions or consensus. Furthermore, "environment" has become a term brimming with political overtones. The rise and appeal of translocal and transnational environmental causes in recent decades have only raised the political stakes surrounding definitions of "environment" and the terms of its salvation. This conceptual murk nevertheless emphasizes the complexity of these questions and their importance to anthropologists.

The troubled lexicography of anthropologists and others on this topic reflects the difficulties of speaking clearly about the world around us. As comprehensively explored in the introduction to this volume as well as elsewhere (e.g., Kirby 2001, ch. 1, 2), social action occurs in settings that may, to disparate actors, be termed "nature," "environment," "landscape," "architecture," "city," and so on, and the mere choice of terms can resonate with social and political nuance. This perspectival fluidity of our surroundings is, in a sense, an inherent characteristic of what Tim Ingold (2001) calls "inhabiting the land" itself: "place" changes with perspective and position and history, and life is more a process of moving *around*, *toward*, and *between* places than an existence *in* any particular place. Indeed, the abstract, Cartesian notion of "space" belies the constantly dissolving horizons, the profusion of surfaces, and the flowing habituation of lived experience that transpires through action.

The study of human relations with surroundings has produced an important and varied body of work that deserves brief comment here. In response to the long-standing Western bifurcation of experience into Mind and Body, and the clear priority of the former over the latter (e.g., Descartes 1992), philosophers began to aver in the 1920s that our experience of the world is dominated by phenomenological immersion in our surroundings, repositioning bodily perception at the forefront of life (Merleau-Ponty 1995; cf. Leder 1990). This focus on the body was eventually seized upon and reinterpreted in the antiocularcentrist writings of the Situationists (e.g., Debord 1983), and important perspectives on bodies in social spaces later surfaced in both Foucault's (1991) writings on discipline and Bourdieu's (1977) work on practice. But these two latter writers, for example, produced somatic theories that remain peculiarly disembodied (cf. Turner 1994). And phenomenologists' emphasis on the lived body was only fully to reenter the purview of the human sciences when "embodiment" engulfed anthropology and much of the rest of academia in the 1990s. Much of this work, of wildly uneven quality, spiraled off into writings on anything and everything related even distantly to bodies. (A good example of robust embodiment scholarship would be the work of Csordas, e.g., 1993, 1994.) But the interrelation of bodies and social surroundings has surfaced in solid work, often focussing on the interplay between language, culture, and bodies in social spaces (e.g., Pandolfo 1989).

Ingold's work on human-environment relations (Ingold 1992, 1995, 1996) chooses a different tack, rigorously exploring the liaison of humans and "the land" and amassing important critiques of Western and anthropological approaches to the study of "nature," "culture," and "environment." Due to the fact that his work has been relatively underexamined with reference to social environments, and particularly due to its important points of correspondence with my analyses of urban Japanese environmental consciousness, I delve into his engrossing work here in relatively greater detail. In contrast to what he calls the "building perspective" (Ingold 1995, 58, 66; Ingold 1989), which along with most Western scholarship posits "an imagined *separation* between the perceiver and the world, such that the perceiver has to reconstruct the world, in the mind, prior to any meaningful engagement with it" (Ingold 1995, 66), he emphasizes the salience of the "dwelling perspective," where "the forms people build, whether in the imagination or on the ground, arise within the current of their involved activity, in the specific relational contexts of their practical engagement with their surroundings" (1995, 76). Rather than positioning human relations with their surroundings as the actions of "disembodied intellect[s] moving in the subjective space delimited by the puzzles [they] set out to solve" (1995, 76), Ingold stresses that humans are immersed in the world and their engagement with their surroundings stems from this immersion.

Though this model of positionality and relationality comes closer to conveying the embodied experiences of social actors' lives, Ingold's theorizations of engagement seem far less well suited to complex, developed urban settings so common in human settlements, as opposed to the hunter-gatherer contexts where he conducts his fieldwork.[2] Japanese urbanites were, admittedly, intensely concerned with their surroundings in culturally specific ways: conceptions of hygiene, notions of health and illness, attunement to weather, shifting boundaries of place and the home, mappings of the community—all these elements interspersed to shape the cultural "climate" of my Tokyo field sites. Yet "environmental engagement" in cities like Tokyo seems dominated by levels of varying *disengagement*. Tokyo's urbanscape typically ranges from extremes of constructed intervention—where overlaying strata of development such as thoroughfares chiseled through densely built areas, extensive subterranean passageways and arcades, and interconnected elevated promenades and other edifices obscure where "the ground" is—to residential areas where distinctions between the built environment and the natural milieu seem more straightforward. Denizens do become bodily and mentally habituated to this built ecology, a kind of "second nature,"[3] but they remain at a distance from less mediated ecologies.

Below, I briefly describe the striking extent to which Japanese urbanites participate in intensive discourses surrounding "Japanese nature" by giving a snapshot of community engagement in leisure activities in one Tokyo field site, Horinouchi. Then, having established a baseline of sorts, I detail the effects of toxic illness on urban engagement in the toxic protest site of Izawa in order to demonstrate the profound influence of toxic symptoms on experiences of urban life, and their articulation, in Japan.

Immersion and Detachment

"Nature" is a prevalent trope in contemporary Japanese society. Along with the pervasive notion that Japan is a homogeneous society with distinctive universal characteristics, such as groupism, and bearing a uniqueness that distinguishes it from all other nations, Japan resonates with the belief that the unique characteristics of Japanese culture derive from particularities of Japanese nature (Berque 1997*b*, 105; Dale 1986). The Japanese *idea* of the Japanese love of nature is one firmly embedded in a wide range of contexts; yet it seems particularly notable in its most teeming cities. Indeed, a deluge of media and advertising typically immerses urbanites in a "sea of signs" (Yatsuka 1990) that subtly and yet inexorably influences constructs of "the natural" in the relative absence of a corresponding ecological referent. One example among many others that helps demonstrate the peculiar resonance of natural-cultural symbols in Japanese society, in turn illustrating typical forms of urban engagement with surroundings there, is that of the cherry blossom.

Hanami (literally, "flower-viewing") seizes the nation every April or so. The focus of attention, particularly media attention, is the brief efflorescence of these trees; *mankai*, or full bloom, lasts only a short time, and due to idiosyncrasies of climate, contiguous areas may at times find themselves at different points in the strictly coded progression of the *sakura*. Television news programs broadcast nightly, with color-coded maps, on the *sakura* blossoms' progress across the nation. Print media join in as well, and advertisements featuring *sakura* bedeck metro trains, billboards, gigantic buildingside television screens, and other sites of hypersemiosis. The national bank Sakura, named after the cherry blossom, stepped up its commoditization of this natural-cultural symbol with huge advertisements of its own at a branch not far from Horinouchi (cf. Moeran and Skov 1997). In public parks and riverside walks all over Japan, groups of friends, colleagues, and family descend on stands of cherry trees in order to drink and eat at night under the illuminated, radiant blossoms. In Tokyo parks well-known for the quality and vistas of *sakura*, nearly every patch of available ground might be claimed by raucous seated groups of revelers in their stocking feet on blue plastic tarpaulins, and it is frequently impossible to walk except on crowded pathways. Some groups bring generators to run electric lights and portable stereos and karaoke machines.

During my fieldwork, Horinouchi commemorated the coming of the *sakura* with two *hanami* celebrations, the first at night and the next the following afternoon. Because the evening *hanami* was unseasonably cold (and therefore sparsely attended), I will focus on the daytime *hanami*. The *chōkai*, or neighborhood association, for the third district sponsored a barbecue in a grove of cherry trees near the river. Residents counted themselves lucky to have this resource available for the purpose; the stand of five mature *sakura* was located on land owned by the nearby Buddhist temple, and it was through the temple's largesse that use of the land was granted to the *chōkai* for the morning and afternoon. (A high chain-link fence ringed the grove to prevent rowdy interlopers from gaining access to this rare Elysium.) *Chōkai* members spent the evening and morning preparing for the few hundred residents who came to spread their plastic sheets and blankets under the cherry trees. The congregating Japanese consisted almost exclusively of families with children, elderly groups, and the (male) organizers; teenagers and unmarried young professionals tended to prefer natural-leisure sites like the trendier and more scenic and romantic Inogashira Park located a fair distance away.

In contrast to the noisier celebrations around Tokyo, roughly simultaneous with the arrival of *mankai*, Horinouchi's *hanami* was a muted affair. While adults were drinking beer, *shōchū*, and *sake*, emphasis was on relaxing in small groups and eating lunch. As with most excursions into the natural milieu in Japan, residents had their cameras out to commemorate the occasion. Though children wandered and played with (and sometimes nearly destroyed) the snow-white blossoms on low-lying branches, most residents engaged in *hana yori dango*. The phrase, used with more than a hint of self-irony, captures the often clear priority in Japan on social relations in nature rather than over the nature itself: literally "dumplings instead of flowers," the phrase *hana yori dango* winks at how Japanese will often tend to pay more attention to the social exchanges taking place under the trees (metonymically encapsulated in the *dango*, grilled dumplings, common at *hanami* among the clustered groups) than the blossoms that constitute the central aim of the gathering. Indeed, Japanese engagement with nature often resembled a person holding aloft two mirrors: one with which to regard the "nature" in question, and one for looking at *oneself* looking at nature.[4]

In the community of Izawa, which resembled Horinouchi before Izawa became riven by toxic controversies, residents participated in cherry blossom viewing just as avidly as the families described above. Yet the advent of toxic illness disrupted the lives of many in Izawa, irreversibly transforming their ability to "engage" in natural-cultural activities typical of Tokyo communities. Indeed, their conceptions of nature underwent a sea change, and this had wide ramifications for the protest against toxic pollution there and for how afflicted residents expressed their suffering.

A Punctured Calm

In the spring of 1996, Mrs. Shinoda felt as if she were going to die. For two months, she had been unable to sleep, save fitfully. Her eyes burned. She had severe skin rashes and a hacking cough. And she suffered from a migraine that made her head feel as if it would split open like a melon. To make matters worse, in recent days her breathing had become labored and she had shooting pains down her leg. It became all but impossible for her to walk. One day, it got to be too much and she called an ambulance to take her to the hospital. Wincing, she recollects this agonizing period before she was forced to call for help:

> Back then, the air was truly awful. You couldn't believe it. . . . At first, we would go outside and think "That's strange, the air seems bad, doesn't it" (okashīnā, okashīnā, kūki ga warui ja nai kashira). But then it just got worse. . . . I couldn't eat, I couldn't drink the water, I couldn't take a bath, I couldn't sleep a wink. . . . I would cough and the phlegm (tan) that came up smelled terrible. I couldn't believe that something that smelled so bad could come out of my own body.
>
> Around that time, I went out to visit my daughters, and [where they lived] the food tasted good, the water tasted good, the air was good. But when I got back home, everything was just the same, and my condition kept getting worse (chōshi ga waruku natteta).

She was eventually diagnosed with blood poisoning (*haiketsushō*) and extreme respiratory problems, in addition to her other complaints.

Over the next couple of months, it began to dawn on Mrs. Shinoda and others in her community that their failing health might not be a coincidence. The fact that they shared common symptoms was the first clue: burning eyes, respiratory problems, skin outbreaks, headaches, lack of taste, acutely swollen lymph nodes, and so on.[5] Originally through informal personal networks, and by virtue of an extended discourse among the community that began largely through gossip and hearsay, the most seriously afflicted of the *higaisha* (or "victims," who constituted roughly 10 percent of the community's population) began to meet up and discuss their health problems. Though the exact cause of the illness was at first a mystery, residents began framing their discourse about the disease in terms of toxic chemical substances (*kagaku bushitsu*) and environmental hormones (*kankyō horumon*), partly due to growing informal evidence that a waste facility, newly constructed in the center of the community, was implicated in their afflictions.[6] By July of 1996, embodied engagement with a changed milieu had transformed into political engagement: these locals organized into a formal protest group named the Group to End Azuma Disease (*Azuma-byō wo Nakusu-kai*, hereafter designated by the English acronym GEAD), an entity that began to lobby the ward and metropolitan governments to close down the reviled waste facility in question.[7] But before exploring important themes embedded in the articulations and tactics of the Izawa protesters, and the discursive shift their articulations eventually underwent, I air residents' descriptions of their symptoms below in order to help convey the magnitude of the life transformations with which they were confronted, as well as the intensely personal nature of these complaints outside activist fora.

Responses to the GEAD questionnaire[8] span from the mundane to the touching: for example, a woman might rather superficially complain of the brownish film covering her white balcony railing, then later reveal that "[e]ver since I stopped hanging my laundry outside to dry, my skin condition has disappeared" (GEAD Study 1998, no. 160). Most of the accounts are poignant and somehow humble; through sheer weight of numbers, responses impress upon the reader that this is a widespread phenomenon that has disrupted many lives. One woman in her twenties, who had recently moved to the area, relates the devastation of her condition: "I just had a miscarriage. Lately, I've increasingly been having unexplained bodily illness. Lack of energy, weariness, dullness (*darusa*), but even when I get a [medical] examination, there's no abnormality" (GEAD Study 1998, no. 18). Another woman of the same age states, "[e]ver since I left the family house and moved here by myself, my eyes have become itchy, I get constipated, and my back and shoulders have stiffened up severely. My body feels dull and weary (*darui*) and my energy doesn't rise (*okinai*)" (GEAD Study 1998, no. 166). A woman in her thirties confesses: "In the past I've been prone to terrible allergies . . . during the summertime. But this year, worse than any time before, it's been so severe that

I can't sleep at night. . . . I have two children, ages 11 and 2, and both of them have slowly started becoming allergy-prone as well (nose and skin). I'm very worried, thinking that my children will inhale things that are even worse in the future" (GEAD Study 1998, no. 91). A woman of approximately the same age has this to say: "Since I moved here (it might just be the fault of aging), my dependence on headache medicine and other medicine has increased sharply. Since I have a small child and I am thinking about having another, I'm hoping we can live in an environment where we'll feel at ease (*anshin shite kuraseru kankyō*)" (GEAD Study 1998, no. 216).

Contrary to the criticisms of detractors in the community (those who did not suffer symptoms, and who possibly had ulterior motives in discrediting the claims of the afflicted), the epidemic was not limited to women—in the critics' minds, hypochondriac women. For instance, a man in his twenties who had moved to the area recently reports: "From the beginning, I've had a weak stomach, but [these days] I've got terrible diarrhea. I often catch colds. There have been times when I've had a cough for two months. [Now] I always suffer from diarrhea and a throat that feels out of sorts (*fukaikan*). . . . Since I work at home all day long, I'm very worried about this" (GEAD Study 1998, no. 70). A man in his thirties, who had lived in the area only two years, reports these symptoms: "I tire easily, and I've become prone to lose my temper. I've lost eight kilos. . . . I've also noticed that the trees in front of the facility's ventilation tower are withering" (GEAD Study 1998, no. 142). A man in his sixties who had lived in the area for thirty-five years, for his part, has this to say: "This year, it has become easier for me to catch cold, and moreover, it has got harder to get better. In particular, when I get a cough, it becomes extremely painful and hard. This August, I got sick three times. . . . In the morning when I open the window, a strange, bad smell comes from outside" (GEAD Study 1998, no. 141). Hundreds of residents within 500 meters of the facility reported grave symptoms along the lines of these responses.

The gradual, yet dramatic, realization among Izawa residents that there existed a toxic problem in their midst was, it should by now be obvious, a deeply affective one. Once the affliction began to take its toll, people in the community found it very difficult to separate their feelings of ill health from their attitudes toward Izawa as a whole. And over time the toxic defilement and the facility that was its root became closely wedded in the protesters' minds with the community itself. Echoing Watsuji's (1940, [1935] 1975) notion of "betweenness," Japanese informants viewed Tokyo as comprised of sites of intensive relationality. Between the familiarity of a person's home or community and the familiarity of his or her place of work can exist an indeterminate, uncontextualized liminal zone of "colourless indifference" (Berque 1997a, 90–95) where a lack of relations led to a lack of emotional engagement. The flip side of this social coin is that, when one's community is afflicted by this pollution, the relational mapping and emotional ties of the area are changed utterly. That is to say, if toxic pollution attacks local health, disrupts patterns of relations and movement, and pits neighbor against neighbor in disagreement over the logic and politics of activism versus consensus, then a community can begin to lose the warmth, security, and sociality that Japanese often associate with home.

Such was the case in Izawa. Toxic damage transformed the topography of the community irrevocably for those affected by Azuma disease. In their minds, their suffering became equated with the waste facility's operations, the full toxic effects of which still remained unknown. Because of their distrust of the facility, they closed their windows even in summer, when in the past they would have relished the evening breeze. They tended to hang their laundry inside to dry as an attempt to limit toxic exposure of their clothes. (Japanese rarely use dryers for their clothes and linens, mostly due to the fact that sunlight is believed to have an extremely healthful effect.) And with the waste facility located directly in the middle of their community, the routes of walks they would have taken in the past now diverged; they might forgo a nightly constitutional around that part of the neighborhood, or choose a lengthy detour around the area to visit a friend's home. If, as Lynch (1960) suggests, the spatial experience of living in a community can be understood through the landmarks by which people choose to orient their (practical and mnemonic) navigations, then the waste facility itself became a negative landmark, a site to be avoided, and yet which loomed in the mind as an undesirable specter of insalubrity.

But though the source of the problem could, according to the facility's opponents, be specified, the effects of the problem, for residents, diffused throughout the area. For with the residents who actually felt the symptoms of toxic pollution, anywhere within a reasonable distance led to direct deterioration of their condition (the most often cited range was a half-kilometer radius, but this was also, perhaps not coincidentally, the range that the GEAD survey employed). Early on, those with acute cases (like Kōzō-san, a male retiree in the area) might wait to go outside until they thought the wind had changed direction, so as to decrease their exposure to the "smoke" (*kemuri*) coming from the facility.

This perception among the afflicted that the community itself was contaminated had an immediate and lasting effect on their participation in emblematically Japanese community activities, such as local cherry blossom viewing of the sort described above in nearby Horinouchi. And while disaffection with local community evocations of "Japanese nature" (and Japaneseness) was widespread among sufferers, this transformation took time and was closely intertwined with the developing protest against the waste facility and the state apparatus that operated the facility.

As toxic damage exacerbated afflicted residents' engagement with their surroundings, the need to "translate" the particulars of their plight, like those aired above, into political capital via activism led to a transformation in the way the afflicted represented their suffering. Below, I describe the facility and the Forest Park, delving into protesters' tactics and discursive shift with regard to the controversy.

Troubles with a "Trouble Facility"

First, a few words on the origins of the facility and its operations. The waste transfer facility was the result of a concerted Tokyo metropolitan effort to make the burgeoning waste problem more cost-effective and manageable. With the millions of tons of waste that the Tokyo area produces each year, waste is a serious issue that looms over government planning, if only because remaining landfill space in the middle of Tokyo Bay is swiftly diminishing, leaving Tokyo with few options for local disposal of waste. In spite of Japan's reputation as a global environmental villain, relative lack of space and resources back home have forced cities like Tokyo to enforce strict waste protocols: residents divide household trash into burnable (*moeru, kanen*) and unburnable (*moenai, funen*) categories, as well as into recyclables (or "resources," *shigen*) and bulky waste (*sodai gomi*). The state has, in recent years, attempted to limit the amount of burnable waste that finds its way into unburnable collections and channel this waste into incinerators, of which they are attempting to build more. Furthermore, one way to deal with unburnable waste more economically is to compress it with extreme force and then either deposit it in metropolitan landfill or, better yet, transport it out of the city, where distant rural communities charge by the truckload.

This, in a nutshell, explains the waste facility in Izawa. As a waste transfer facility, or *gomi chōkeisho*, the Izawa plant served as a relay station between the relatively small trucks that collect waste throughout the labyrinthine byways of neighborhood Tokyo and the much larger container trucks that take the waste to its final destination. The smaller trucks dump the waste into enormous rectangular compressors that violently pound the waste together before sliding the compacted mass into a container on the other side. These containers are, then, what is lifted onto waiting larger trucks to be whisked away beyond the city limits. Recyclables such as plastic bottles, glass containers, and metal cans are also sorted and taken away for processing.

The mystery of this facility, and source of the bitter controversy surrounding Azuma disease, is that there is no incineration of waste there despite the advent of symptoms of Azuma disease amongst some residents. That dioxins and other dangerous toxins are typically released into the atmosphere through the incineration of plastics has long been averred in scientific studies (more on the claims of technoscience below). The members of the GEAD, by contrast, claim that, *somehow*, toxins are released through the extremely forceful compression of plastics deep within the bowels of the Izawa waste facility. GEAD members reason that, as the air leaving the facility through the ventilation tower was from the beginning treated only to filter odors rather than more dangerous substances, the alleged toxins have been discharged directly into the air and have blanketed the community. And as the facility is said to be the first of its kind in the world, the protesters go on to claim that science has not had a chance to verify the dangers of compressing plastic in order to protect such residents as themselves.

One complicating factor in their argument is that, in the protesters' lay calculus, not everyone responds to the toxins in the same manner. The GEAD claims that over 400 of the residents living within 500 meters of the waste facility (or roughly 10 percent) had manifested aggravated symptoms common to Azuma disease since the facility became operational. Protesters explain this as the result of the vagaries of *kagaku-bushitsu kabinshō*, or chemical sensitivity. Some individuals, like Mrs. Shinoda, with a low tolerance fell prey to the alleged toxins almost immediately. Others carry on with their lives as though nothing had changed in their environment (though their health still suffers, according to the claims of GEAD protesters and environmental scientists, as a result of daily exposure). Most of the rest of the population, including the 400-odd residents afflicted with varying levels of Azuma disease, fall somewhere between these two extremes. Due to the vicissitudes of chemical sensitivity, then, a facility might have a grave effect on a fraction of the population while seeming relatively innocuous to the majority. Such was the case, protesters reasoned, in Izawa.

To be sure, theirs was a controversial claim, one that was at first mocked and then more systematically discredited by government officials since the protesters' campaign began. But even in cases where more conventional arguments prevail, toxic pollution and the illnesses that result from it are extremely difficult to prove to recalcitrant government officials: cause and effect are not nearly so wedded in the skeptical mind as in those of the victims of toxic pollution. Since most chemicals, even such lethal substances as dioxins, are statistically rather harmless in small amounts, the assessment of risk comes down to scientific analyses and shifting definitions, many of which are open to interpretation, influence, and downright sabotage (cf. Berglund 1998).[9]

The protesters arrayed a convincing amount of indirect evidence that goes a long way toward supporting their claim that the facility was unhealthy and that the Public Cleansing Bureau was behaving underhandedly both in its running of the facility and in its dealings with the public. This was not merely a compilation of data, but a conversion of personal, individual experiences into a more respectable, clinical format that was deemed to have a greater chance of success in promoting the protesters' cause; this translation process echoes that discussed in the introduction and several other contributions to this volume, and seems an important element of efficacious environmental activism broadly conceived. The study that the GEAD conducted on residents living within 500 meters of the facility (the product of written questionnaires) is filled with testimonials to a decline in health and an increase in the symptoms that have become associated with Azuma disease. The activist group did the best they could with the methodology to make the study "scientific": assigning random numbers to the respondents, preserving anonymity, and ranking participants with regard to the severity of their condition. The questionnaire and other GEAD materials, in addition, are filled with clinical medical terminology of the sort that helped imbue their efforts with biomedical legitimacy. Poignant personal accounts are leavened with respondents' answers to specific queries and then organized for maximum impact.

The other prong of the study was the atmospheric testing they requested from a Tokyo scientist who had first been commissioned by the Public Cleansing Bureau, Arasaki-sensei.[10] Arasaki-sensei, here representing the GEAD, sampled the air quality in over thirty sites around Tokyo; some of them were places where high levels might be expected, others were residential neighborhoods thought to be relatively free of such toxins. Arasaki-sensei's research determined exactly what the GEAD had believed from the beginning: the dioxin levels for the neighborhood in Izawa were dramatically higher than in the other residential neighborhoods tested, and far higher than in other sites tested in Tokyo. This was damning evidence, and most importantly, it had been compiled in technoscientific terms that would make the GEAD's case harder to refute out of hand.

The obvious need for the protesters to substantiate their claims in legitimate technoscientific terms led to a marked discursive shift in how protesters articulated their sufferings and depicted their surroundings. Contemporary Japanese society is, by and large, highly predisposed to respect scientific and mathematical information and methods. So these residents of Izawa were for the most part already operating in a discursive universe where scientific descriptions and statistical data yielded deference and approbation. But as members of the GEAD began to crave the raiment of legitimacy that would buttress their case against the waste facility, individuals such as Arasaki-sensei, for example, took on a kind of aura and celebrity that made their importance to the GEAD quite evident. Both before and after the formal studies undertaken by the GEAD, protesters and afflicted residents soon found that their complaints in the community bore far greater weight when peppered with scientific language and bolstered by reference to "hard" evidence. Most of the members became highly conversant with the figures and tables that constituted their study, and most knew at least passably well the points in the

Public Cleansing Bureau's study that could be considered gross manipulations of the otherwise impartial data. Of course, it practically takes a physicist like Arasaki-sensei explaining the data in person to understand some of the places where the Public Cleansing Bureau twisted the data in their reports, so most of this information came secondhand: there were individuals whose judgment had been deemed trustworthy, particularly those who had spoken out publicly against the actions of the Public Cleansing Bureau and the waste facility. And these individuals' voices carried a great deal of weight in shaping the convictions of the GEAD members.

In Japan there was simply no critique of the use of technoscience as the final arbiter in disputes surrounding Truth. Those who were adept at handling science (such as Arasaki-sensei, Mr. Yamada, and Mrs. Miyamoto to some extent, and others who chose a quieter, advisory role, such as local doctors) used technoscientific language and data with calm certainty; those who were less comfortable with science, but who swaddled themselves in its discursive raiment, came to view technoscientific evidence in an almost religious light, imbuing the data (and the practitioners) with a respect that bordered on blind reverence. Somewhat similarly to Berglund's informants (Berglund 1998), in Izawa among the residents there was a sense in which the polarization of "good" science versus "bad" science was symmetrical to that of "our" science versus "their" science. This distinction resonated with more than a little of the group identity and inside-outside distinctions that crop up often in Japanese organizations. But without a doubt, the conflict over the facility and the alleged toxic damage it produced played out as a battle between camps arrayed with the weapons of technoscientific knowledge. And the front lines of the contest lay in the Forest Park where the "trouble facility" (*meiwaku shisetsu*) was located. Below, I show how this (re)constructed natural domain became a locus of controversy not only over toxic pollution, but also over divergent views of what nature should be. And I delve into the ways in which the arguments invoked by different sides reverberated with discursive elements that help demonstrate the shifts protesters' claims underwent during the course of the conflict.

Conflicting Views of "Nature"

The Izawa Forest Park, euphemistically named after its transformation, had for decades been a rather dense stand of trees and undergrowth ensconcing a small agricultural facility. Residents in Izawa had often specifically chosen to live near this modest woodlands due to the extreme rarity of such sylvan spaces in the world's most populous conurbation (Cybriwsky 1998). And therefore, when the state had proposed to build a waste facility underneath the area, some residents were apprehensive that this verdant domain would be under threat. The state's assurances that the proposed facility was only to be a waste transfer station rather than an incinerator belching out smoke helped placate many members of the community; but the government's proposals to "improve" the woods with sculptured greenery, a sports ground, a recreation center, a playground, a stroll-through rock garden, and more extensive meadow space for cherry blossom viewing were what eventually sealed the deal for most residents. In their minds, the Forest Park plan would enhance the beauty of the area while contributing these substantial amenities to the community, and the waste facility, hidden underground, seemed a small price to pay. Yet "nature" here was not the thick, lush forestland and sometimes almost impenetrable *sasa*-grass underbrush of the Japanese hinterland.[11] Rather, the nature that government authorities chose (and which was warmly received by residents) was a zone of highly mediated nature, landscaped to accord with urban Japanese tastes.

When the last of the landscaping vehicles had rumbled away, a significant number of residents admitted that they had expected far fewer of the trees to be cut down. And they acknowledged that the forestlike feel of the woodlands had been changed, transforming not only the views out their windows, but also the character of much of the surrounding community. But the minority of residents who were more vocally upset by the extent of the damage to this erstwhile trove of verdure were far outnumbered by those who welcomed the abundant leisure facilities at the disposal of themselves and their families.

From most of the park, a nine-meter ventilation tower standing at the top of a small rise is the only visible sign of the four floors of the subterranean waste facility buried under Izawa Forest Park. The tower's rendering, somewhat reminiscent of the architecture of I. M. Pei and matching the two pyramidal skylights embedded nearby in the grass and hedges of the hillock, uses transparent plastic panels and an angular crown design to give these elements the veneer of high tech. At the same time, these protrusions also appear autonomous, as if they were not appendages of the facility but rather sculptural features of the park.

The entry to the facility from the street behind the Forest Park is obscured by trees and the ramp leading down into the facility lies well below the level of the hillock, itself ringed by hedges, thereby frustrating all but the most intrepid of observers. Trucks rumble in every few minutes, but the sound of their engines is muffled by this simulated natural insulation. Early on, this environmental veil of greenery and landscaping prevented the facility from seeming obtrusive to parkgoers. But when the *gomi chūkeisho* embarked fully on its waste operations, the resulting stench emanating from the Forest Park was sharp and pervasive, and in addition to presenting a local annoyance struck residents as being contrary to the idea of a green oasis of natural calm in the city.

Still, Japanese urbanites are well accustomed to ignoring the unseemly in the not infrequently crowded world around them, and those in the community who felt no concrete decline in health steeled themselves against any offense to their senses and sensibilities. The attraction of having a large recreational space, custom-tailored to prevalent Japanese ideals of tamed, artifice-laden conventions of the natural and boasting numerous leisure facilities over the previous avatar of the "Forest Park" was simply too irresistible to most residents. The irony of the fact that the vast majority of Izawa residents reveled in the new Forest Park's contrived natural spaces, while ignoring the detrimental effects that dioxins and other toxins were having on the health of members of the community, was not lost on GEAD members. For most of the protesters, community health was inseparable from that of the flora and fauna within the Forest Park. And riddled with the debilitating symptoms from which they suffered, leisurely immersion in falling cherry blossom petals in the middle of the same Forest Park that was churning out the toxins that had contaminated their bodies was simply out of the question.

The protesters painted the Forest Park itself as a sylvan sham whose function was to disguise the toxic effects of the waste facility on the community: they pointed to the fact that, early on, there was a considerable amount of dying and wilting foliage surrounding the facility until park groundskeepers, on the alleged strict orders of the Public Cleansing Bureau, began to cut it away. Mr. Kimura, a GEAD member in his forties who worked at the local primary school, put it this way: "You couldn't believe the poisons coming out of [the transfer facility]. Nature can bear a lot, but this kind of toxicity was too much. . . . People [here] could reject our pain, but could they ignore the dead leaves, the smell, the decline in birds and animals?" Typical of the GEAD's ecological sensitivity and technoscientific focus, protesters also complained that, once the Public Cleansing Bureau decided to install filters in the same ventilation system contaminating the park and the community, the bureau would not allow them to have the filters analyzed scientifically for the agents of toxic pollution. These and other matters led the protesters to view the claims of their adversaries in the Public Cleansing Bureau with an extremely jaundiced eye.

To hear the protesters tell it, the Forest Park was the scene of an ongoing battle to keep the park looking "healthy" and "natural" (my inquiries with park staff and other locals on this theme indicated that the above was somewhat the case, especially early on, but might have been exaggerated along the way). Whatever the true state of toxic degradation, the Forest Park was without doubt a public relations exercise in improving the image of the waste facility and in heightening the aura of the natural in the community. And in parallel with the protesters' campaign against the government with the weapons of "scientific" data and methods, they gathered a wide range of circumstantial evidence to lend credence to their central point.

In particular, protesters kept careful watch on the state of the flora of the Forest Park, eager for further ecological reflection of their own bodily suffering. They amassed and distributed photos—of consistently dead or dying foliage and even a dead cat found near the waste facility—that were widely viewed by those against the facility to constitute clear evidence of toxicity. They also tried to document the efforts of the waste facility to disguise this defilement of the park's ecology: they took photos over time of the same shrubs around the ventilation tower and other orifices of the waste facility, and tried to show how groundskeepers routinely attempted to "hide" this toxic damage to the greenery and the community.[12] Mirroring this concern with the park, protesters accumulated photographic evidence of the devastation of their bodies, and the mingling of proofs of ecological and somatic damage was telling. For example, one woman showed me numerous photographs of dying leaves and bushes in the park and then brought out photos of her and her family members' bodies with their swollen lymph nodes, swollen joints, acute skin rashes, discolorations, and so on. On that and other occasions, both she and others of the afflicted regularly mixed together references to body and ecology, and it was clear that the interlinkage of the root cause of their afflictions had translated into something of an affective blurring of their subjectivities. For not only was the Forest Park's "nature" a vital part of the community, but it was also visible to all in a way that protesters' bodies, often shut up in their homes or recovering far from Izawa, were frequently not.

In a related process, protesters began to display a more global consciousness in voicing concern over ecology and health that is, typically, less common in Japanese society than in, say, Europe or North America, where identification with abstract global causes is far more widespread.[13] Though there has been some rise in interest in environment in the Japanese media during the previous decade, GEAD protesters were very much on the leading edge of this gradual social shift. Not only did a marked change in bodily environmental engagement translate into earnest political engagement, but in choosing to phrase their suffering in the terms of the technoscientific discourse, and in searching for other regional, national, and international cases where the toxic damage with which they grappled had been discerned and handled, protesters became bathed in global environmentalist discourse as well. GEAD members, like Mrs. Shinoda and Mrs. Miyamoto, found themselves communicating their plight at environmental and scientific conferences in Tokyo, Osaka, and elsewhere in Japan; here, not only were they immersed in this discursive realm through participation in colloquia and symposia, but they came into lasting contact with a wide range of global environmentalists at these venues. Soon, they were using the Internet to exchange information on waste and toxins, communicating via their own set of e-mail lists, and even broadcasting their case, in specific terms, with a sophisticated website.

This kind of concern for the global came out in protesters' many references to what they perceived as the Forest Park's beleaguered ecology: for example, many GEAD members and others in the community spoke eloquently of the problem of "unsustainable" development and waste processing in developed areas, making reference to globalism in a myriad of ways yet frequently playing rhetorically off of the recycling slogan "gentle to the earth—protect [our] greenery" (*chikyū ni yasashī—midori wo mamoru*) that had become common there. Moreover, it came out as well in their discussion of wider environmental problems for which their plight had galvanized them. For instance, Mrs. Shinoda complained of increases of pollution in Tokyo, in Japan, and all over the world in railing against the causes of her suffering: "Think about all these factories, businesses, consumers, the cars on motorways. And all the waste, the plastic, all these electronic goods—we have to do something! Let's think about our children, let's think about the planet, let's think about the future. I'm just a grandmother, but this problem will last longer than I will!"

As protesters began to explain the world in terms of a nature in which humans should participate as partners rather than conquerors, they cast their eyes beyond the microcontext of the protest and its narrow goals in sparring with recalcitrant government officials to consider what their wider impact might be. And, in the process, their ways of representing the ecology and the community underwent conspicuous change. Mr. Kimura, briefly mentioned above, serves as a telling example. He worked as a playground monitor at the local primary school located near the waste facility. He decried Japanese urbanites' lack of engagement with the ecology; he claimed, furthermore, that "Japanese children think nature is dirty. . . . [They] don't understand how fragile nature can be." Amid the controversy surrounding toxic pollution in Izawa, Mr. Kimura used his link to the school to become a self-styled nature and ecology instructor to these children. Behind the school playground there were slimy concrete pools filled with algae and plants. In this unlikely setting, he carried on daily lessons on the micro-ecology there. Children would take plastic cups and nets and catch small animals and insects. Mr. Kimura, in turn, would identify the specimens, describing what they ate, how they survived, and how they fit in the larger ecosystem. The most important lesson of all, though, was the care with which these specimens had to be handled. In Mr. Kimura's outdoor classroom, what was taken out of these slimy pools and patches of dirt had to be returned unharmed. And Mr. Kimura's adolescent pupils tended to learn respect for their tiny companions, not to mention fascination, though with occasional destructive outbursts typical of young children the world over. This instruction in conceiving of, and speaking about, the world around them was a conscious attempt to transform the thinking of younger Japanese that could endure as an additional activist legacy in this community that had experienced the devastations of "unsustainable" policies. And it demonstrates as well the distance GEAD members, and others, have journeyed beyond the mediated, cherry-blossom-style interventions into nature that most Japanese urbanites experience.

Conclusion

What I have described in this chapter is a provocative case of emergent engagement with surroundings, through extreme embodied toxic illness, of erstwhile disengaged Japanese urbanites. It demonstrates how environmental engagement was converted into political engagement, and it depicts the discursive shift that protesters' articulations of their plight underwent as they translated highly personal experiences into the "legitimate" and more instrumental terms of the technoscientific discourse. This was, in addition, a shift from deeply socially embedded ideas of "Japanese nature" to the terms of global environmentalism, with important ramifications for how protesters came to describe their homes not as contained, particular zones of personal history and affect, but as components in the planet's wider ecology. This was of course closely related to the conditions of the protesters' health and their relations to the community where they had been ravaged by toxic defilement.

While Mr. Kimura chose, for his part, to stay on in the community to teach engagement and ecological consciousness to this new generation of young Japanese, many of his compatriots in the GEAD protest group were forced to leave Izawa entirely. Their debilitating toxic symptoms, not to mention the unpleasant associations of the place, made it impossible to continue living there. Some moved to areas ten or twelve miles away from Izawa, close enough to return to visit friends and fellow activists on a regular basis. Others, like Mrs. Miyamoto, chose to relocate far away to sparsely populated mountain areas, where they say they breathe cherished clean air and can continue their protest activities long-distance. But while rejection of their erstwhile home environs constitutes an extreme disengagement of sorts from the specific environment of Izawa, most of these self-exiles continue their political engagement by lobbying the local and metropolitan governments for change and by participating in environmental activities that seek to transform Japanese interventions in their ecology into more sustainable behavior. In becoming entangled in discourses of technoscience and global environmentalism that their cause led them toward, these Japanese urbanites learned to translate their bodily destabilization into a pursuit of environmental justice that continues to alienate them from some of their erstwhile neighbors, but knits them tightly together as a network of shared memory. And the balancing of particularism and abstraction binds these Izawa activists together in wider networks of agitators and sufferers, linked by the poignancy of individual narratives, and at the same time trussed in the threads of environmental activist discourse—in touch with the local, but in tune with the global.

Notes

1. These forms of engagement, and these patterns of translation from the particulars of personal experience to the abstract, bear important similarities to those described by James Carrier in his chapter in this collection.

2. Ingold's work also neglects the extensive power-vectors that radiate throughout social domains, which surface clearly in the highly charged protest setting of my Izawa field site, below, and are important in many of the chapters in this collection.

3. I use this phrase as the French commonly do, to refer to "the built environment" (cf. translator's note in Berque 1997a, 119).

4. Hoffman (1986, 19–20, 39) uses this image exclusively to describe the self-reflexivity of *tanka* poets in Japan, but it is applicable to wider relations with nature in Japan.

5. Based on interview findings and details in the study commissioned by those who had contracted Azuma disease in order to bring their case against the ward government. I will delve into some more specific descriptions of the condition below.

6. Cf. Kirby (2003) for the wider ramifications of toxic pollutants and their politicization in late-nineties Japan.

7. Due to conditions of anonymity agreed to prior to interviews with some informants, as well as related ethical concerns, I have opted to use a pseudonym for Azuma Ward, as well as other pseudonyms and biographical adjustments. While some of my informants were willing to "go on the record" with their comments, others definitely were not, and I tread with great caution here to avoid creating more of a burden than I already have through persistent fieldwork.

8. Since the initial onset of symptoms dates back several years for many of the afflicted, I will focus below on excerpts from residents' responses to the GEAD questionnaire to attempt to capture some of the immediacy of the local health crisis and the anxiety that an unknown threat can engender.

9. One important difference in Izawa was that toxic damage was experienced bodily by the afflicted, taking it beyond the level of language that Berglund describes in German activist circles. These Japanese protesters themselves had no doubt that they were suffering from the ravages of toxic pollution and illness; their task was to convince others, and this was to involve language a great deal, as I show below.

10. This physicist earlier took atmospheric measurements for the Public Cleansing Bureau's Izawa survey and found a very high level of dioxins and other toxins in the air at several points in the community while he was on the government payroll. He gave these and other data to the Public Cleansing Bureau, who then systematically warped the information in their official reports. (The warping of these data is patently obvious to anyone presented with the initial measurements and the later reports of the Public Cleansing Bureau, who methodically used selection, omission, and distortion to obfuscate Arasaki-sensei's clearly undesired findings.) These substantiated distortions, and his participation in the initial tests, gave his subsequent testings and testimony greater weight.

11. Indeed, some forms of nature were simply *too* natural for the comfortable consumption of most adults in Izawa. Instead, engagement with "nature" more often took the form of culturally sanctioned interventions, such as a trip to a hot springs resort nestled in the forest, a hike up Mount Fuji in the summer, or the aforementioned indulgence in *sakura*-viewing.

12. That the clearing of dead foliage is part of any groundskeeper's job was not by itself a mitigating point for most protesters, given the nature of their grievance.

13. For example, in referring to group-focussed Japanese social dynamics and health, Lock (1980, 255) points out, "The average Japanese is interested in the problem of pollution, for example, not in its global aspects, but only insofar as it affects one of the groups to which he or she belongs."

References

Berglund, E. 1998. *Knowing nature, knowing science: An ethnography of local environmental activism.* Cambridge: White Horse Press.

Berque, A. 1997a. *Japan: Cities and social bonds,* trans. C. Turner. Yelvertoft Manor, Northamptonshire: Pilkington Press.

———. 1997b. *Japan: Nature, artifice and Japanese culture,* trans. R. Schwarz. Yelvertoft Manor, Northamptonshire: Pilkington Press.

Bourdieu, P. 1977. *Outline of a theory of practice.* Cambridge: Cambridge University Press.

Csordas, T. J. 1993. Somatic modes of attention. *Cultural Anthropology* 8: 135–56.

———. 1994. *Embodiment and experience: The existential ground of culture and self.* Cambridge: Cambridge University Press.

Cybriwsky, R. 1998. *Tokyo: The shogun's city at the 21st century.* Chichester: Wiley.

Dale, P. 1986. *The myth of Japanese uniqueness.* New York: St. Martin's Press.

Debord, G. 1983. *The society of the spectacle,* trans. M. Prigent and L. Forsyth. London: Chronos.

Descartes, R. 1992. *Meditations on first philosophy,* ed., trans., and with an introduction by G. Heffernan. Indianapolis: University of Notre Dame Press.

Foucault, M. 1991. *Discipline and punish: The birth of the prison.* London: Penguin.

Hoffman, Y. 1986. *Japanese death poems.* Rutland, Vt.: Tuttle.

Ingold, T. 1989. The social and environmental relations of human beings and other animals. In *Comparative sociology,* ed. V. Standen and R. A. Foley, 495–512. Oxford: Blackwell Scientific.

———. 1992. Culture and the perception of the environment. In *Bush base: Forest farm: Culture, environment and development,* ed. E. Croll and D. Parkin, 39–56. London: Routledge.

———. 1995. Building, dwelling, living: How animals and people make themselves at home. In *Shifting contexts,* ed. M. Strathern, 57–80. London: Routledge.

———. 1996. Hunting and gathering as ways of perceiving the environment. In *Redefining nature,* ed. R. Ellen and K. Fukui, 117–55. Oxford: Berg.

———. 2001. Against space. Plenary lecture presented at the "Space, culture, power" conference, University of Aberdeen.

Kirby, P. W. 2001. Environmental consciousness and the politics of waste in Tokyo: "Nature," health, pollution, and the predicament of toxic Japan. Ph.D. thesis, University of Cambridge.

———. 2003. Troubled natures: Toxic pollutants and Japanese identity in Tokyo. In *Synthetic planet: Chemical politics and the hazards of modern life,* ed. M. Casper, 3–24. New York: Routledge.

Leder, D. 1990. *The absent body*. Chicago: University of Chicago Press.

Lock, M. 1980. *East Asian medicine in urban Japan*. Berkeley: University of California Press.

Lynch, K. 1960. *The image of the city*. Cambridge, Mass.: MIT Press.

Merleau-Ponty, M. 1995. *Phenomenology of perception,* trans. C. Smith. London: Routledge.

Moeran, B., and L. Skov. 1997. Mount Fuji and the cherry blossoms: A view from afar. In *Japanese images of nature: Cultural perspectives*. Nordic Institute of Asian Studies, Man and Nature in Asia, No. 1, ed. P. Asquith and A. Kalland, 181–205. Richmond, Surrey: Curzon Press.

Pandolfo, S. 1989. Detours of life: Space and bodies in a Moroccan village. *American Ethnologist* 16: 3–23.

Turner, T. 1994. Bodies and anti-bodies. In *Embodiment and experience*, ed. T. J. Csordas, 27–47. Cambridge: Cambridge University Press.

Watsuji, T. 1940. *Rinrigaku.* (Ethics). Tokyo: Iwanami Shoten.

———. [1935] 1975. *Fūdo.* (Milieux). Tokyo: Iwanami Shoten.

Yatsuka, H. 1990. An architecture floating on the sea of signs. In *The new Japanese architecture*, ed. B. Bognar, 38–41. New York: Rizzoli.

Environmental Conservation and Institutional Environments in Jamaica

5

JAMES G. CARRIER

THIS CHAPTER is concerned with understandings of the environment, especially as they are revealed in marine conservation projects in the developing world. The specific projects I will consider are two national parks in Jamaica that oversee coastal waters. I use the parks and activists to address a set of points concerning how people understand their surroundings and how scholars have thought about those understandings. As I hope to show, these activists and parks embody a range of understandings of their surroundings, a range that calls into question the scholarly assumption that people in Modern (industrial, capitalist) societies have a single characteristic view of the environment. Also, I hope to show that the view of the natural environment found in the activists and parks is shaped by the institutional environment that they confront, a shaping that is one example of the process of translation that I described in the introduction to this collection. These institutions are an instance of the sort of power that concerns Macleod in his chapter in this collection. In a sense, then, this chapter complements Macleod's description of Bayahibe, in the Dominican Republic. Looking at a different part of the Caribbean, my chapter can be seen as investigating many of the points that concern him.

I will begin by describing a common and influential model of understandings of the environment. After describing this model, I will turn to environmental activists in Jamaica. Having studied these two parks and the activists involved in them intermittently for a few years, I will use them only to illustrate, rather than demonstrate, the point I want to make about that model, that it may simplify a more complex reality. I then turn to aspects of the practical experience of these activists as they pursue their conservationist goals. In doing so, I will show how pressures on them make it likely that they will end up approaching the environment in particular ways and translating their concern with the environment into terms that reflect these pressures. Accommodating to these pressures in turn affects their relationships with previous users of the marine environment, local fishers, who are likely to see the marine environment in different ways. This mismatch in perceptions, similar to what Theodossopoulos describes in his chapter, is prone to lead to miscommunication and perhaps animosity between fishers and activists, which reduces the likelihood that conservation projects will succeed.

A Model of Understandings of the Environment

The scholarly model of understandings of the environment that concerns me reflects the growing appeal of phenomenological and bodily orientations within anthropology. The model asserts that it is people who are engaged with their surroundings in material and practical ways who have a meaningful and consequential relationship with their environs, and that over the course of human history, and especially with the rise of Modern society, this sort of engagement and relationship has faded. The result is that Modernism is the realm of the disengaged person, the flaneur, the tourist gaze. My concern here is with this construction of Modernity.

This model is found in the influential and insightful work of Tim Ingold, whose extensive writings on the topic revolve around a distinction between two polar views of the natural surroundings, which define a continuum. One pole is what he calls the sphere view, which locates people in the center of their surroundings, with which they are intimately and practically engaged. The other pole is the globe view, which locates people at a distance from their surroundings, which they approach as an object of contemplation or consumption. Ingold (1993, 35) summarizes this distinction when he says "the lifeworld, imagined from an experiential centre, is spherical in form, whereas a world divorced from life, that is yet complete in itself, is imagined in the form of a globe."

Those with the globe view see their material environment as alienated from themselves, and they "can describe their environment, and report on their actions within it, as though they had themselves stepped outside it, posing as mere spectators" (Ingold 1992, 52). This resembles the conception of the surroundings that Macnaghten and Urry (1998, 1) call "environmental realism," a conception of the environment as "essentially a 'real entity' . . . substantially separate from social practices and human experience." To say that such people are alienated from their natural environment does not mean that they see that environment as without meaning or power. For instance, Veronica Strang (1996) reports that urban Australians immerse themselves in a natural environment and see themselves as being strengthened and rejuvenated by it. However, the process she describes entails people standing apart from that environment and voluntarily entering it, experiencing it and extracting something of value from it. This is very different from the intimate practical engagement that characterizes those with a sphere orientation.

The historical-developmental dimension of the shift from sphere to globe orientation is marked when Ingold (1993) relates the sphere to Medieval European imagery, and the globe to a very Modern artifact, a photograph of the earth taken from the moon. This dimension is developed more explicitly in the work of another influential scholar, Arturo Escobar (esp. 1999). He describes three "regimes of nature," ways that people relate to their surroundings: organic nature, capitalist nature, and technonature. The first is characterized by "the fact that nature and society are not separated ontologically" (1999, 7), with no clear separation of "the biophysical, human, and supernatural world" (1999, 8). This echoes Ingold's sphere view, and springs from people's material, practical engagement with their natural environs. Capitalist nature is Modern and looks like Ingold's globe view. Its core is the objectification of "nature," which Escobar links to the spread of patriarchal capitalism and the commodity form. The result is an alienation of the natural environment, which is approached through the frame of capitalist rationality and control (1999, 6). Escobar's third regime, technonature, is one where the boundary between nature and culture is blurred through such things as genetic engineering (1999, 11–12). However, even though the boundary may be blurred, under this regime the relationship to the natural environment is mediated by technologies, and hence indirectly by the drive for profit that motivates their development, rather than the more immediate practical engagement that characterizes organic nature.

Although the influential works of Ingold and Escobar differ in detail, they share an important distinction between what they take as pre-Modern and Modern views of the surroundings. The pre-Modern relationship (the sphere view, organic nature) is characterized by a close practical and material engagement with the surroundings and no clear separation of self and environs, culture and nature. Alternatively, the Modern relationship (globe view, capitalist nature) is characteristically mediated by the apparatus of industrial capitalism, and entails a marked distinction between self and environs, culture and nature.

I said that this model of people's understandings is a common one. For instance, Nicholas Green describes just the transition from the pre-Modern to the Modern in his argument that around the middle of the nineteenth century the Parisian bourgeoisie came to revalue the countryside as a landscape to be visited and consumed. According to Green (1995, 39), this was rooted in the socioeconomic position of "those social constituencies who not only had the economic resources and leisure to make country trips and buy tourist guides, but who identified personally both with dynamic urban modernity and with environmental threat." Green is pointing, then, to the appearance among these Parisians of a Modern view of rural France. For them, this was a natural realm that had meaning precisely because it was so distinct from urban Paris. The result, facilitated by advertisements catering to these people, was a rendering of the rural as an object of the tourist gaze: something to be seen and experienced, but not something to be engaged with in any material, practical way.

Bruno Latour (1993) argues that the separation between the cultural and the natural, of the sort that Green describes, is a core of Modernity. The separation that Latour describes, though, appears to be only part of what was happening. For instance, Felicity Edholm (1995) describes a different change that occurred in Paris at about the same time that concerned Green, the rebuilding of parts of the city in the second half of the nineteenth century. She says that one consequence of this was that the Parisian poor became visible to the bourgeoisie in a way that they had not been hitherto. They came to be seen but not engaged with, and hence were an object of contemplation on the new boulevards. They became an abstract category, an object of dismay and fascination, particularly sexual. And Edholm's argument echoes a point that Richard Sennett (1976) made much earlier. He said that the rise of capitalism led to an increasing separation of the better-off London and Paris residents, which he described, from their urban milieu. For these people, public space was something they passed through on the way elsewhere, rather than something they engaged with directly.

The separation that Sennett, Latour, and the rest describe indicates that the model of understandings of the environment that concerns me resonates with an important common assumption. With Modernity comes the separation of parts of life from the activities and relationships with which they had been implicated previously. And as a corollary, with Modernity comes a more abstract and intellectual relationship, not just with nature or the natural environment, but with many aspects of the world (e.g., Polanyi 1957; specifically on the environment, see Hornborg 1996; more generally, see Carrier 2001b). This assumption has been a powerful one in the social sciences, and indeed can be seen to be central to the work of Marx and Weber. In the hands of Escobar and especially Ingold, it has helped motivate interesting and thoughtful work on people's understandings of their surroundings. However, it also has important limitations.

By being concerned with broad types of societies and with historical moments that the typology defines as significant, this assumption makes it difficult to see diversity, whether that is diversity among Western people in the ways that they approach their environs, or diversity within Western individuals, who may have more than one view of their environs. A consideration of individuals in the context of their different activities can help show the link between their understandings and their situations, and so help fracture the uniformitarian image that this influential model projects.

Understandings of the Environment in Jamaica

The individuals I want to look at are some of those who have been involved in in-fluential ways in environmental conservation in Jamaica. While they are concerned with the marine environment in Jamaica, these people are from Europe and the United States, and have a range of backgrounds, including engineering, computer communications, advertising, nursing, and so on. The conservation projects that have concerned them are in Montego Bay and Negril. These are the sites of the first two marine parks in Jamaica, and they were authorized by the Jamaican gov-ernment in the 1990s.

Negril

The Negril Marine Park was established through the efforts of the Negril Coral Reef Preservation Society (NCRPS), an organization primarily of Europeans and North Americans involved in tourism in Negril. The NCRPS was formed in 1990 and the Jamaican government authorized the park in 1998. Two women were especially influential in the NCRPS, and I will focus on them. One, whom I will call X, effectively founded the NCRPS, served frequently as its president, and took charge of the park when it was established. The other, whom I will call Y, was a close friend of X and also served as president. Both of these women are from the United States and both were born around 1950. I begin with X.

When X works to protect "the environment," what concerns her is the coastal waters in the immediate area of Negril. Reasonably, she sees these waters as hav-ing become increasingly polluted over the time that she has been in Negril. For her, the deteriorating health of the coastal environment is marked by the increas-ing death of the coral in the area. X points, again reasonably, to the shrinking of Negril's sandy beach as an indicator of that deterioration, as healthy coral forma-tions both protect the shore from erosion and contribute to beach sand.

As this indicates, she sees the marine environment in abstract, scientific terms, Macnaghten and Urry's "environmental realism." This approach sees the coastal waters as a neutral space (see, e.g., Gupta and Ferguson 1997; Hirsch 1995), de-fined by the processes of marine ecosystems, which in principle apply everywhere. She is no specialist, but she is familiar with the science of coastal ecosystems, and especially about the properties and effects of terrestrial runoff, which seem to be significant in Negril.[1]

While this approach to the environment is clearly Modern, it is not the only way that X sees Negril's coastal waters. Her dispassionate, objective description and understanding of the area's environmental degradation is matched by clear, strong emotion. And as she tells it, she is not alone in this emotional involvement. She said that she showed some pictures of the Negril beach to a group of local fishers, pictures taken in the 1950s. She told me that older fishermen cried when they saw how much things had changed for the worse.

Thus it is that X's orientation to her surroundings is complex. The Modern, objectivist approach is complemented by a non-Modern personal, emotional involvement, one that sees Negril not in terms of neutral space, but as a local and personal place. To understand how she came to have these complementary views, it is necessary to understand what brought this American woman to Negril, and what she did once she arrived.

X was married and living in the United States in the 1970s. At that time she became gravely ill. She was treated for her illness and recovered. At the same time, she was divorced, and it appears that an important factor ending her marriage was the strain of her disease and its treatment. She said that she had seen pictures of Negril from an acquaintance who had been there, and she decided that she would leave the U.S. and go to Negril to recover from her illness and from the collapse of her marriage. She paid for the move from her divorce settlement, and lived on that money without working until it ran out, which took about five years.

During this time, she said that she swam several miles each day. She was not exploring the coastal waters, for her route did not vary: up and down the shore of the area of Negril called the West End. At the time, then, her relationship with her marine surroundings was clearly indirect. She was not engaged with them in any practical, material way, as a Negril fisher might be. She was not even viewing them as a tourist might. Rather, these waters were the backdrop against which she was passing her days as she recovered from the disastrous recent events of her life, gradually rebuilding herself physically and mentally and trying to figure out her life. Although X's initial relationship with her surroundings was so indirect, gradually she began to take an interest in the waters where she was swimming, and she told me stories of octopuses changing color and the other things she saw during her swims that intrigued her. She said that gradually she got to know what she described as the personalities of different sorts of marine life, and this led her to find books on the subject.

Eventually X exhausted her divorce settlement. After a false start, when she tried working at the profession in which she had been trained, she went to work for Y. X had been renting lodgings from Y, who owned a dive shop in Negril, a business that rented and refilled air tanks, taught people how to dive, and provided boats to take people out on dives. X told me that business was booming at Y's dive shop, and that Y was wearing herself out trying to deal with it, coming home late and exhausted, still in her wet suit, complaining that she needed an additional instructor. X decided to assist her friend and to earn some money. She trained as a diver and as an instructor, and as she became more concerned about the marine environment, she recruited Y to her cause.

I have argued that, contrary to the uniformitarian approach of the model I described earlier in this chapter, X held more than one understanding of her surroundings. As I have noted, one of her understandings is Modern, speaking in terms of an abstract, scientific construction of the natural environment. However, X also had a close personal identification with the waters of Negril, so that she saw those waters as both space and place. And again contrary to that model, this personal identification did not spring from the sort of practical, material engagement with the environs that underlies Ingold's sphere orientation and Escobar's organic nature. X was no Negril fisher engaging with the waters to survive. Rather, she was a middle-class American émigré to Negril, and her intimate relation with those waters emerged from the vagaries of her personal life. Those waters were interwoven in the way she rebuilt herself after her grave illness, the collapse of her marriage, and her flight from home. And in this rebuilding, the waters off the West End and the marine life she saw there took on a distinctive personal meaning for her.

Certainly I am not arguing that X's case is typical, or even all that common, among people with a Modern orientation. However, X is important for two reasons. The first is that she became an environmental activist and was instrumental in setting up the Negril park, so that her understanding of the environment has been consequential. Second, the very extremity of her case makes visible engagements and processes that, in less extreme form, may be more common than the construction of a Modernist view would lead us to expect. X's emotional engagement is echoed in the sort of people Kay Milton (2002, ch. 4; her chapter in this collection) describes. These are people for whom aspects of the surroundings are implicated in their emotional lives, so that self and surroundings inflect each other in significant ways. And as with the sort of people Milton describes, for X this personal engagement led to a greater interest in those surroundings, and the adoption of a scientific environmentalist approach.

If X is the sort of person who contradicts the portrayal of people in a Modern society, Y (who was X's landlady, employer, and supporter) appears to conform to that portrayal. Y liked diving and the coastal waters, but she lacked X's emotional involvement. The way she presented herself, Y's main engagement was with her business. She was absorbed in and enjoyed running her dive shop, and the fact that the shop was in Negril was almost incidental. She enjoyed the organization of the business, and she enjoyed dealing with people and working with her staff. In other words, in good Modern fashion, her relationship with Negril's waters was indirect, for it was mediated by her relationship with her dive shop, which was her primary concern. It is not too much of an exaggeration to say that, for Y, those waters were simply the background in which she pursued the activities that she enjoyed and that provided her livelihood. This emotional distance is clear, almost striking, in what Y said about her swimming. Whereas X swam for years as part of her emotional, personal process of recovery, Y said that when she herself swam, she did so as part of her work, for the exercise, or to get from point A to point B. Why did Y, then, become an environmental activist, get involved with the NCRPS, and become one of its leading officers? She said that conservationist concern was not the issue. Rather, X was a close friend whom she wanted to support, and she enjoyed the administrative side of the job.

X and Y, then, present very different approaches to the marine environment in Negril. For X, that environment took on important personal meaning over the years that she recovered from her illness and divorce, and this affective engagement led her to learn more about Negril's waters and to become an environmental activist. For Y, there was certainly the potential for a close relationship with those waters, but this potential was not realized. From the perspective of her dive shop, Y's approach to the waters was simply instrumental. However, the waters did take on an indirect emotional meaning for Y, through her friendship with X.

Montego Bay

The history of the Montego Bay Marine Park is more complex than that of the Negril park. As a result of the work of local activists, a small protected area was established in the waters of Montego Bay in the middle of the 1970s. Activists continued their agitation and established the Montego Bay Marine Park Trust. In the 1990s this agitation resulted in the massive expansion of the protected area, which is now the Montego Bay Marine Park. As in Negril, activists have generally been people from Europe and North America involved in the tourist industry. Although more people have played important roles in Montego Bay than in Negril, those that I have spoken to said that one man was the most important early force. He is Z, and I will sketch Montego Bay primarily from his perspective.

In some ways, Z resembles X. For him, as for her, "the environment" is effectively the marine environment, here the waters of Montego Bay. Like her, he was aware of scientific findings about Jamaican coastal waters, and like her he had worked with marine biologists in Jamaica. So, like X, Z had an orientation that construed the surroundings in terms of the abstract Modernist frame of environmental space. However, and yet again like X, Z's Modern orientation was only one of the ways that he understood the coastal waters. He had another important orientation, one that reflected his personal history in Montego Bay, a history in which the bay's waters played an important part. This history lacks X's drama, but the events in it laid the basis for an important personal identification with those waters.

Z was born in Ireland. He first went to Jamaica in 1957, and in 1964 went to Montego Bay, where he became involved with two other divers in the area, one of whom ran a dive shop at a hotel. Around 1970, these people learned that a group of British divers wanted to go to Montego Bay. This group was larger than existing dive organizations could handle, so Z and his fellows decided to form their own company to cater for them. Like Y, with her dive shop in Negril, Z's involvement with the Montego Bay waters rested on commercial enterprise. However, there was more at work than business interest. Patently, Z enjoyed Montego Bay as a place to dive, took pride in it, and wanted others to enjoy it as well.

At about the same time that Z and his fellows set up their dive company, a popular American diving magazine carried a story that the waters of Montego Bay were not as clear as they had been. After initial disbelief, Z and his fellows concluded that the story was correct, and they decided to try to do something about it. They organized a workshop in 1974 to consider the state of the bay and what might be done. The result was a proposal for a relatively small marine protected area in the bay. This was recognized by the Jamaican government late in 1974 (O'Callaghan, Woodley, and Aiken 1988). Z continued his environmental activism, and his commercial interest in diving, through the 1990s, and around 1995 he left Jamaica to return to Ireland, though he frequently returned. (I spoke with him when he was on one of his visits to Montego Bay.)

In his relationship with the coastal waters, Z stands somewhere between X and Y. Like Y he is linked to those waters through commercial interest. That interest should mark Z as having a Modern view of the waters. From the perspective of his business, the bay's waters were a commodity, part of capitalist nature, the consumption of which Z's company sold to tourist divers. However, this is not an adequate description of Z's thinking. Rather, and like X, Z also had a personal orientation to those waters; he took a personal pride and interest in them, even though they appear to figure in no intense personal crisis in the way that Negril's waters did for X.

Z's commercial interest sprang from and fed into his personal and pragmatic involvement with the marine environment. So, while his decision to form a dive company was a business decision, it also rested, as I have said, on his pleasure and pride in diving in Montego Bay. And running this dive company was a context within which Z engaged practically with aspects of his environment. This was not the engagement of a Montego Bay fisher, but even so it was a practical engagement, reflected in things like the 1974 workshop and Z's repeated efforts to protect and improve the bay's waters. And because Z was living in Montego Bay and diving there for many years, bay waters were likely to figure in events that he saw as shaping his life in important ways. For instance, around 1970 two of Z's diver friends tried to set personal depth records. Both bodies were recovered eventually, one from a depth of over 300 feet. Z said that this helped to change the way that he thought about the waters at Montego Bay.

The result of this engagement was an approach toward the waters of Montego Bay that was not simply utilitarian or Modern, for Z took a personal interest in the bay and in what others said about it. He did not seem to see the American diving magazine's criticism simply as a sign that business might fall off, though he was aware of its commercial implications. In addition, it dented his pride in the bay's waters and saddened him. Montego Bay was part of his world and work, and what affected it affected him, both professionally and personally.

I have described some of the people associated with marine conservation projects in Jamaica with a simple end in view. I have argued that such people can have a close personal relationship with their environs. This is striking in the case of X, and apparent in the case of Z. The presence of these personal engagements raises questions about the model of views of the environment that I described at the beginning of this chapter. These people saw their coastal waters in Modernist terms, but they also saw them in personal terms. For X and Z, those waters were both space and place, construed in terms of both abstract science and personal engagement.

This personal engagement is what led these people to become environmental activists. And in their activism they came to confront a different sort of environment, an institutional one. In confronting this new environment, they confronted structures of power that were alien to them; hence they confronted the problem of translation in a way that they had not previously. I now turn to their dealings with that environment.

Realizing Understandings

As a result of their activism, these people were instrumental in the creation of national parks intended to protect the bodies of water that concerned them. This very success meant that they were obliged to deal with a set of institutions that were shaped by and hence expressed the sorts of power relations that Macleod describes in his chapter in this book. These institutions included Jamaican state government agencies and bureaucratic officeholders, government ministers and MPs. In addition, these institutions included NGOs and national and supranational agencies in Jamaica and elsewhere. The most noteworthy of these was the United States Agency for International Development (the USAID).

To echo a point made in the introduction to this collection and illustrated in Kirby's chapter, when they were trying to generate support for their conservation projects, these activists had to recruit others, and had to socialize their desires into terms that made sense to the individuals they were trying to persuade. The invocation of a scientific view of the coastal waters was part of this. On the other hand, once they started to deal with these institutions, the activists had to socialize their desires in a different way; they had to translate things into a different conceptual language; and they had to present their conservation projects in terms of a different set of issues. Put most broadly, those issues and that conceptual language reflected the political-economic ideology that goes under the name of neoliberalism. This ideology was intrusive in two ways. First, its practical consequences obliged activists to approach agencies like the USAID. Second, those agencies were themselves shaped in important ways by neoliberalism.

Neoliberalism is based on an idealization of the free market (see Carrier 1997). Further, as that ideology has taken institutional form, it has led to what can be called "virtualism" (see Carrier and Miller 1998). That refers to efforts by powerful institutions to make the world conform to the virtual reality defined by that idealization. The most notorious vehicle of neoliberal virtualism has been structural adjustment regimes, typically imposed by the International Monetary Fund. Like other countries in the Caribbean, Jamaica has been subject to such regimes (see Klak 1998). The processes that lead to the development and imposition of these regimes are complex. Although their criteria are putatively economic and fiscal, IMF negotiators appear to be as much concerned with political, even party-political, factors as they are with economic or political-economic ones (for Jamaica and other Caribbean countries, see Edie 1991). Further, the influence of neoliberalism is sufficiently pervasive that countries without formal structural adjustment regimes are constrained to conform fairly closely to the ideology. For example, Jamaica rejected further IMF regimes late in the 1990s. However, the effect of this rejection was insignificant in terms of state policies, because that rejection was not accompanied by any marked reversal of earlier IMF-induced policy changes, and because Jamaica was seeking to be included in the North American Free Trade Agreement, which obliged the state to maintain its IMF-type policies.

While neoliberalism has many aspects, perhaps its core is a radical rejection of the state in its political and economic guises. The rejection of the state in its economic guise is manifest as a growing pressure to curtail state financial power and regulation. In poorer countries like Jamaica, this is coupled with a denial of the legitimacy of state-based models of economic development, and the granting of legitimacy to market-based models (see Bromley 1994; McMichael 1998; Toye 1993). The rejection of the state in its political guise is manifest as a rejection of central governments and state agencies, which are seen as corrupt, or at least lethargic, grossly inefficient, and unresponsive. This is coupled with growing faith in "the community" (Etzioni 1993; see also Moore 1993), and local institutions and organizations, which are seen as energetic and efficient. In the field of environmental conservation, this meant a growing stress on participatory or community conservation, part of a rhetoric of "empowering" people (see Adams and

Hulme 1998; Adams and McShane 1996; Christie and White 1997; Leach and Mearns 1996; Roe 1991).

In Jamaica, the central state agency that oversaw environmental and conservation projects was the Natural Resource Conservation Department, and it nicely illustrates these two strands of neoliberalism. Early in the 1990s, this switched from being a Department to being an Authority, largely in response to pressure from the USAID. This change in name marked a change in status, for the institution went from being a government department to a quasi-autonomous agency, a change intended to take conservation out of the political hands of the state and put it in the putatively nonpolitical hands of local activists and specialists. (The supposed apolitical autonomy of the reconstituted NRCA was illusory at least in part. The Authority was a creature of the USAID, which occupied the top floor of the NRCA building for some years and which carried out extensive guidance and training of NRCA staff under the development rubric of "capacity building.")

I said that the political side of neoliberalism is the denigration of state institutions and the elevation of local groups and institutions. This aspect of neoliberal thinking seems to govern the NRCA, and it was summarized by some environmental activists in this way:

> The Natural Resources Conservation Authority (NRCA) . . . recognizes that officials in the capital are less able than locally-based organizations to identify local problems, propose solutions, or implement them. Central control over environmental policy has historically resulted in decisions favouring short term financial interests of individuals and institutions which are well connected in the capital. Decision making is often protracted and may not address local concerns. Residents of the area feel increasingly dispossessed and powerless to control access to resources or halt degradation from development that adversely affects their quality of life, causing increasing alienation from the political process. NRCA has decided to increase the power of local communities to decide which forms of development, conservation, and environmental management best meet their long term needs. (Goreau et al. 1997, 2093)

The other side of neoliberalism is economic, which in this case means the belief that states should oblige local groups to fund their own conservation projects. The NRCA illustrates this side as well. The Agency disbursed money for Jamaica's parks, but the neoliberal restriction of state finances and their redirection to debt repayment meant that the NRCA's budget was cut sharply in the last years of the 1990s, and the amount of NRCA money going to parks dropped accordingly. Thus, funding for the Montego Bay Park was J$2.7 million in 1997 and again in 1998 (about U.S.$75,000). In 1999 it fell to J$450,000 (about U.S.$12,000) and remained at that level in 2000, supplemented each year by about J$125,000 (about U.S.$3,000) from an NRCA fund based on user fees collected at all the installations that the NRCA oversees. (This supplement was about a quarter of what the NRCA collected at the Montego Bay Park: J. Williams, personal communication.)

This collapse in government support obliged the Negril and Montego Bay parks to look for other sources of funding, and it was no surprise that at the two meetings of the Montego Bay park governing body that I attended in 1999, the primary topic was ways of getting money. The Negril and Montego Bay parks tried to secure money in two different but intertwined ways. One way is applying for money from international donors; the other is charging people, directly or indirectly, to enter the parks. I will describe each of these.

Although the Negril Park got money from the European Union, the EU's presence in conservation in Jamaica is fairly insignificant compared to the USAID's in terms of the amount of money distributed, the number of staff present in the country, and activists' impression of who has the most influence. In attempting to get support from the USAID, these organizations felt obligated to understand and present themselves in distinctive ways, though some aspects of neoliberalism were so pervasive that any substantial donor would expect the same sort of self-presentation. The core of this was portraying these parks as rational bureaucratic organizations. The most visible form of this portrayal was the obligation to draw up management and business plans, something the parks were doing annually by the last part of the 1990s. The Montego Bay park management plan for 1998 is about seventy pages long. It begins with a list of park "goals," which is followed by statements of the park's "mission" and "vision." What follows is the vast majority of the management plan, a set of five "action plans," each with a set of associated "strategies," themselves broken down into a set of "activities": "Marine ecosystem management," "User management," "Community relations," "Administration," and "Financial sustainability." The Negril park management plan for 1998 is broadly comparable, though it is about twice as long.

The logic behind management plans is that drawing up such a plan obliges people to think through just what it is that they want to do and how they want to go about it. However, imposing such plans is an exercise in power of the sort that concerns Macleod in his discussion of Bayahibe. This is because the plans are not simply frames to encourage people to think, but devices that oblige them to think in certain ways. They do this because they oblige people to translate their desires and motivations into a particular language that is socially powerful (see Carrier 1997, 47–54; 2001a). For instance, the management plan for the Negril park could not begin with X's illness, divorce, and years spent swimming off the West

End; likewise, the management plan for the Montego Bay park could not refer to people who died trying to set depth records, or even Z's pride in helping divers enjoy the bay's waters. At least, they could not begin that way if either park wanted to be taken seriously as an organization that deserved support. Thus, preparing these management plans obliged these activists to silence, and hence deny, their personal histories, and hence silence a crucial aspect of their understanding of the surroundings and the reasons why they want to protect them. In place of what is silenced, the expectations underlying the demand for these plans obliged the people who ran these parks to think of themselves and their goals in terms of things like biodiversity, ecosystem, consultative groups, and the like. So, the obligation to produce a proper management plan can be expected to affect the ways that these people think about and engage with their marine environment; what had been a feature of personal history and scientific knowledge becomes as well an object of administrative planning.

The other way that parks try to get money also affects the ways that people are obliged to think about and present the coastal waters that concern them. As I have said, that other way was attracting ecotourists to the parks and charging them user fees, either directly or by charging companies that cater to tourists. This is not a new idea, and it is an attractive one at a number of levels, an attraction that is almost wholly economic. Received wisdom is that there are a vast number of ecotourists: global estimates for as long ago as 1988 range between 157 and 236 million; received wisdom is that they spend a vast amount of money: estimates for the revenue they generated in those years ranged up to about U.S.$1.2 trillion (Ceballos-Lascurain 1996, 46–48). In the Caribbean, it is commonly assumed that ecotourists can provide substantial income for parks. In the published literature and in regional conferences and workshops, X and Z and others involved in these two parks were told repeatedly of places like Saba Marine Park and Bonaire Marine Park (see Dixon, Scura, and van't Hof 1993), both in the Netherlands Antilles and both catering primarily to divers. There, user fees generated substantial income and even financial independence (for detailed analyses, see Framhein 1995 for Saba, and Scura and van't Hof 1993 for Bonaire).

While ecotourism was attractive to park mangers, it was also attractive to those in the tourist industry.[2] In Jamaica, partly as a result of neoliberal pressure for open markets, local industries were deteriorating, agriculture was increasingly uncertain as an export sector, and tourism became increasingly important both as a commercial activity and as a source of foreign exchange. However, the country's position in the tourist market and the benefits it gained from tourism were increasingly uncertain. Like most Caribbean countries, Jamaica found itself in the commodity tourist sector, for it was selling sun, sand, and sea, and these are available not only throughout most of the Caribbean, but also throughout most of the tropical world. As a result, the industry in Jamaica had become dominated by all-inclusive resorts competing on price for the largely North American tourist market (as Macleod's description indicates is also the case for the Dominican Republic). One consequence of this for Jamaica was the increasing domination of the industry by large corporations and fewer linkages with the Jamaican economy (see generally Pattulo 1996): tourists in the larger all-inclusive resorts around Montego Bay were eating chicken, beef, lettuce, and even fruits shipped in from the U.S.

Attracting ecotourists was often thought to be a way out of the commodity market, for they were assumed to be wealthier than mass tourists, less sensitive to price, and more likely to be attracted to local organizations and products. While these supposed benefits of ecotourism rest only on anecdotal evidence, they increased the attraction of ecotourism both for the Jamaican tourist industry and for the Jamaican state. And though these benefits may have been reported only in anecdotal evidence, there were published reports that indicated that ecotourists brought money. The recreational use of the Virgin Islands National Park in the early 1980s brought benefits totaling U.S.$23.3 million annually (Dixon, Scura, and van't Hof 1993; this ignores social and political drawbacks: see Olwig 1980); Tobago's Buccoo Reef and Bon Accord Lagoon Restricted Area are said to have brought approximately U.S.$510,000 in revenues per year (van't Hof 1985, 554); the use of Bonaire Marine Park is thought to have generated annual revenues of over U.S.$23 million in total, nearly half the island's entire income (Scura and van't Hof 1993, 37–39).

I said that ecotourism had been attractive for some time. In a study of possible sites for marine parks in Jamaica, carried out late in the 1980s, ecotourism was an important consideration in the evaluation of the different locations considered in the study. The report stated:

> [M]arine parks can be pretty much self-supporting through a number of activities: snorkeling, SCUBA diving, glass bottom boat tours arranged for a fee. Usually the marine park organization will leave most of these activities to commercial diver operators and watersport centers. In that case, however, substantial revenues may be obtained from concessions. . . . If basically all commercial activities in a marine park are subject to permits, then a variety of activities can be hired out to concessionaires. (O'Callaghan, Woodley, and Aiken 1988, 37)

Using this criterion of potential ecotourism revenue, the report selected Montego Bay as a desirable park location. Montego Bay was then, as it continues to be, by far the largest tourist location in Jamaica. In the late 1990s it was the country's second largest city, with fifty-six hotels and over 5,000 rooms (Bunce and Gustavson 1998, 75). Here it is possible that economic considerations overruled more purely ecological ones. Some of those in Jamaica who dissented from the report's selection of desirable sites argued that the resources available to run a marine park were likely to be small, and that because the waters of Montego Bay had deteriorated so badly, a park realistically could make no real difference there. Instead, they argued, it would be better to pick a site where a small effort could make a difference.

I am not arguing that it was solely because of neoliberalism that these national parks needed to find their own sources of income. However, that ideology was an important factor. And as a consequence, activists and managers had to present these parks not just as bureaucratic, rational organizations, but also as commercial organizations. A manifestation of this is that, of the five action plans in the Montego Bay park 1998 management plan, the longest is the fifth, "Financial sustainability." The goal of that plan is: "To become financially sustainable through utilizing all possible sources of revenue, cost sharing and partnerships including fees, donations, grants, volunteerism and sales of goods and services, locally, nationally and internationally, from private, corporate, government and institutional organizations." The associated substrategies are: opening a visitor center at the park headquarters, establishing an ecotourism program, merchandising and franchising, generating park products and services, placing collection boxes in the area, corporate fund-raising, setting up a donor organization, issuing user permits, holding public events, participating in existing public events, and establishing a park trust fund.

These institutional pressures led people like X, and the successors to Z in Montego Bay, to think about their marine environment in novel ways that conform to the Modernist model. In accord with Escobar's model of capitalist nature, these people were obliged to see that environment and the things in it in terms of a commodity, access to which was to be traded for money.

Thus, senior park management in Montego Bay was concerned to enhance those aspects of park waters that it thought would attract ecotourists, and hence generate user fees. Management probably would not have stated what it was doing in just this way, but it embraced any opportunity to learn about consumer demand: What is it that divers, a particularly salient body of ecotourists, are looking for in a dive site? Another sign of this pressure to see their park and its waters in this way is the link that some Montego Bay activists made between tourism, money, and the environment. One activist with a substantial history of involvement in conservation organizations in Jamaica made the point bluntly. The tourist industry should pay a levy for environmental protection. He said that their situation is "Just like in any business. It [the environment] is a maintenance cost."

These commercial and economic orientations and pressures could be insistent. In Negril, X said that hotel operators thought that she should ban all fishing in park waters. She said that hotel operators said that their guests were complaining about the presence of Jamaicans in small fishing boats in park waters, apparently believing that any fishing was bad for the marine environment and that no Jamaican fishing boat had a legitimate reason to be in park waters. From what X said, hotel operators seemed to think the same. Two points are worth noting here. First, the Negril park has not banned all fishing in all its waters. Second, access to the Negril town landing beach is through park waters, so that fishermen necessarily traverse those waters on their way elsewhere. X resented this pressure from hotel operators and tourists, but she recognized that it was a real pressure, an important factor springing from commercial interests, and it is reasonable to expect that this affected the ways that she saw the marine environment.

These activists did not respond to the pressures of their institutional environment by seeing the marine environment only in commodity terms. Rather, these pressures led to new problems of translation and new forms of understanding. Early personal orientations to coastal waters had been supplemented by scientific orientations, and these became supplemented in turn by bureaucratic and commercial orientations. However, activists appear to have seen these institutional pressures as an intrusion in the way that they did not see the pressure to adopt a scientific orientation. At least, activists complained about their institutional pressures, often in the form of stories about the USAID and the iniquities and idiocies of its policies and projects (for similar tales from elsewhere in the Caribbean, see Nietschmann 1995).

Practical Consequences

These stories reflect the activists' sense that these institutional pressures were making it harder for them to achieve their conservationist goals because of the additional time and effort required in dealing with the demands of that institutional environment. There is another way that those pressures appear to have been reducing the likelihood that activists would achieve their conservationist goals: institutional pressures and the larger political-economic environment affected local fishers. These people are important both because their use of the coastal waters is restricted by these parks, and because their cooperation is important for successful marine conservation: the truism is that fisheries management will be only as good as the fishers allow it to be.

Local fishers should not be seen as a group that could claim to be indigenous and unified (the following paragraphs draw on Polunin et al. 2000, esp. 55–64). Some fishers were the children of fishers, but, especially in Montego Bay, fishers were a disparate set of people brought into being by Jamaica's economic position in the last quarter of the twentieth century. During that period, the conventional sectors of the Jamaican economy deteriorated, while Negril and especially Montego Bay turned into boomtowns driven by the expansion of tourism. One activist says that from about 1970 to the end of the 1990s, the city grew from about 25,000 people to about 125,000 (see also Bacon 1987, 105; a smaller version of this elsewhere in the Caribbean is described in McMinn and Cater 1998, 689–91). As a result, many Jamaicans moved to these places to look for work. Some of those unable to find or keep work took to fishing as a way of generating a bit of food and money. (These people tended to become spearfishers, since spearfishing could be learned easily and required little initial outlay. This technique was looked down upon by some others as not being "real" fishing.) In this situation, the relationship between fishers and the parks was likely to be problematic. To protect coastal waters, parks relied on restricting fishing, and both parks introduced zone systems, which divided park waters into distinct areas and prohibited different activities (including types of fishing) within different areas. The success of these restrictions required the cooperation of fishers, for the alternative was the sort of massive and oppressive policing effort that the parks did not want and could not afford.

Securing the cooperation of fishers was never likely to be a simple task. For one thing, it seems likely that many of them saw the coastal waters as something like "family land," which is common in much of the Caribbean, including Jamaica. It is land that belongs to all the descendants of the ancestor who acquired it, often at the end of slavery. Having family land is a form of identification, marking a person as belonging to a particular group of kin. However, it also has an economic aspect. Most family land is too small to support any significant portion of those with rights to it. However, a claimant who is in dire economic circumstances can return to the family land and live on it while looking for another job. As Karen Fog Olwig (1997, 151) puts it: "For the greater part of family members, the land has been a place where they might go whenever they are in need, but not a place where they actually have chosen to live." The rise of opportunistic fishing with the growth of Montego Bay and Negril indicates that coastal waters were used in a way analogous to family land, and the parallel between the two is reasonable. To ban fishing, then, was to deny economically hard-pressed Jamaicans a resource that they thought themselves entitled to because they were Jamaicans.

The difficulties caused by the enclosure of what I have described as being like family land are serious. However, the fact that these parks were obliged to seek revenue through attracting tourists made matters worse. The resulting association in people's minds of the parks and the tourist industry led to important points of tension between parks and the fishers whose support they needed. This tension revolved around contrasting views of the nature of the threat to coastal waters.

Local fishers' main concern with the marine environment is the state of fish stocks. To fishers in Negril and Montego Bay it was clear that stocks had deteriorated markedly in past years, and that their fishing harmed these stocks. However, this did not mean that fishers supported the parks. Rather, fishers rejected the parks' conservationist message and policy, because they disagreed with the understanding of the causes of the deterioration of the marine environment that these messages and policies expressed. While fishers said that fishing harmed stocks, they also said that they were a relatively minor influence on local waters, when compared to the systematic degradation of the environment that had been going on for some time. (Both X and Z also thought that environmental degradation was important.) The case is clearest in Montego Bay. Fishers there argued that the growth of the city, and the nature of the tourist industry that has fed that growth, were the main causes of the deterioration of coastal waters.

Montego Bay fishers were right in asserting that the growth of the city was important. The extensive building of beachfront hotels led to the destruction of a substantial amount of the original coast. This not only destroyed a substantial portion of the shoreline, but it also eliminated a number of large and environmentally beneficial mangrove stands. Fishers argued that the damage caused by these hotels was not limited to their construction. Some fishers, as well as at least one environmental specialist, said that it is likely that some of the beachfront hotels were dumping their sewerage directly into the bay, rather than processing it themselves or introducing it into the city's sewerage system. Fishers also pointed to the construction of a new port facility in the bay in the 1970s, which included significant dredging and land filling very near an important and environmentally sensitive area of the bay, the Bogue Lagoon. This new port was built to serve the increased volume of shipping required to supply the growing city, and to attract more and larger cruise ships. Also, both to attract and to cater to tourists and commercial interests, a section of the bay was filled in and a portion of the shoreline modified near the center of the city, causing further degradation.

From their perspective, then, fishers were being asked to give up their fishing, while nothing was done about the tourist industry, the main cause of the deterioration of the marine environment. This struck them as unjust, and reaffirmed their belief that these two parks were not so much about improving the coastal waters as they were about benefiting the tourist industry. Thus, while the larger political-economic environment obliged these parks to associate with and accommodate to the tourist industry, the result made fishers less likely to support conservation measures and so reduced the likelihood that these parks would achieve their conservationist goals.

Conclusion

I have presented a set of linked themes in this chapter, revolving around the ways that people understand their surroundings and the factors that affect those understandings. Along the way, I have sought to extend important existing anthropological work on people's understandings of the environment.

Concerning that work, I have used a handful of environmental activists to illustrate the point that it may be unwise to see people's material engagement with their surroundings as the key to their understandings. Engagements can be of different sorts, as X, Y, and Z's cases illustrate. Indeed, as X illustrates, one can end up with a complex, non-Modern understanding of the environment in situations where the surroundings are little more than the background against which important aspects of one's life take place. These cases also show that it may be unwise to think of a Modern view of the environment, for that implies that such a view is the only important view that people in modern societies have. Rather, X and Z show that such people can have more than one view, affirming Barbara Bender's (1998, 34) point that "landscapes—even as experienced by a single person—are multiple and contradictory."

These different understandings do not necessarily arise unbidden in people's minds as a result of their dealings with the environment. Rather, some of them can develop as a result of relationships with other people. So, for instance, X and Z were conversant with scientific knowledge about coastal waters, but this distanced view arose in part because of their interest in being able to speak and think about those waters in ways that would persuade others. Put differently and in terms used in this collection's introduction, these people may have been motivated by personal reasons to protect their environs, but they were constrained by social factors to socialize their motivations, to translate their care and understanding into public, persuasive terms. Those are the terms of environmental science.

This sort of constraint became pronounced when these activists and the organizations with which they were involved confronted funding agencies and the broader institutional environment. As I described, dealing with this environment obliged these people to adopt yet another set of understandings of the coastal waters, as an economic resource to be exploited through ecotourism and as an administrative object to be managed by environmental organizations. These activists were not happy to adopt these views of the waters, their conservation organizations, and themselves. However, they did adopt them.

Finally, it is important to recognize that the processes by which these different views are linked to conflict. At times, these activists described their relationship with their institutional environment as one of conflict, complaining especially about the USAID and its requirements. This conflict is more apparent when one considers local fishers, who confront conservationist regimes that appeared to see the coastal waters in terms very different from their own. In a sense, what granting agencies were doing to activists, those activists were doing to fishers, using their superior power to impose a set of meanings on the environs.

I want to close by using what I have said here to point to yet another way that conventional anthropological work on people's understandings of their surroundings might be extended. When it accounts for those understandings, that work tends to focus on factors internal to the social group being described, as indicated by the focus on people's practical engagement with their environment. However, the situation that I have sketched in this chapter suggests that entities outside of that group can have significant power over local people, and oblige them to adopt or conform to sets of understandings that they would not otherwise have held. In short, it is important to recognize not just the possibility that people will hold more than one view of their surroundings, but also the possibility that the larger social setting will constrain individuals and groups in important ways.

Notes

Some of the field research referred to here was carried out as part of ODA (later DFID) project R6783, "Ecological and social impacts in planning Caribbean marine-reserves." Among those I spoke to in Jamaica, I thank particularly Jill Williams and Jeremy Woodley, as well as Gordon Glave, Malden Miller, and Teo Schmidt, and of course the anonymous X, Y, and Z. In the midst of their own concerns, they were forthcoming and hospitable in ways for which I am most grateful. I am also grateful for helpful comments from Simon Coleman, Eric Hirsch, Daniel Miller, Kay Milton, Adam Reed, Veronica Strang, and Dimitrios Theodossopoulos. Aspects of this chapter have appeared in Carrier (2003).

1. Her approach is effectively that in Goreau et al. (1997). Aspects of this approach are not universally accepted among marine biologists who have worked in Jamaican waters.

2. Recall that Macleod noted that the Gulf and Western corporation donated land to the state for the creation of a park. This donation made more attractive the land that Gulf and Western was selling to private investors, while assuring that the cost of maintaining the attraction would fall on the state rather than those investors. A similar strategic donation is described at St. John, in the U.S. Virgin Islands (Olwig 1980).

References

Adams, J. S., and T. O. McShane. 1996. *The myth of wild Africa*. Berkeley: University of California Press.

Adams, W. M., and D. Hulme. 1998. Conservation and communities: Changing narratives, policies and practices in African conservation. Working paper 4. Manchester: University of Manchester Institute of Development Policy and Management.

Bacon, P. R. 1987. Use of wetlands for tourism in the insular Caribbean. *Annals of Tourism Research* 14: 104–17.

Bender, B. 1998. *Stonehenge: Making space*. Oxford: Berg.

Bromley, D. 1994. Economic dimensions of community-based conservation. In *Natural connections*, ed. D. Western and M. Wright, 429–47. Washington, D.C.: Island Press.

Bunce, L., and K. Gustavson. 1998. *Coral reef valuation: A rapid socioeconomic assessment of fishing, watersports, and hotel operations in the Montego Bay Marine Park, Jamaica and an analysis of reef management implications.* Report, Project RPO 681-05. Washington, D.C.: World Bank.

Carrier, J. G. 1997. Introduction to *Meanings of the market: The free market in Western culture,* ed. J. Carrier, 1–67. Oxford: Berg.

———. 2001a. Diplomacy and indirection, constraint and authority. In *An anthropology of indirect communication,* ed. J. Hendry and B. Watson, 290–301. London: Routledge.

———. 2001b. Social aspects of abstraction. *Social Analysis* 9: 239–52.

———. 2003. Mind, gaze and engagement: Understanding the environment. *Journal of Material Culture* 8: 5–23.

Carrier, J. G., and Daniel Miller, eds. 1998. *Virtualism: A new political economy.* Oxford: Berg.

Ceballos-Lascurain, H. 1996. *Tourism, ecotourism and protected areas.* Gland, Switzerland, and Cambridge: IUCN.

Christie, P., and A. T. White. 1997. Trends in development of coastal area management in tropical countries: From central to community orientation. *Coastal Management* 25: 155–81.

Dixon, J. A., L. F. Scura, and T. van't Hof. 1993. Meeting ecological and economic goals: Marine parks in the Caribbean. *Ambio* 22 (2–3): 117–25.

Edholm, F. 1995. The view from below: Paris in the 1880s. In *Landscape: Politics and perspectives,* ed. Barbara Bender, 139–68. Oxford: Berg.

Edie, C. J. 1991. *Democracy by default: Dependency and clientelism in Jamaica.* Boulder, Colo.: Lynne Rienner/Kingston: Ian Randle.

Escobar, A. 1999. After nature: Steps to an antiessentialist political ecology. *Current Anthropology* 40: 1–30.

Etzioni, A. 1993. *The spirit of community.* New York: Fontana.

Framhein, R. 1995. *The value of nature protection: Economic analysis of the Saba Marine Park.* Summary for the Government of Saba.

Goreau, T. J., L. Daley, S. Ciappara, J. Brown, S. Bourke, and K. Thacker. 1997. Community-based whole-watershed and coastal zone management in Jamaica. *Proceedings of the Eighth International Coral Reef Symposium* 2: 2093–96.

Green, N. 1995. Looking at the landscape: Class formation and the visual. In *The anthropology of landscape,* ed. E. Hirsch and M. O'Hanlon, 31–42. Oxford: Clarendon Press.

Gupta, A., and J. Ferguson, eds. 1997. *Culture, power, place.* Durham, N.C.: Duke University Press.

Hirsch, E. 1995. Introduction: Landscape: Between place and space. In *The anthropology of landscape,* ed. E. Hirsch and M. O'Hanlon, 1–30. Oxford: Clarendon Press.

Hornborg, A. 1996. Ecology as semiotics: Outlines of a contextualist paradigm for human ecology. In *Nature and society: Anthropological perspectives,* ed. P. Descola and G. Pálsson, 45–62. London: Routledge.

Ingold, T. 1992. Culture and the perception of the environment. In *Bush base: Forest farm,* ed. E. Croll and D. Parkin, 39–56. London: Routledge.

———. 1993. Globes and spheres: The topology of environmentalism. In *Environmentalism: The view from anthropology,* ed. K. Milton, 31–42. London: Routledge.

Klak, T., ed. 1998. *Globalization and neoliberalism: The Caribbean context*. Lanham, Md.: Rowman & Littlefield.

Latour, Bruno. 1993. *We have never been modern*. London: Prentice Hall.

Leach, M., and R. Mearns, eds. 1996. *The lie of the land: Challenging received wisdom on the African environment*. London: Heinemann.

Macnaghten, P., and J. Urry. 1998. *Contested natures*. London: Sage.

McMichael, P. 1998. Development and structural adjustment. In *Virtualism: A new political economy*, ed. J. G. Carrier and D. Miller, 95–116. Oxford: Berg.

McMinn, S., and E. Cater. 1998. Tourist typology: Observations from Belize. *Annals of Tourism Research* 25: 675–99.

Milton, K. 2002. *Loving nature: Towards an ecology of emotion*. London: Routledge.

Moore, M. 1993. Good government? Introduction. *IDS Bulletin* 24 (1): 1–6.

Nietschmann, B. 1995. Defending the Miskito reefs with maps and GPS. *Cultural Survival Quarterly* 18 (4): 34–37.

O'Callaghan, P. A., J. Woodley, and K. Aiken. 1988. *Montego Bay Marine Park: Project proposal for the development of Montego Bay Marine Park, Jamaica*. TS.

Olwig, K. F. 1980. National parks, tourism, and local development: A West Indian case. *Human Organization* 39: 22–31.

———. 1997. Caribbean family land: A modern commons. *Plantation Society in the Americas* 4: 135–58.

Pattulo, P. 1996. *Last resorts: The cost of tourism in the Caribbean*. Kingston: Ian Randle.

Polanyi, K. 1957. *The great transformation: The political and economic origins of our time*. Boston: Beacon Press.

Polunin, N., I. Williams, J. Carrier, and L. Robertson. 2000. *Final technical report: Ecological and social impacts in planning Caribbean marine-reserves*. (DFID project number R6783.) TS.

Read, P. 1996. *Returning to nothing: The meaning of lost places*. Cambridge: Cambridge University Press.

Roe, E. 1991. Development narratives, or making the best of blueprint development. *World Development* 19: 287–300.

Scura, L. F., and T. van't Hof. 1993. *The ecology and economics of Bonaire Marine Park*. The World Bank, Environment Department, Divisional Paper 1993-44. Washington, D.C.: World Bank.

Sennett, R. 1976. *The fall of public man*. New York: Vintage Books.

Statistical Institute of Jamaica. 1996. *Statistical yearbook of Jamaica 1995*. Kingston: Statistical Institute of Jamaica.

Strang, V. 1996. Sustaining tourism in Far North Queensland. In *People and tourism in fragile environments*, ed. M. F. Price, 51–57. Chichester: John Wiley and Son.

Toye, J. 1993. *Dilemmas of development*. 2nd ed. Oxford: Basil Blackwell.

van't Hof, T. 1985. The economic benefits of marine parks and protected areas in the Caribbean region. *Proceedings of the Fifth International Coral Reef Congress* 6: 551–56.

A Situated Global Imperative: Debating (the Nation's) Forests in Finland

6

EEVA BERGLUND

> Given that recently Rio's environment summit has been taken to oblige Finland
> radically to transform its forestry and to discipline its forest owners, it is worth
> quoting Rio's first principle: "States have, in accordance with the UN's charter
> and with international law, the full right to exploit their own natural resources in
> accordance with their own environmental legislation.". . . Citizens, we can, after
> all, decide our environmental policy ourselves! (Prof. Matti Kärkkäinen 1995)

THIS QUOTATION comes from one of the leading champions of industrial
forestry in Finland, the onetime Head of Research at the Finnish Forest
Research Institute. He was responding to claims by Finnish environmentalists that a global ecological imperative means that the exploitation of the country's expansive boreal forest must be curtailed. His words are expressive of a key
conflict of our times, that between global ecological health and global economic
growth.

Within anthropology, questioning global imperatives has become commonplace. On the following pages I will rehearse the familiar argument that so-called
global environmentalism is indeed situated and thus in some important sense
local. However, the above quotation also captures the resonance of the national in
debating policy, and so I will further suggest that social scientists would do well
to explore how the nation and the national are a framework for environmental policy, management, and activism. Even in an era of globalization and globality, the
national has enormous salience in ecopolitics.

Claims to identities and resources are everywhere increasingly tied together, not
least in countries like Finland, which have been economically dependent on one
natural resource. In the mid-1990s, Finnish policy on its primary natural resource,
forests, became a focus of intense public debate. Environmentalists whose concern

was the fate of specific tracts of forest invoked the global imperative with considerable success. The fact that the Earth Summit of 1992 made environmental concerns appear as a global preoccupation, and not just as the locally occurring campaigns of easily frightened technophobes, was a victory for ecowarriors of all varieties around the world. Environmental problems were no longer to be explained away as local accidents, but as integral to the operations of a global or international community. However, as the quotation above demonstrates, the Summit still meant that implementing the global imperative to save nature would remain in the hands of national governments and that there would be no worldwide ecopolice. In other words, specificities such as Finland's decades-old economic reliance on the forest products industries could not be overridden through appealing to global ecological crisis and the related urgency of protecting biodiversity.

Implicit in the quotation above is the fact that ecopolitics unfolds not only in relation to nature conservation agendas, but also in the context of another noteworthy imperative: to organize social life as a race for economic supremacy. The Finnish case material shows that, whether articulated in ecological or economic terms, the apparently global imperatives become salient as national preoccupations. It is the national that continues to link the personal to the political, but it is frequently also the national that hinders constructive debate. This chapter will argue that one reason for this is that the slippery terms "local" and "global" can both be opportunistically mapped onto the national. Finally, it suggests that anthropologists look again at the links between nationalisms and economics.

"[O]nly time will tell," writes Arjun Appadurai, "whether our current preoccupations with the nation-state are justified" (1996, 188). Given the empirical ubiquity of the national as a self-evident justification, despite the reality of diaspora and global flow that are Appadurai's concerns, it remains something that anthropologists cannot sidestep.

My chapter is in three parts of unequal length, beginning with a discussion of Finland's so-called forest wars in the last years of the twentieth century. I then discuss anthropological insights into the global, arguing that the discipline already has conceptual resources for tackling the seemingly intractable problems associated with global environmental politics. The chapter concludes by endorsing a standard anthropological position, arguing that the salience of the local, the global, and the national for ecopolitics is always relational, never absolute, and never beyond reasoned debate, but also always consequential.

Environmentalism in the Nation's Forests

Everywhere that logging is economically significant, conservationists and industrial users have long had disagreements over the proper management and use of forests. In the 1990s the politics of logging was increasingly cast in global terms. Nevertheless, the conflicts at the heart of what many still call Finland's forest wars were place-focused insofar as they unfolded in a series of on-site clashes pitting activists against police and representatives of the forest sector. The media portrayed the situation as a battle between state-sanctioned and nationally advantageous industrial forest use on the one hand, and romantic and economically foolhardy conservationism on the other. Usually, these sides were also represented within a framework that pitted the "local" interests of forestry-dependent rural communities against the "global" interests of urban activists, that is, against something abstract and possibly unrealistic. The values attached to each side differed according to medium and context. In reality, though, "locals" and "activists" were rarely easily distinguishable groups. Despite this, the "global" imperative of conservationists was often contrasted not only with "local" needs, but with the national (that is, collective) good of Finns. Gradually, however, this configuration was turned around, so that today national interest in the forest sector appears more and more as the need to project an ecologically benign image of its forestry practices, highlighting that new conservation areas have been established (see Berglund 2000), and informing customers of ever-"softer" management practices. The global ecological imperative seems to have become a Finnish national imperative too. It has displaced, significantly if not completely, the older view according to which environmentalism is an unwelcome intrusion from the outside world and a threat to local ways of life.[1]

In Finland, debating forest politics has always been a feature of public life, but in the first years of the 1990s it took on a new intensity as the whole country was faced with sudden economic hardship.[2] Conservation issues inevitably appeared together with other political imperatives. Questions of internal distributive justice were raised with increasing frequency, and, in contrast to earlier economic downturns, it even became possible to query the country's commitment to a strong welfare state. Adjustments to the end of the Cold War in the European Union's economy, and consumer pressures for environmental sensitivity, led to reorganizing, or "restructuring" as it was called, the forest sector.

Finland gained independence from Russia in 1917 and has, as the slogan says, "lived off the forest." Export revenue from forest products has always been remarkably high. Before the Second World War there were years when they accounted for well over one-half of exports, and even in 1990 they accounted for almost 38 percent, although by 1999 their share went down to under 30 percent, with the trend continuing downwards since (Lehtinen 2002). These figures reflect the way that state policy treated forests in a utilitarian way geared toward paper and pulp manufacture, and which was frequently labeled "forest fundamentalism" (Lehtinen 1991, 148–49; see Berglund 2000) because of its narrow interpretation of a "good" forest as an easily exploitable forest. Against the background of this hegemonic understanding, environmentalists have aimed to reeducate those responsible for Finland's forests. A broad environmentalist coalition, domestic and international, has been successful in transforming policies, not least by passing new legislation in 1997 and securing over 300,000 hectares of newly protected lands since 1993. Furthermore, it has succeeded in swinging public opinion in its favor, as well as in shifting the terms of consumer demand. Less polluting manufacturing methods and less intensive forest management[3] have now become marketing tools for the paper and pulp industry, leaving some environmentalists frustrated that despite their relative success, the consumption of timber-based products shows no sign of falling.

The forest sector across the world is still undergoing economic transformation. Constant mergers lead to regionalization and even globalization, and new preoccupations like shareholder value and some foreign ownership have entered the previously rather state-corporativist forest sector (see Donner-Amnell 2001). Although forest industries are unlikely ever to disappear from Finland, the profile of the country projected abroad is now not that of a world leader in paper and pulp, but that of a superpower in information technology, NokiaLand! Secondly, Finland's entry into the European Union in 1995, together with Sweden and Austria, meant that the EU became a net exporter rather than importer of forest products. Being in the EU also gave vigor to environmentalist views that saw Finland's old-growth forests as "Europe's last wilderness." These structural disjunctures are partly responsible for the relative gains enjoyed by environmentalists over the last ten years even though their language obviously highlights ecological rather than economic aspects. Nevertheless, biodiversity-speak was a relative novelty in early 1990s forest politics (Berglund 2001).

In boreal forests, biodiversity is said to be located in dead and rotting wood. In the politics of old-growth protection, the discovery of practically invisible allies was something of a revelation for activists. Until the mid-1980s, conservation in Finland was either a depoliticized discourse of water management and recreational services, concretized for instance in the creation of an Environment Ministry in 1983, or the highly politicized discourse of the Green Party. A shift occurred when the term "biodiversity" entered into English-language ecological discourses and a little later into Finnish. At the same time, hiking, a favorite pastime of Finnish environmentalists, became a scientific act undertaken on behalf of global nature, because it could be combined with surveying forests for endangered species (Berglund 2000, 2001). Photogenic megafauna they may not be, but the grubs and polypores that can be found in unmanaged or old-growth forests, of mixed species and of varying ages, are indices of forests' ecological value. But they are among the creatures that professional foresters, keen on "legible" (cf. Scott

1998) stands of even-aged trees, regarded with horror as destroyers of the raw material of paper and pulp. Effectively, what the forestry establishment considered a crime, namely, leaving a tree to rot standing up (Berglund 2001, 839), was seen as the epitome of nature's value by activists.

The mostly young activists[4] who became involved in conservation organizations calling for limits to industrial forest use had a variety of motivations for their work. For some an interest in flora and fauna was what had brought them into such organizations in the first place, and it was only subsequently that they found their expertise and their passion to be at the heart of a political battle. For others, politics was itself an overt motivating factor. By the mid-1990s, the global language of ecological science was definitely center stage in the debates as activists joined university groups as well as ministry-sponsored project teams, whose aim was to inventory Finland's forests and to establish how much of the landscape could still be set aside for protection on legitimate grounds, especially because of the presence of valued species. Like many biologists (Takacs 1996), activists represented themselves as resolutely scientific or objective at the same time as they appealed to absolute moral imperatives (e.g., "extinction is for ever" or "destroying forests equals killing life"), and to the global imperative (compare the description of Greek environmental activists in Theodossopoulos's chapter, this volume).

The result was often that in their zeal to save the planet activists appeared to have little or no concern for the livelihoods of forest-dependent communities. They were easy to represent as arrogant and out of touch with reality. It is noteworthy that the values attached to different stakeholders and their perspectives in the debates were associated with spatial scales. "Reality" was often coded as pertaining to local or national economic realities, biodiversity as something global and therefore distant. In pronouncements closer to environmentalist sensibilities, the perspective was switched: reality is the flora and fauna right here, perhaps even Finland's forests, whereas the economy is an unwieldy abstraction, and, as many activists pointed out, part of a utopian and romantic worldview.

The most vehement disagreements appeared to be not over global imperatives or even specific forests, but over the correct perspective from which to view "the nation's forests." Phrased like this, the tendency was for ecology to become pitted against economics, or, as elsewhere, conservation against jobs. The most striking feature of the debates in the mid-1990s was that both nature and the economy were almost always discussed as national property: Finnish forests or Finnish nature in opposition to Finnish ways of life or Finnish exports. This is typical of Western ideas of property relations, where an individual or quasi-individual (e.g., corporate) subject is considered the most natural owner of an individual object. However, there are interesting features of Finnish land ownership that make the idea of Finnish forests as Finnish collective property even more resonant.

Throughout the twentieth century, well over half of the forest used by the industry was (as it still is) in private, small-scale ownership. Thus, most timber was sold to the industry by owners easily considered part of the ordinary public, and for whom forest revenue formed a calculable and steady, though often small, part of total household income. Particularly in the dramatic recession of the early 1990s, the forest conflicts were also conflicts about the rights of individuals, particularly rural men and women, to dispose of their property as they wished. (The broad argument about Finnish forests as Finnish property is complicated but also strengthened by the fact that despite private ownership of forests, their management has effectively remained in the hands of a forest administration whose task has always been to look out for the interests of the industry: see Berglund 2000, 2001.) If legislation on forests was to be changed, this meant real effects on the social and biological environments that most Finns inhabit.

The forest sector's significance in the economy had already begun to decline in relative terms in the 1970s. The social and ecological transformations associated with this continue (Donner-Amnell 2001), but despite the growing prominence of high tech as an export item, forest-based production is and will continue to be of major significance to Finland. So, it is not surprising that by the middle of the decade the debate had become a conflict about how best to respond nationally to a new external, that is global, economic situation. What was at stake was the future of the national economy: the country as a whole had to choose which fork in the road to take, and this meant that the nation's forest politics was being redrawn or recast in a new mold. Such metaphors of construction are all prominent throughout the public debates and the documents that accompanied them (e.g., Palo and Hellström 1993).

Even before the start of the recession, employment in the forest sector, both forestry and related manufacturing, was down substantially from the heyday of the 1960s and even the 1980s. Furthermore, benefits from the forest sector began to be less equally distributed than they had been earlier in the century (Donner-Amnell 2001). Despite such economic shifts, a powerful narrative of Finland as a forest-state and Finnish culture as forest culture (Berglund 2000) regularly conflated the forest sector's interests with national interests. Images of wise management proliferated for domestic and foreign consumption, and new books began to get published with titles like *The Green Kingdom*, celebrating the fact that over 150 years of state forestry and state support for the forest products industries had woven the landscape, the people, and the infrastructure into an integrated, but also impeccably surveyed and governable, whole (Berglund 2000). As I write in 2002—when Nokia and other high-tech sectors have become dominant economically and more visible culturally—publications, TV, and film, and, indeed, the everyday lives of most Finns still partake of the forests. In short, although the real economic significance of forestry has been declining, it is still not too difficult to talk up the nation's historical dependency on its forests.

The above sketch of the defining features of Finland's recent economic history and the key characteristics of the forest debates allows some comparisons to be made. North American environmentalism, of which so much has been written (e.g., Cronon 1995b; Nash 1973), is often identified as a model for the global politics of biodiversity (e.g., Takacs 1996). Classifying environmentalisms is not the task here, but by any definition, American environmentalism has undoubtedly been a key inspiration for what is now thought of as global environmentalism. It echoes the vague but powerful notion that the "global" is something distant and far away. Numerous conservation initiatives in the past, as well as today, attest to the fact that saving nature is often an agenda whose implementation takes place somewhere distant. However important long-distance alliances are in efforts to prevent the destruction of nature, the long-distance character of "global" environmentalism has often meant that it easily appears arrogant. If agenda-setting in Washington, D.C., influences the global South, by the same token agenda-setting in Helsinki shapes rural Finland. To that extent at least, conservation wields central power in the periphery.

Some of environmentalism's arrogance can be traced to the foundational role that nature plays in Western thought (Cronon 1995b; Latour 1998; Takacs 1996). In the dualistic frameworks characteristic of Western philosophy, nature is simply the Other. As Other, nature is as easily objectified as industrial raw material as it is as sacred and timeless Arcadia. The generally unproblematic argument is that for urban dwellers, daily engagement with forested landscapes tends to be mediated by images and expectations that emphasize either the purely recreational and the aesthetic on the one hand, or the purely instrumental on the other. Whether as nature to be consumed or nature to be exploited, such a view of nature as Other is often analyzed as a construct of the bourgeois, and above all, the colonizing mind, but also as a legacy of Judeo-Christian visions of humanity as inescapably fallen. Such combinations of Western cultural beliefs have led to conceptualizing nature as timeless, perfect, and empty of humans. It has also led to writing conquest and genocide out of the history of the so-called great outdoors. For example, in his analysis of environmentalism in the USA, William Cronon (1995a, 79) writes, "[t]he removal of the Indians to create an 'uninhabited wilderness,' uninhabited as never before in the human history of the place, reminds us just how invented, just how constructed, the American wilderness really is."

As inheritors of such a history, and part of the expansive and fossil fuel–dependent organization of space in North America, no wonder American nature lovers could also become convinced that there is an absolute dividing line between the cultural life of the city (whether valued or devalued) and the absolutely pristine nature of the world beyond it. And no wonder that this separate world came to be valued not unlike a beautiful portrait might be, as an aesthetic experience, providing temporary respite from the more real labors of everyday life in the city. And no wonder it appears passive rather than active. From this perspective, one can take this visual metaphor quite literally: saving nature is indeed about meddling in other people's lives.

As inspirational as U.S. environmentalism has been, it would be absurd to assume that the country's violent and resource-exploiting expansion, and its development into a fossil fuel–dependent territorial power without equal, would generate a "global" template for environmentalism any more than it has enabled a "global" model for economic and military supremacy. Finnish experiences of the nature out there are historically quite different from North American ones and so Finnish activism reflects such differences. Whether privately (within the household) or collectively (through the idea of the forests as Finland's shared property), natural resources have been experienced as part of everyday life, not only as identity-forming, but as economically significant over several generations. This was true for some activists too.

On the other hand, despite the fact that "nature" is more present in quotidian life in Finland, Finnish activists have found common cause with peers in the United States and elsewhere. Aesthetic appreciation and scientific interest, as well as environmentalism's resistance to the encroachment of capitalist relations into every corner of the world and every aspect of life, certainly combine to create alliances that can in turn generate global networks and a global social movement. No doubt the mutual understanding and the recognition of shared problems increased the sense of justification of environmentalism as a specifically global task. Beyond the practice of activism and the social interaction it has fostered, the salience of global arguments about needing to protect (good) nature from (bad) humanity and its exploitation rests also in part in the history of modern resource management, which, along with the expansion of capitalist social relations, has only reinforced the pervasive dualism between nature and culture-society.

This situation alerts us to the salience of the national. Many forest activists knew the economic importance of forests from their own experience, and framed their work as a question of how all Finnish landowners must now face the global challenge. Finland is hardly unique in the way its debates over resources are articulated in terms that highlight national ownership at the same time as they talk about "global" imperatives. This case study, however, can yield insights into what kinds of questions anthropologists concerned with environmental relations more generally might be posing. This is because the sticking point of these debates seems to be less the nature-culture dualism than the issue of national proprietorship of a resource.

A Short Ethnographic Illustration

The following ethnographic illustration highlights the salience of the national. It also shows that debating it can have a debilitating effect on the discussion.

Activists have explicitly pitted their demands against a historical legacy of a century of self-consciously modern state-sanctioned forestry in the name of the national good. They appeal to several dimensions of this, for instance: a historical connection between people and forests in Finland, the experience as individual human beings of being protected by a forest, the shame of living in such a potentially rich yet actually degraded environment. They contrast Finland's protected areas unfavorably with neighboring countries (Sweden's higher proportion of protected land, Russia's untouched wilderness areas) and they cite percentages of territory demarcated as national parkland as evidence of a lag in the international competition to be ecofriendly.

In the mid-1990s, Kuusamo Common Forest, a cooperatively owned old but loggable area of forest[5] in remote eastern Finland, was identified by activists as spectacular in biological terms. But it was also seen by local owners as revenue for an ailing local economy. Over the weeks and months during which the conflict spilled out into the media, both sides appealed to the national interest. In activist discourse the Kuusamo forest was a microcosm of Finland and its fate was emblematic of the fate of the whole country. In local accounts, the forest was part of the national economy, in which it was local people's right as well as duty to participate. There was mutual learning, and some locals were willing to enter into discussion with outsiders. Nevertheless, in their opinion, what Kuusamo Common Forest had already done to promote conservation should be seen as pioneering in the national frame, not as backward, as conservationists implied. For other locals, the fact that volunteer conservationists had succeeded in bringing the area onto the agenda of the state environmental administration was taken as a sign that the nation had forgotten them, and bitterness ensued.

The debate thus invoked a number of understandings of the national, not all of which were compatible. For some the nation as a source of economic and political security seemed to be eroding; for others national economic competitiveness was either trivial compared to threats to biodiversity or a cynical front for profit-hungry global capital. For many activists, the national was the level at which Finland's conservationist credentials would be measured. But for everyone, the national was the level at which conflicting interests should be reconciled.

However, it was at an international meeting convened in Kuusamo in October 1996 by the Taiga Rescue Network, an umbrella organization of nongovernmental organizations, focused on boreal forest, that the national issue came up most poignantly. Despite efforts to engage with rather than confront the townspeople via the conference, the environment in the form of forests was again quickly pitted against the economy in the form of local jobs. Many interests were represented: industry, shareowners of the Common, and trade unions, as well as voluntary and governmental organizations. Over and over again, conservation was represented as a threat to the rights of people living in Kuusamo. According to at least one local landowner, Finland had neglected this peripheral region and now, by seeking to take the forest out of commercial use, the rest of the country was effectively sacrificing the region on the altar of green images to help promote Finnish forest products as ecofriendly. According to another landowner, what was at stake was the fate of Kuusamo's "indigenous" people, whose forefathers had migrated there 400 years ago, and who had worked in the forests ever since, so that "claims concerning ancient and primeval forests lack a factual basis. . . . Certainly there are individual old trees there, but a tree and a forest are different things" (Kuusamo Common Forest, address 26 October 1996). Workers and trade unions were critical of a national policy that failed to add value and create skilled jobs through the industry. They also compared their wages to those of woodworkers beyond Finland, and found them wanting.

According to my notes, one of the strongest audience reactions came during a panel discussion involving a number of very different representatives under the heading: Can the ecological and socioeconomical interests of the remaining old-growth forests in Kuusamo be combined? A representative of the Common Forest reiterated the familiar phrase, "Finland lives off the forest," and proceeded to outline the real economic importance of forestry for the area's population and to underline the need for compensation if any more forests were to be set aside. When a representative of Greenpeace responded that Finland no longer actually lived off the forest, that electronics was bigger, there were several shouts from the audience that he was wrong. The discussion moved to one of how regional and national problems could be solved together, since whether or not Finland lives off the forest, the fate of Kuusamo's Common Forest is of statewide interest. Tony Jupiter of WWF-UK pointed out that, in fact, Kuusamo was of interest to the EU and that it should be EU taxpayers who compensate Kuusamo for any losses. As the debate threatened to move onto yet another exchange of facts and figures, of local jobs and revenue lost, a young activist cut in, protesting that thinking about jobs versus environment would inevitably lead to losses in both areas. Furthermore, she insisted, activists like herself were not merely interested in saving "creepy crawlies" (biodiversity) nor were they part of a global conspiracy of urbanites seeking to undermine rural economies. In the end, she said, what is important is Finnish heritage. And that, she pointed out, could not be reduced to facts and figures.

I have invoked this as an example of the salience of the nation even at moments where one least expects it. This young woman had frequently made it clear that her knowledge of worldwide biodiversity loss was exemplary and that she was as critical of green agendas of a blood-and-soil variety as anyone. The effect of such interventions on the debate is, however, often debilitating in itself, for the focus of the debate then shifts. The interlocutors' reciprocal claims to be more patriotic than their opponents displace, for a while at least, the possibility of mutual learning, negotiation, and thus political breakthrough.

The idea of the nation provided a fetishlike point of reference for people with a variety of political agendas and personal interests. Like polyvalent symbols everywhere, "the nation" is emotionally and socially powerful but analytically weak, leaving those with power more likely to succeed in pursuing their interests even if the intellectual grounds for doing so are lacking. When national interest is invoked it is automatically virtuous, unquestioned as grounds for action and for assessment of risk and of benefit. But it means different things to different people, and even different things to the same people in different situations. Where the nation is represented as part of an international economic order, it emerges as just one among many local actors all operating at a global level. At other times, the nation stands for shared and cherished commitments and is contrasted to the abstract and impersonal calculations of economists as well as counters of endangered species. At yet other times, the nation itself is the external power, the abstraction against which local and urgent needs have to be claimed. (In the context of Kuusamo, the nation as an abstraction was a focus of bitterness and resentment: we here on the periphery have once again been ignored!)

The national is then unreflectively deployed in real-life conflict situations. In practice, the national may provide more realistic coordinates for policy, and even for narrating what is important, than the global. The national also operates as a surrogate, possibly a conduit, for the global or the abstract. Reflecting on the polysemic qualities of the national, one might argue pragmatically and constructively that it has the capacity to mediate between the personal and the planetary. But it is also used in ways that confuse. As deployed in rhetoric as well as in law or policy, there are elements of the national that make it intellectually as well as emotionally compelling, but also obfuscating, and it is these elements that the rest of my chapter will examine. In this respect there are striking resemblances between uses of the global and uses of the national.

Anthropology and the Global

> While it is easy to render local whatever passes for globalspeak, anthropologists cannot close their ears to it either. (Strathern 1995, 168)

The ability to make the epithet "global" stick goes together with the power to define oneself as part of the international community. So the idea of the global reflects the preferences of those in that community; say, comfortable if clonelike hotels across the world, market forces, ecofriendliness, and latterly also Islamophobia. Seen like this, the global is always a situated affair, but, as Strathern's quotation above reminds us, it is still consequential. Often enough, the parochialism of the "global" perspective has been presented in relation to environmentalism. In a poignant essay on the politics of whaling, Niels Einarsson cites a twelve-year-old American conservationist's letter to the government of Iceland. The child's use of global ecospeak captures the imagination, but his proclamation also demonstrates the parochialism (and immaturity) of his position, and his inability to "get a perspective" on anything but the cuddly whales iconic of Western conservation imagery. The passage from the letter provided by Einarsson ends in an expression of disgust at all Icelanders: "You are lazy savages who do not wish to work at other things but prefer to kill innocent creatures. You make civilized children sick. I am sure God hates you all" (quoted in Einarsson 1993, 73).

A noteworthy anthropological point here is that the imagery and language of the quotation do not remain detached from practical decisions or from tangible consequences. There is, however, still a tension in this kind of exposition and analysis of environmentalism, in that anthropological engagements with ecopolitical struggles have often been interpreted as turning away from the material consequences of ecological degradation. They have, obviously, focused on the cultural and symbolic aspects of life at the margins. Conventionally, they have also concentrated on the minutiae of a place rather than the big picture. As a profession, we also struggle to come to terms with the fact that our work has meant the implicit romanticization and dehistoricization of those whose lives we have interrupted for the sake of academic research (see Berglund and Anderson 2002). Anthropologists have blamed their own discipline for the binarism that divides the world into modern and traditional societies and that polarizes knowledge into technoscientific and indigenous (e.g., Dove 2000). Notwithstanding these issues, I will suggest that the discipline actually offers important and influential arguments about place and scale, which explode any easy dichotomies between the abstractions of the global versus the concreteness of the local and which make the tussle between proponents of big pictures and defenders of local context seem anachronistic.

The basic points are unchallenged within social sciences, but still important to make explicit. In one sense, a global view cannot be achieved by everyone because defining what is global is a question of power. In another sense, a global view is available only to those who believe they have access to completely unbiased, disinterested knowledge, especially modern science. It also remains the case that to claim one's view as global is still to attribute value to an embodied, concrete, and located something. The example with which environmental anthropologists are most familiar is the Amazon, which is taken by many across Europe, North America, and Australasia to be part of humanity's, not just Brazil's, natural heritage: the lungs of the world. However, it is the case that what counts as global is only one aspect of the region, its biodiversity and "ecological services," whereas the Amazon's history and politics, its human life, is routinely overlooked. Similarly Finland (along with parts of Russia) is treated by many overseas environmentalists as Europe's last wilderness.

Analyzing ecopolitics almost always invites addressing questions of place, scale, and power. Working out of the Finnish material, it is necessary to explore how it is that, under the weight of whatever is more encompassing (global, or European), the national vanishes only to reappear with vigor. What I have described is how spatial boundaries tend to come back into debate as that which cannot actually be debated: a question of national sovereignty. To move on, what is needed is another set of coordinates to enable mutual learning and transformation.[6] The point of getting a new perspective, of highlighting that what appears as the "global imperative" itself emerges "in context," is not to undermine claims to knowledge or truth, that is, to relativize and confuse, but the exact opposite. If anthropology takes neither the global nor the national as given, perhaps those beyond anthropology should and could be made to take note. What follows is a selective survey of some of the anthropological work that has already helped to foster such debate.

The framework which Tim Ingold has elaborated in a number of texts (collected in Ingold 2000) lends itself to reflecting on Finland's old-growth conflicts. Here I only touch on one aspect of Ingold's influential and broad-ranging work, his critique of the global perspective. According to Ingold, in European thought true knowledge is considered to be available only through vision and transmissible through representation, whereas one who is fully engaged with the world and "dwells" within it finds his or her knowledge "regarded as illusory and incomplete" (2000, 211). The irony Ingold highlights is that the notion that space travel and images of the fragile blue planet heralded a key turning point for environmental politics, an event which humbled humanity and forced the global environment onto everyone's political agenda, is in fact completely to misunderstand the philosophical legacy of Western, dualistic thought. Rather than the global perspective providing humanity with a sense of togetherness and an appreciation of its common destiny, Ingold suggests that the concretization of the global perspective in the photographs of planet Earth was, in fact, a culmination of a process in which Western civilization separated itself from its materiality and took itself out of the process of living (2000, 209). As a way of constructing a relationship with one's surroundings, the global perspective, as Ingold's work elucidates it, has been extremely powerful but needs to be, and is increasingly being, challenged (2000, 217).

Ingold's work finds echo among self-consciously feminist authors. Acknowledging Ingold's inspiration, *Global Nature, Global Culture* (Franklin, Lury, and Stacey 2000) brings politics more explicitly back into the discussion about the local and the global, focussing on the violence and the inequality involved in conceptualizing the natural environment as a global commons. Specifically they link the image of the fragile blue planet to similarly disseminated images of the fetus and of the cell, the building block of the human body. They highlight the point that despite certain differences, both the globe and the cell are represented as self-regulating, and their proliferation also conveys a normative message. These understandings of the planet and of the cell as building blocks of the human body are attached to certain imperatives: "the responsibility to maintain balance, the need to keep oneself informed, the duty to calculate risk" (2000, 41).

Such a self-consciously politicizing and specifically feminist reading of these widespread icons and metaphors adds some important elements to the discussion. Thus, if the planet is in danger, not all societies or all humans are equally to blame. If imagery is fundamental to creating and upholding norms and value systems, the imagery of global nature erases differences and inequalities or alternatively renaturalizes them. Planet, fetus, and cell as key metaphors travel across scales. This means that the hegemonic interpretation of the imperative associated with the images, to ensure health, operate as much on the cellular and bodily level as they do on the planetary level. The argument can also be applied to spatial scales: individual people, specific neighborhoods, nations, even the planet, have come to be treated not only as self-regulating subjects with the power to determine their future, but as responsible for their own fate. Finally, *Global Nature, Global Culture* draws attention to the way the global and the local are produced through processes of commodification. The promise that consumer goods will transcend cultural difference and spatial distance is no longer at issue, as brands and logos circulating through exchange networks make the world seem ever smaller. Indeed, it is the "global" of so-called world trade, of course, that is the focus of the critiques, along with the way global capital treats locality as an opportunity for niche-marketing and the commodification of (superficial) diversity.

While these authors warn against taking the global as given, Arjun Appadurai (1996) warns against taking locality and the local as given. His treatment of the issue is above all political, and he foresees only further disjunctures in the production of reliable social futures, as complex and contradictory forces—economic, cultural, political—at different scales are simplified into a standard formula: the tussle between the indigenization or primordialization of the local on the one hand and global commoditization (or equivalent external enemy) (1996, 32) on the other. Like globality or the global, locality too needs constantly to be produced, materially for example, in gardens, fields and forests, and house construction (1996, 180), as well as in images. The political dimension of Appadurai's work is ever present, for instance as he links the existence of such practical activities to the expectations associated with them. Writing in the flux of modern and postmodern abstractions, he proposes the term "neighborhood" to denote the kind of sociality that is produced and reproduced in a place. This can be contrasted to the notion of ethnoscape, a community that is created across several locations. Places in effect are produced through local knowledge, something that produces "reliably local subjects as well as . . . reliably local neighbourhoods" (1996, 181). In Appadurai's vision, the nation-state appears as a counterforce to this kind of production of locality that, for the modern nation-state, is "either a site of nationally appropriated nostalgias, celebrations, and commemorations or a necessary condition of the production of nationals" (1996, 190).

Notwithstanding their differences, these discussions draw out the complexity in how spatial relations are experienced and narrated. They suggest dynamic or historical and metalevel theoretical frameworks of the kind that social science in an age of ecological crisis might find useful. They also make room for analyzing the fraught questions of difference and identity, which, as the potential for nationalist impasse demonstrates, need to be addressed in relation to environmentalism too.

Finally, a word about one of the best-known anthropologists to have elaborated on the relationship between the local and the global, Ulf Hannerz. His work on the topic (e.g., 1996) affirms the existence of a global culture as well as of local cultures, but he wishes to destabilize the implicit value judgment involved in the local-global opposition. What is significant about his essays in the present context is their continued attention to the role of the national in the way such value judgments are made. Among his more resonant examples (Salman Rushdie in literature and Robert Reich in corporate management are among them) are those that highlight hybridity, fluidity, and translocality as key characteristics of our era, and yet which evoke a sense of pain at not being able to be unhybrid, fixed, or local. Analytically too there is a desire for a replacement of some kind: "If the nation as an idea is culturally impoverished . . . we cannot be quite certain whether it is replaced by anything else" (1996, 88), though Hannerz's own conclusion is that the nation is less withering away than changing (1996, 89).

Discussing the production of localities and identities, Hannerz does come up against the ubiquitous role of the global economy, and suggests that the big question for an increasing number of people is "what can your nation do for you that a good credit card cannot do?" (1996, 88). The mischievous example is apposite to my current concerns, since it incorporates all three terms at play in the ecopolitical struggles that this book is about: the local market where the credit card will buy anything from a good (ethnic?) meal to tourist trinkets (or at least the cash to purchase them) in any location across the globe; the exchange networks that are themselves global in the sense that capital today is allowed free movement across the world; and the nation.

In this brief survey I have wanted to indicate, firstly, that the same spatial instabilities that become so visible and problematic in ecopolitical struggles are already being tackled by anthropologists who are not overtly discussing anything ecopolitical as such. This does mean that if anthropology wants to address the ecological disasters that color the lives of so many it studies, it need not start from scratch, nor indeed need it worry about transposing ethnographic methods onto questions of spatially dispersed action, such as resource politics. The global and the local are both amenable to analysis as products of sociality (Strathern 1995). Secondly, I have wanted to suggest that the spatial issue must be seen in relation to social and cultural activities. These authors have begun to highlight that spatial coordinates and spatial mythologies, for instance that the global is everywhere and it is neutral and homogenous, are tightly linked to coordinates that allocate resources and recognize identities as legitimate or not. In effect this means that as anthropologists we recognize, and must tackle, the fact that the material and the symbolic or imaginary are always linked. As anthropologists we also appreciate the double fact that the global is never "simply" all that is universal and the local is never "merely" the local.

The National as Both Global and Local

New political spaces—alliances, networks, administrative branches, international agreements, and so on—proliferate through ecopolitical struggles. At the same time, ecopolitics connects claims over identities to claims over resources at all scales (Strathern 1999). This is evident in the rhetorics of national values, not only in self-consciously patriotic nation-states such as Finland or in contemporary indigenisms where pristine nature maps onto primitive humanity, but also in self-consciously modern states like the United States and even the United Kingdom, where Welsh, Scottish, and English heritages are increasingly meaningful realities. A logic seems to be at play that intensifies the identification of resources, or heritage, with national or quasi-national identification despite countervailing globalizing forces.

If the previous section stressed that locality and globality are social achievements, ethnography alerts us to the conditions of institutionalized commercial competition and a heightened sense of differentiation that impinge on such processes. These tendencies are regularly referred to in the work of Franklin, Lury, and Stacey, of Appadurai, and of Hannerz. They are also ubiquitous in regional politics as localities compete with each other to attract investments. Above all, they appear in ecopolitics, which is to say, wherever the distribution of goods and bads, specifically of natural resources, is center stage. However, it seems that the imperative to compete and national difference both come out of the way that life is imagined as a race for supremacy between "economies," and these in turn ideally map onto nation-states. Despite globalization, what falls within the borders of a state is thought about and talked about as an economy (Mitchell 1998), and the resources therein, both human and natural, are easily treated as national property.

Elsewhere I have argued that history accounts for the strength of national thinking in Finland (Berglund 2000, 2001). Here, though, I want to suggest that the trope of the national, specifically of national property, is salient not only because of its empirical (historical) integrity, but also because it operates as a mediating term between the local and the global. I shall further suggest that it mediates an economic relationship between the local and the global whose material and social reality is far more complex and vibrant than appeals to national competitiveness suggest. Drawing on Marilyn Strathern's suggestive analysis of the qualities of local and global as coordinates for organizing knowledge (1995), I argue that both are combined in the national. Rhetorically, this makes it appear utterly unassailable. At issue is not simply a polarity with global as the opposite of local (Strathern 1995, 158–59). For instance, locals appear to be fragile things, defined by contrasting them with other locals. Of course locals are also conceptualized in relation to the global, but asymmetrically, so that the global operates with a force of its own, irrespective of the multiplicity of locals. "Global influences may be locally expressed, but the force that drives whatever appears as global is assumed to have its own origins" (Strathern 1995, 159). Rhetorically, then, global and local are in a hierarchical relationship. There is only one global, it transcends all locals, and above all, there is nothing beyond it to provide an external context, a way of getting a perspective. The global is global is global and that's it; it requires, indeed it affords, no further explanation.

Envisioning "the local" for a moment as abstraction, rather than as the location of the anthropologist's endeavors, brings some interesting features into view. In that way it is possible to envisage the nation, at least in some cases, as a local in contrast to other locals—that is, to other nations—displaying not similarity but above all essential difference. The United Nations and countless other conventions already enshrine this view and map it, quite literally, onto territorial boundaries (the work of Liisa Malkki, e.g., 1995, provides compelling analysis). It is then also possible to see what happens when the national is contrasted to what anthropologists more habitually consider local: say, a municipality like Kuusamo. In relation to Kuusamo, the national operates in the same way as the global. In that situation it is the national which is irreducible; it has its own origins, its own ubiquity that is not reducible to the vicissitudes of mere localities, neighborhoods, or places (though this is not something that can be said of supranationals like the European Union).

In Finland, the nation parallels the irreducible global in the sense that to try to imagine not having a nationality is as impossible as trying to imagine no nature. Nationality is equated with citizenship and an individual's automatic entitlement to universal human rights. But although the idea of universality was key to early nationalisms, it has been the localizing and thus exclusionary aspect of nationalism that has generally been highlighted in the literature (Appadurai 1996; Gupta and Ferguson 1997). This is hardly surprisingly, given the intensity and expansion of the violence associated with contemporary identity politics. However, when the nation stands for universal principles as it does in law and policy, including environmental or resource-use policy, it appears with the universalizing qualities of the global. Perhaps it helps to think of it as the global-national.

What I am getting at is that the nation can still, despite talk of multiculturalism and globalization, provide the same kinds of irreducible coordinates as the global. It provides its own justification, the outer limits of itself; and also like the global, the national provides its own imperative, its own context and its own arena of self-fashioning. But it does more than this. At the same time as it denies that it is embedded in a context, it constantly highlights that very context, making a virtue of the difference between itself (compatriots) and the other (foreigners). Inward-looking, it embraces the specificity of the here and now only to acknowledge that, beyond its borders, there are other, equivalent but different, specificities. Effectively, the national takes the features of the global and the features of the locally specific and combines them to create a self-referential whole powerful enough that the internal contradiction or paradox of nationalism, simultaneous universality and specificity, turns into strength, not weakness.

Conclusion

I have argued that by the mid-1990s, Rio's Earth Summit had made the environment a global imperative even Finns could not ignore, however much the country struggled in the post–Cold War upheaval. Two global imperatives became public preoccupations. One was increased competition in the global market, which, for Finland, was taken by many to require continuation and even intensification of industrial forest use. Incompatible with this, the other was the need to protect biodiversity and retreat from industrial forest use.

And so a specter that has haunted this chapter but has not been fully revealed must now be named: the economy. Rhetorically and implicitly with respect to the economy, the national and the global regularly slide into each other. In Finland a domestic economy really was constructed in the early twentieth century: railroads, manufacturing plants, banks, state-sanctioned professional bodies like the forestry services. Arguably, without such a national economic infrastructure political independence would not have been possible for Finland. And wealth grew through the twentieth century literally on the lands of hundreds of thousands of small-scale landowners, and via the workplaces of further thousands in the various parts of the forest products industries. Although it was not the only source of wealth, industrial forest use was instrumental in transforming Finland in three or four generations from a colonized, obscure, and above all poor place to an icon of technological and economic success. However, the goods and services that are accessible to citizens increasingly shade into something far more abstract, namely, the economy of the theorists and policy makers. In this economy only timber sold on the market counts, but not that collected for domestic use or berries and mushrooms that are consumed outside monetary relationships. The official national economy then easily slides into the economy of global markets. The global economy is then the irreducible that provides the context for national competitiveness. There seems no inconsistency in the fact that although "the economy" is neither contained within the borders of the nation-state nor imagined as self-sufficient, it is consistently talked about as if it were its own irreducible entity. The consistency would seem to emerge out of the sense that "the economy," wherever it is, is just too powerful, too encompassing, for any other system to challenge it.

Indeed, the specter of the economy is truly frightening in its ability to change shape and size and yet at the same time maintain its power. In this chapter, for instance, I have talked of the construction of Finland as a political unit whose landscape reflects economic history on the one hand, while on the other I have referred to the ideas of global competitiveness and global commerce that have served as implicit backdrops to the people, places, and resources mentioned. The idea of a global economic reality lurked in the background of the debates all the time so as to make national competitiveness the unquestionable political goal of all fully human and rational Finnish people. Nevertheless, it is imperative not to ignore the fact that the backstage utterances of many activists, unsurprisingly, challenged this ("what's truly utopian is the belief in continuing economic growth"), and some wanted to redefine what the national good might be: perhaps not first place in OECD league tables, but good quality of life. Despite this, the very idea that one might overtly want to erode the link between Finnish identity and Finnish natural resources, let alone fail to maximize economic growth, was unutterable if not unthinkable.

I have argued that the resonance of the national, at least in the Finnish case, rests on both the abstract and implicit qualities of the global-national imperative, but also on the visible and tangible traces left by a history that naturalized nationalism. The quotation at the beginning of this chapter underlines the way the global-national imperative has been naturalized. The point of my analysis has been to suggest that even if political independence and Finnish identity appear as the key motives for the outburst, these were long ago subordinated to narrower imperatives. The "we" the author refers to may well appear just as abstract as global humanity; its use is certainly even less warranted than twenty years ago, given that the "benefits of the [national forest use] project have not spread as evenly and broadly as before" (Donner-Amnell 2001, 114). As we know, this fact can actually lead to further intensification of nationalist politics and sentiment.

Given the way the economic and the cultural are fused in the territorial nation-state, more conceptual work on this nexus should be done. If activists and stakeholders in emotionally charged confrontations find themselves stuck when national identity is invoked, social science can demonstrate slippages and ambiguities in politically salient claims and arguments. We can draw attention to and even account for the often limiting impact of explanations and exhortations made in the name of the national or the global. We can begin to show that it is the global economic environment that has come to encompass and thus contextualize all decision making, but also that the god of globalization is not the countervailing force with which to combat nationalisms and other forms of exclusion and violence.

Notes

1. Forests mostly remain in small-scale ownership. They are fundamental to economic life at all scales, from households to state coffers, as well as to local identities.

2. There is a wealth of literature in Finnish that treats the roots and consequences of the crisis. An overview is available in English on the net on NATO's information site (http://www.nato.int/ccms/general/countrydb/index.html), consulted in August 2002.

> The economy, which experienced an average of 4.9% annual growth between 1987 and 1989, sank into deep recession in 1991 as growth contracted by 6.5%. The recession—which continued in 1992 with growth contracting by 4.1%—has been caused by economic overheating, depressed foreign markets, and the dismantling of the barter system between Finland and the former Soviet Union under which Soviet oil and gas had been exchanged for Finnish manufactured goods. The Finnish Government has proposed efforts to increase industrial competitiveness and efficiency by an increase in exports to Western markets, cuts in public expenditures, partial privatization of state enterprises, and changes in monetary policy. In June 1991 Helsinki had tied the markka to the European Union's (EU) European Currency Unit (ECU) to promote stability. Ongoing speculation resulting from a lack of confidence in the government's policies forced Helsinki to devalue the markka by about 12% in November 1991 and to indefinitely break the link in September 1992. The devaluations have boosted the competitiveness of Finnish exports to the extent the recession bottomed out in 1993 with renewed economic growth expected in 1994. Unemployment probably will remain a serious problem during the next few years, with the majority of Finnish firms facing a weak domestic market and the troubled German and Swedish export markets.

3. Finnish forestry practice has gone through many changes in the last 150 years, but although most of the forest land has been managed with industrial uses and maximum

profitability in mind, clear-cuts for instance, have tended to be relatively small and even infrequent in some areas and geometrically laid out plantation forests are rare. Biologists have mostly complained that prevailing management practices may have resulted in more trees or timber, as the industry likes to point out, but also in less intact and viable ecosystems with minimal biological diversity.

4. From the mid-1980s there has been a steady but constantly changing network of activists, many of whom have gone on to have careers in various voluntary organizations as well as in governmental environmental protection. Helsinki has been the network's central node, but its operations have extended across the country and even beyond into Russian old-growth forests (Berglund 1997). A sense of the work can be gained, for example, via the website of the Nature League: http://www.luontoliitto.fi/forest/.

5. Although much of Finland's forest is managed as small woodlots by individual farmers or their heirs, whether living locally or not, there are a number of cooperatively owned and run forests across the country. These are generally thought of as privately owned as opposed to state owned, and so conservation has been seen as a curtailment of rights to make profit from them. The Kuusamo Common Forest is owned by representatives from 6,000 families either currently or formerly living in the region.

6. At the conference where these papers were first presented, Kay Milton noted that reasoned (or reasonable) argument must maintain a significant place in environmental conflicts. It is argument, not entrenched positions on axioms of belief, that can dislodge what look like impasses in ecopolitics.

References

Appadurai, A. 1996. *Modernity at large*. Minneapolis: University of Minnesota Press.

Berglund, E. 1997. Clear-cut madness in Russian Karelia. *The Ecologist* 276: 237–41.

———. 2000. Forestry expertise and national narratives: Some consequences for old-growth conflicts in Finland. *Worldviews* 4: 47–67.

———. 2001. Facts, beliefs and biases: Perspectives on forest conservation in Finland. *Journal of Environmental Planning and Management* 44: 833–49.

Berglund, E., and David G. Anderson. 2002. Introduction: Towards an ethnography of ecological underprivilege. In *Ethnographies of conservation: Environmentalism and the distributing of privilege*, ed. D. G. Anderson and E. Berglund, 1–15. Oxford: Berghahn.

Cronon, W. 1995a. The trouble with wilderness; or, getting back to the wrong nature. In *Uncommon ground: Rethinking the human place in nature*, ed. W. Cronon, 114–31. New York: Norton.

———, ed. 1995b. *Uncommon ground: Rethinking the human place in nature*. New York: Norton.

Donner-Amnell, J. 2001. To be or not to be Nordic? How internationalisation has affected the character of the Nordic forest industry and forest utilisation in the Nordic countries. *Nordisk Samhällsgeografisk Tidskrift* 33: 87–124.

Dove, M. 2000. The life-cycle of indigenous knowledge, and the case of natural rubber production. In *Indigenous environmental knowledge and its transformations: Critical anthropological perspectives*, ed. R. Ellen, P. Parkes, and A. Bicker, 213–51. Amsterdam: Harwood Academic.

Einarsson, N. 1993. All animals are equal, but some are cetaceans. In *Environmentalism: The view from anthropology*, ed. K. Milton, 73–84. London: Routledge.

Franklin, S., C. Lury, and J. Stacey. 2000. *Global nature, global culture.* London: Sage.

Gupta, A., and J. Ferguson. 1997. *Culture, power, place: Explorations in critical anthropology.* Durham, N.C.: Duke University Press.

Hannerz, U. 1996. *Transnational connections: Culture, people, places.* London: Routledge.

Ingold, T. 2000. *The perception of the environment: Essays on livelihood, dwelling and skill.* London: Routledge.

Kärkkäinen, M. 1995. Ympäristöpolitiikka on Suomen metsätalouden kannattavuuden suurin uhka. *Käytännön Maamies* 1: 41.

Kuehls, T. 1996. *Beyond sovereign territory: The space of ecopolitics.* Minneapolis: University of Minnesota Press.

Latour, B. 1998. To modernise or ecologise? That is the question (trans. C. Cussins). In *Remaking reality: Nature at the millenium*, ed. B. Braun and N. Castree, 221–42. London: Routledge.

Lehtinen, A. A. 1991. Northern natures: A study of the forest question emerging within the timber-line conflict in Finland. *Fennia* 169: 57–169.

———. 2002. Globalization and the Finnish forest sector: On the internationalisation of forest industrial operations. *Fennia* 180: 237–50.

Luke, T. W. 1995. On environmentality: Geo-power and eco-knowledge in the discourses of contemporary environmentalism. *Cultural Critique* 31: 57–81.

Malkki, L. 1995. *Purity and exile: Violence, memory, and national cosmology among Hutu refugees in Tanzania.* Chicago: University of Chicago Press.

Mitchell, T. 1998. Fixing the economy. *Cultural Studies* 12: 82–101.

Nash, R. 1973. *Wilderness and the American mind.* (Rev. Ed.) New Haven, Conn.: Yale University Press.

Nugent, S. 2000. Good risk, bad risk: Reflexive modernisation and Amazonia. In *Risk revisited*, ed. P. Caplan, 226–48. London: Pluto Press.

Palo, M., and E. Hellström, eds. 1993. *Metsäpolitiikka valinkauhassa.* Helsinki: METLA (Finnish Forest Research Institute).

Scott, J. C. 1998. *Seeing like a state: How certain schemes to improve the human condition have failed.* New Haven, Conn.: Yale University Press.

Strathern, M. 1995. The nice thing about culture is that everyone has it. In *Shifting contexts: Transformations in anthropological knowledge*, ed. M. Strathern, 153–76. London: Routledge.

———. 1999. *Property, substance and effect.* London: Athlone Press.

Takacs, D. 1996. *The idea of biodiversity: Philosophies of paradise.* Baltimore: Johns Hopkins University Press.

A Changing Sense of Place: Direct Action and Environmental Protest in the U.K.

7

KAY MILTON

MANY COMMENTATORS AGREE that environmentalism in the U.K. underwent a dramatic change in the 1990s. Until then, disputes about the environmental impacts of development had been largely local. Arguments and issues were focused on local concerns and fought out in local public inquiries and the pages of the local press. The only exceptions to this pattern were cases involving sites that were officially designated as nationally or internationally important, and that therefore attracted wider attention. During the 1990s, environmental protest was transformed into a nationwide movement through direct action. Disputes that would previously have attracted only local attention were reported in the national media and participants in these disputes became national heroes. What is more, they had a significant impact on national policy. The Conservative government, before its dramatic downfall in the 1997 general election, radically changed its policy on road building, abandoning a number of schemes and putting many on hold (Porritt 1996). Doubts were publicly expressed by politicians about the wisdom of building large out-of-town shopping centers, and plans for new housing shifted slightly away from greenfield (rural) sites to brownfield (urban) sites. In this chapter I consider what happened, during this period of change, to the sense of place, and attachment to place, that had previously claimed overriding importance in environmental disputes and given them their essentially local character.

A useful analytical model for describing this process is Roland Robertson's concept of globalization, which he (1992, 8) defined as consisting of two parts, "the compression of the world and the intensification of consciousness of the world as a whole." By "compression of the world," I take him to mean the process through which distant parts of the world become connected through their inclusion in single economic, political, and communications systems. Anthony Giddens

(1990, 64) described this process well: "the intensification of worldwide social relations which link distant localities in such a way that local events are shaped by events occurring many miles away and vice versa." For instance, the act of buying a mahogany door in Europe or America supports the logging of Malaysia's rain forests, which deprives indigenous forest peoples of their homes and livelihoods.

By "intensification of consciousness of the world as a whole," I take Robertson to mean the process whereby we come increasingly to see the world as a single place. This is a change, not in what people do or in the scope of their social relationships, but in what they think, feel, and know about the world. We might expect these two processes to be interdependent. The compression of the world through increased transnational activity and communication leads us to see it more as a single place than as a collection of separate countries and localities, and the more we think of the world as a single place, the more inclined we are to treat it as such, to travel, deal, and communicate over long distances. But it is important not to allow this expectation to conflate the two processes. We need to keep them analytically distinct so that we can investigate the relationship between them, so that we can ask questions about how social actions in the world are related to knowledge and understanding of the world (see Milton 1996).

The kinds of processes identified by Robertson as contributing to globalization are taking place at many different levels. The phenomenon we call "globalization" is, in a sense, the broadest expression of these processes (at least for the moment, in the absence of interplanetary communication), but it is not just "the world as a whole" that is undergoing compression and being seen increasingly as a single place. This is also happening to continents, countries, and regions. In this chapter I examine the operation of globalizing processes in a national context. I am interested in how the actions of direct activists engaged in environmental protest in the 1990s reflected and reshaped people's sense of place. Drawing mainly on published accounts,[1] I suggest that the direct action movement, which connected events taking place in different parts of the U.K., was accompanied by an expanding sense of place. Love of and attachment to particular localities came to be encompassed by, or derived from, love of and attachment to the country as a whole.

I shall also suggest that there was a subtle but significant change in the perceived legitimacy of environmental protest. Whereas, in the past, local attachments were seen as giving people a right to protest, in the 1990s the legitimacy of protest came to depend partly on a freedom from local connections, so that, in some contexts, not being "a local" increased one's credibility as a protester. I shall begin by describing the importance of localness in environmental debate, drawing examples from before the 1990s in order to establish the baseline for the changes described in the second and third sections of the chapter.

The Local Nature of Environmental Debate

The planning system in the U.K. encourages opposition. The details of the process may vary according to country (England, Wales, Scotland, Northern Ireland), the level of government responsible (local or national), and the type of development project involved (agricultural, industrial, or residential use), but the basic pattern is the same. A particular development scheme is proposed, objections from interested parties are invited, and the relevant authorities weigh up the evidence and make a decision. Thus, in each instance the system tends to establish an opposition between those for and those against the proposed scheme, with the decision-making authority somewhere in between, though rarely impartial.

Given that development schemes affect the environment, it is inevitable that many of the objections raised are couched in environmental terms. This has been particularly so since the 1970s, which saw a rapid increase in the number of national and international mechanisms for environmental protection. As the U.K. became a signatory to various international conventions and subject to a growing body of European environmental legislation, the provisions of these various mechanisms were translated into national law and began to influence local debates. For instance, the designation, by national authorities, of particular areas for the protection of scenic beauty or nature conservation (which, in some cases, dates from before the 1970s) has helped many opposers of development schemes to construct, if not win, their arguments. A particularly significant change was heralded by the 1985 European Community (now European Union) Directive on "the assessment of the effects of certain public and private projects on the environment" (85/337/EEC). Many proposals for development schemes have to be accompanied by statements of their likely environmental impacts, statements which can be scrutinized and challenged by objectors.

However, despite the nationalization and internationalization of environmental protection mechanisms, much of the debate surrounding specific development schemes focuses on local issues. This is inevitable given that nationally and internationally designated areas are always part of someone's local environment. It is local environments that undergo the most immediate and devastating changes due to development projects, and it is local populations that experience these changes, whatever their national or international implications may be. There are countless examples that could be used to demonstrate the local character of opposition to development schemes. The first two cases presented below have been selected because I know them well through my own research on environmental issues. Twyford Down is included because it played a pivotal role in the changes described later in this chapter.

Belfast Harbour Estate

In 1987, Northern Ireland's Planning Service published its draft of the Belfast Urban Area Plan (BUAP), which would form a basis for the development of the city up to 2001. Under this draft plan, much of the land around Belfast harbor was zoned for industrial development. There was nothing remarkable in this, since a large proportion of this land had been claimed from the sea for precisely this purpose. However, the land claim operations, which had begun in the 1930s, had created a series of lagoons that had become important roosting and feeding habitats for wild birds. In addition, there was an adjacent wetland area that held a rich variety of wildflowers and was used as nesting habitat by wading birds. The area was important enough for part of it to be declared an Area of Special Scientific Interest (ASSI) by the Department of the Environment in November 1987. Local conservationists agreed that it was the most important wildlife habitat within the Belfast urban area.

The Royal Society for the Protection of Birds (RSPB), a national organization with an office in Belfast, and the Ulster Trust for Nature Conservation (now the Ulster Wildlife Trust) both objected to the proposed destruction of the habitat. They were joined by two groups, the Belfast Urban Wildlife Group (BUWG) and the Belfast Lough Nature Conservation Committee (BLNCC), formed specifically to oppose the environmentally damaging proposals in the BUAP. The BUWG was a small group of concerned individuals who came together in order to scrutinize the BUAP's potential impact on the city's wildlife. The BLNCC arose out of a public meeting in November 1987, organized by the RSPB and a local residents' association. Nearly 150 people, mainly local residents, attended this meeting. Some spoke of the land around the harbor as an area dear to them, where they had played and watched wildlife in their younger days. They resented the fact that the Harbour Commissioners, who owned the land, now restricted access to the area, and felt that it should be conserved for all local people and visitors to enjoy.

These four groups led the opposition to the BUAP proposals in what was often a fiercely contentious debate (see Milton 1990, 39). The eventual outcome of a rather complex series of events was a compromise in which two of the lagoons were infilled for industrial use but one was saved, to be managed as a nature reserve by the RSPB. The wetland area, which had been destroyed by infilling in the intervening period, was restored and placed under the RSPB's management as a nature conservation area. Public access has been improved, an elaborate bird-watching hide has been built and is manned by local volunteers, and the area has become what the campaigners envisaged, an important educational resource and a major attraction for local and visiting bird-watchers.

The Harris Superquarry

In 1991 Redland Aggregates Ltd. submitted an application to create a "superquarry" on the island of Harris in the Outer Hebrides off western Scotland.[2] The proposed site was a mountain in the southeast corner of the island. The quarry, which would carve away the eastern side of the mountain, was predicted to operate for over sixty years and create about one hundred local jobs. Local responses were mixed, but initially a significant proportion of the population expressed support for the economic regeneration that it was hoped the quarry would bring. The local authority decided to grant the application.

However, opposition to the quarry on environmental grounds began to increase. An important factor was that it would be within a designated National Scenic Area (NSA). This gave the views of the statutory conservation body, Scottish Natural Heritage (SNH), considerable weight, and they eventually came out against the quarry. Local residents became concerned about the impact of the quarry on their landscape, wildlife, and economy. The local support for the jobs promised by the quarry was countered by local concerns about the effects of pollution on the fishing industry and about the impact on tourism of such a dominant scar on the landscape, as well as the inevitable noise and dust. Once it became clear that some of the quarry's workforce would be imported, there were fears that local cultural traditions, including the Gaelic language, might be diluted. Perhaps the most important concern to local residents was that observance of the Sabbath might be disrupted.

A public inquiry was held from October 1994 to June 1995. There followed several years of waiting, while opinions on both sides of the argument continued to be aired, particularly in the local press. When the report on the public inquiry eventually appeared, it expressed the view that, despite the significant (though far from unanimous) local opposition and the environmental damage that would result, it was in the overriding national interest that the quarry be allowed to go ahead. This recommendation was considered by the Scottish Executive, and in November 2000 it announced its decision to refuse permission, citing its duty to protect the integrity of a designated National Scenic Area. The quarry company lodged appeals and the debate looks set to continue for a considerable time to come.

Twyford Down

In the early 1980s, the Government decided that the M3 London-to-Southampton motorway should run through a deep cutting to be created across Twyford Down, a hill to the southeast of the town of Winchester. The local authorities supported this decision, the one main alternative having proved unacceptable to local citizens. A public inquiry was scheduled for 1985. Until shortly before the inquiry, local opposition to the Twyford Down route had been almost nonexistent, but in the spring of 1985, a small group, led by Barbara Bryant (a Winchester city councillor) and Merrick Denton-Thompson (a landscape architect employed by the local county council), began a campaign of opposition. This brief summary is based on information drawn from Bryant's published account (Bryant 1996).

Bryant and her colleagues suspected that the absence of local opposition was due to the lack of understanding of the consequences if the Twyford Down route was implemented. The scar on the landscape would be huge and dramatic with walls of stark white chalk exposed in the excavation. The models put on public display had failed to show this (Bryant 1996, 31). The road construction would severely damage part of a Site of Special Scientific Interest (SSSI) and two scheduled ancient monuments, and would cut in two a designated Area of Outstanding Natural Beauty (AONB). The campaigners began, through the local media, to bring all this to public attention. Their involvement in the public inquiry helped to do this and generated further opposition. They also drew attention to the possibility of a tunnel as an alternative to the cutting.

During the eighteen months between the end of the public inquiry and the publication of the official report, the campaigners continued to present their views to local groups, and particularly to local councillors. As a result, Winchester City Council changed its position and came out in favor of a tunnel through Twyford Down. The Government decided to reopen the public inquiry in 1987. The earlier inquiry had gone ahead without evidence from the statutory conservation bodies, the Countryside Commission and English Heritage, and the absence of advice and information from them was a potential source of embarrassment to the government. The reopened inquiry gave the opportunity, not only for these organizations to state their views (by now both were opposing the proposed cutting through Twyford Down, though they had not initially done so, at least in public), but also for a much more vigorous expression of local opinion against the cutting and in favor of a tunnel. A survey of local opinion undertaken by the campaigners in 1986 had shown that, of those aware of the proposals, only 9 percent supported a cutting, with the remainder divided between a tunnel through Twyford Down and an alternative route (Bryant 1996, 86–87).

The reopened inquiry continued until March 1988 and a year later there were rumors that the official report would recommend that the cutting proceed, despite local opposition, though this was not finally confirmed until February 1990. From this point on, the campaign to save Twyford Down took on a more national character. The Twyford Down Association was formed, the national media took an active interest, and funds were raised from all over the country. The contract to begin work on the road was awarded in December 1991, and work finally began in February 1992. Symbolic protests took place on the site. Campaigners from Friends of the Earth (FoE), one of only two main environmental NGOs to offer support, chained themselves across the site but withdrew when injunctions were served against them.

Local Association As a Source of Legitimacy

These three cases, along with many others that could have been selected, serve well to illustrate the local nature of environmental debate in the U.K. in the 1980s and early 1990s. Although all three instances involved areas with national designations (SSSI/ASSI, NSA, AONB, and scheduled ancient monuments), and although national and, indeed, international organizations (RSPB, SNH, FoE, the Countryside Commission, English Heritage) often became involved, the debate in each case was focused on local effects, local costs and benefits, local opinions. The underlying assumption was, and still is, that local people (alongside national bodies and other interest groups) have a right to be consulted about and express a view on development proposals because it is their environment that will be most severely affected.

The idea that legitimacy is somehow conferred by local association is reinforced by comparisons with other countries that have similar statutory arrangements for making decisions about development. In the U.S., Canada, Australia, and elsewhere, the rights of indigenous peoples are sanctioned by law, and their views tend to carry particular weight in debates about land use. Hornborg (1994) described the campaign to save Kluscap's Mountain, on Cape Breton Island in Nova Scotia, from a superquarry very similar to that proposed for Harris.[3] Many of the local residents were opposed to the quarry and expressed their concerns in environmental terms. A different dimension was added to the campaign through the involvement of the indigenous Mi'kmaq community, for whom the mountain is sacred. They were able to introduce into the debate arguments about the sanctity of the land that would not otherwise have been admissible. As Hornborg pointed out, "It is as if native people are allowed to say things which non-native people cannot" (1994, 250). As Carrier points out in his introduction to this volume, indigenous peoples, who can claim to have "distinct and autochthonous" ways of understanding the world, have become "a legitimate exception to universalism."

It is the long association of an indigenous population with a particular place, an association going back for many generations, that gives their views legitimacy in a legal process. Their connections with the land, because they are so long-standing, are somehow more authentic than those of populations whose ancestors are known to have arrived more recently. This recognition of authenticity affects the ways in which nonindigenous activists present their case. Satterfield, describing the conflict between environmentalists and loggers over the felling of old-growth forest in Oregon, wrote:

> Both environmental and timber activists recognize that their authority regarding past and future land use depends on the ease with which they can play into publicly salient ideas about past peoples as ecologically instructive due to their relationship with physical territories. Practically speaking, this means that activists affiliated with the more "Aboriginal," or "authentic," tradition wield a distinct political advantage. (Satterfield 2002, 12)

The perceived authenticity of indigenous peoples' connections with the land has also led to their increasing involvement in environmental activism in, for instance, North and South America and Australia, as well as in international arenas (see Conklin 1997). And this involvement, in turn, reinforces the assumption that local associations per se confer rights and legitimize opinions. Indigenous peoples embody the most extreme expressions of localness—they are, if you like, the archetypal "locals"—but other degrees and forms of localness also confer legitimacy. Nonindigenous populations, such as the New Zealand sheep farmers described by Dominy (2000), and even temporary residents, such as the stockmen in North Queensland, described by Strang (1997), can claim to hold particular meaningful relationships with the land (see Carrier's introduction to this volume for a more detailed discussion of these case studies).

NIMBY

There is, however, another side to the local coin. In environmental discourse in the U.K., and no doubt in other countries as well, people who seek to protect their own local environment are open to the accusation that they are concerned only about their personal interests. This is often referred to as "NIMBY" (not in my back yard). As Carrier points out (introduction, this volume), accusations of "NIMBYism" are accusations of selfishness, the implication being that, if the particular road, or quarry, or waste disposal site, or whatever, had been planned for somewhere other than their own immediate location, then the campaigners would not have been concerned about it. It is all right, in other words, to pollute someone else's back yard. The accusation is sometimes intended to imply an interest solely in material wealth. As house prices in Britain rose sharply in the 1980s, and the attractiveness of property as an investment therefore increased, issues of development were often linked to property values, which depend, at least partly, on the quality of the local environment. This issue was considered particularly significant in southern England, where property generally costs more than in the rest of the country, and which was seen as the stronghold of support for the Conservative government.

Accusations of NIMBYism are based on a general presumption, held by developers and planning authorities alike, in favor of economic development. The assumption is that the road or quarry or disposal site has to go somewhere, and if it is not placed in the back yard of community X, then community Y will have to suffer instead. Accusations of NIMBYism are often countered by environmental activists with claims of NIABY (not in anybody's back yard). This implies that government should consider whether a particular kind of development is needed at all, and adopt a more radical approach to economic and environmental planning. For instance, it was claimed that the Harris superquarry was needed to provide material to build roads in southern England. But if the government were to develop a cheap, efficient, and safe public transport system, commuters might be less likely to use their own cars, and the need to build roads in southern England would be reduced. Thus, environmentalists argue, a more radical and more holistic approach to environmental protection removes the need for quarries or roads to pollute anybody's back yard.

Regardless of their validity, accusations of NIMBYism, and the very presence of the NIMBY phenomenon in environmental debate, inevitably undermine the legitimacy of local views. Although people's right to express views on development in their local area is not doubted, the views they express can always be questioned, and so need not actually be given weight when decisions about development proposals are made. The need to insulate environmental protest against accusations of NIMBYism almost certainly influenced the direction taken by environmental activism in the U.K. in the 1990s.

From Local Protest to National Movement

> Long after the Twyford Down campaign was lost, and the Dongas had been brutally routed, Twyford Down continues to work its magic as a symbol of opposition to undemocratic, ecologically wanton road-building, wherever it is taking place. What's more, it has reinforced all the anger and incredulity many people have felt but suppressed for years; it has legitimized a far more explicit avowal of passionate feelings for the British countryside in all its glory and vulnerability. Nothing has ever been the same since. (Porritt 1996, 299)

By the time work began on the cutting at Twyford Down, local campaigners had exhausted almost all the official possibilities for making their views count. They turned their attention to the 1992 general election, feeling that a change of government (which in fact did not take place for a further five years) was the only hope left for

Twyford Down. But as FoE protesters were obeying the injunctions served against them by moving off the construction site, others were moving in. Travelers began to camp in an area known as the Dongas (see below), which was on the route of the cutting. They became known as the Dongas Tribe and stayed until December 1992 when they were brutally evicted. Some of those involved in the Dongas camp and other protests at Twyford Down were members of Earth First!, the group well-known for pioneering direct action against environmental destruction in the U.S. in the 1980s (Wall 1999). Their involvement caused a degree of resentment. The Countryside Campaigner for FoE was quoted as saying, "The trouble with Earth First! is they don't see that this is a local campaign. That's its value. Its strength" (Vidal 1992). As things turned out, this was a significant misjudgment; the value of Twyford Down was to extend far beyond the local context.

The presence of the Dongas and the Earth First! activists and, above all, the publicity they attracted, added another dimension to environmental campaigning in the U.K. This is not to suggest that the Twyford Down protesters invented direct action in Britain. This style of protest has a history going back for hundreds of years. In recent decades it has been most often used in industrial disputes, for instance in the picketing of factories, mines, and ports by workers on strike. Direct action has also been used by campaigners throughout the contemporary environmental movement, most notably by Greenpeace. But events at Twyford Down, and particularly the media reports of violence against peaceful protesters, set the scene for the following years. "Yellow Wednesday," 9 December 1992, when the Dongas' camp was routed by security guards in yellow uniforms, has passed into legend and song.[4] The formal objections to environmentally damaging projects, and their pursuit through the legal process, continued, but defeat in this process was no longer considered the end of the matter. On sites throughout the country, as the bulldozers moved in, so did the direct activists, to set up camps, to live in trees scheduled for felling, to dig and occupy tunnels, and generally to make it impossible for the contractors to continue their work.

Through the 1990s, hundreds of direct action protests took place. Many of these were against road building schemes, the most well-known being the M11 in east London (1993), a bypass at Solsbury Hill near Bath (1994), the M77 in Glasgow (1995), the M65 near Manchester (1995), and the Newbury bypass (1996) (see Wall 1999 for brief descriptions of these protests). Other kinds of development, such as new supermarkets and airport extensions, were met with the same kind of protest. Most failed to stop the specific projects going ahead, but collectively they made a significant impact. Protests significantly increased the costs of development projects and demonstrated to government the potential for public opposition to them. As a consequence, the national road building program was reviewed and many schemes were cancelled or shelved (Bellos and Gibbs 1996).

But it was not just the nature of environmental protest that changed following Twyford Down. The new protests drew in a much wider range of people than had previously been involved in environmental campaigning, "ranging from PhD astronomy students through idealistic youth and the middle classes, to children, the homeless and the old" (Vidal 1993; cf. Plows 1995). And whereas, before, protesters would have been drawn primarily from the local community, direct activists came from throughout the U.K. and sometimes from overseas—one of the Earth First! protesters at Twyford Down was from Montana (Vidal 1992). As they learned from early experiences at Twyford Down and elsewhere, they became better trained and better organized, publicizing protests on the Internet and through their own publications. Protesters moved from site to site, gaining credibility and honor as they went. There were "veterans" of Twyford Down at the M11 protests in East London (Weale 1993) and at Newbury (Griffiths and Vidal 1996), and veterans of the M11 at the M65 protest near Manchester (Ward 1994).

This combative metaphor was taken up by George Monbiot, writing in *The Guardian* about the Newbury bypass protests, who issued a call to the nation. He drew a comparison with the Spanish Civil War, in which idealistic British people pledged their support against the Fascists. He asked, "What did you do in the battle?" and berated his readers for calling themselves green, "perhaps even radical," yet remaining rooted to their armchairs while others were suffering pain, intense discomfort, and imprisonment in defense of the environment (Monbiot 1996). As I read this, I was several hundred miles from Newbury with the Irish Sea between us and a full-time job to attend to, but I still felt soundly reprimanded.

The Changing Basis of Legitimacy

The point I wish to draw out of this is that the broadening of participation in environmental protest brought with it a change in the grounds for legitimacy. Local people had, in the past, been considered the most legitimate protesters, those with the most right to express their views and to have those views addressed in the decision-making process. But many of the direct activists were nonlocal, and some of them were more or less full-time protesters who traveled from one site to another, much as the "flying pickets" had traveled from one industrial site to another during disputes in the 1970s and 1980s. Their right to protest was, of course, questioned by those whose interests were damaged by their activities, and the legality of their actions was threatened by new legislation in the form of the Criminal Justice Act, which came into force in 1994 and created a new criminal offense of "aggravated trespass." But the measures taken against them only served to strengthen their moral legitimacy in the minds of a public largely disenchanted with the Conservative government. There was an understanding that anyone claiming to care about the environment had a moral duty to be involved, if not by actually protesting, then at least by giving support in some way. I am sure that many armchair environmentalists were quite relieved to find, at the end of George Monbiot's article, the suggestion that if they could not go to Newbury they should send a donation (Monbiot 1996).

So what were the sources of the legitimacy accorded to direct activists, and how is it related to the more established legitimacy conferred by localness? I suggest four main contributory factors. First, direct action protests have often been endorsed by local campaigners. This is not surprising given the circumstances in which direct action is most often used. By definition, it can only be used when there is something to take direct action against, which tends to be when contractors are moving onto a site or are about to do so. This only happens when the possibilities of opposing a project through the statutory planning process have been more or less exhausted.[5] Local campaigners are understandably quite desperate at this stage, and have often been willing to welcome, indeed to invite, known direct activists to help them in their struggle. One of the most remarked upon features of the direct action movement was the way in which alliances were formed between activists and local people who welcomed their support. A television documentary about the Newbury bypass protest (entitled "The Battle of Rickety Bridge") emphasized how middle-class suburban dwellers, who would never before have thought of taking direct action, found themselves willingly sitting with the protesters in the path of machinery and being moved on by the police. Several press reports mentioned the support that local people gave to the direct activists, in the form of food, drinks, clothes, and baths (for instance, Griffiths and Vidal 1996).

Second, direct activists have often forged connections between themselves and particular localities through symbolic means. For instance, the protest against the Newbury bypass was called "The third battle of Newbury." The first two battles of Newbury had been fought nearby in 1643 and 1644, during the English Civil War. The Dongas on Twyford Down, from which the protesters took their name, were ancient trackways that crossed the land, worn down by many years of use. According to Bryant (1996, 192), they had acquired this name in the nineteenth century, possibly as a result of Winchester College's colonial connections, given that "donga" is an African name meaning "gully." By calling themselves Dongas, the protesters were expressing their sense of identity with the land they were defending, and also with the area's historical inhabitants, whose feet had created the trackways. Thus the Dongas Tribe, like activists in the logging dispute described by Satterfield (2002, see above), were affiliating themselves with an "Aboriginal" and therefore "authentic" tradition.[6] The parallels with Australian Aborigines, whose ancestors left the traces of their journeys across the land, are quite striking, and Plows (1995, 4), reflecting on her experience with the Dongas, makes the indigenous association explicit: "We felt a part of the land, a physical extension of it, empathizing with indigenous tribes throughout the ages who had felt a spiritual connection with the land they were torn from." The language of "tribalism" (see Carrier's introduction to this volume) thus created and reinforced personal ties which were, in many cases, very short lived.

Third, the protesters declared and embodied a passionate love of the British countryside that touched a chord with many of the public. Reporting from a protest camp on the Newbury bypass route, Griffiths (1995) wrote,

> Someone a way off whistles half a phrase from I Vow To Thee My Country. Not for nothing. This is part of what drives the protesters through these harsh conditions; not nationalism but the passion for country as land, and a feeling for its particularity.

Describing the Newbury protest camps, Griffiths and Vidal (1996) state that Union Jacks were pinned to many of the trees, but stress that this symbol stands not for the political state, but for the land, which is unique, precious, and sacred, embodying personal memories and communal histories. In challenging the security guards and contractors, the protesters used the language of patriotism: "Have you no honour? Have you no shame?" "My grandad didn't die in the war for you to trash this land. He loved this country. He was fighting for this England" (Griffiths and Vidal 1996, 24). This kind of patriotism defends the land against a state that seeks to destroy it in the name of democracy.

> By flying the Union Jack, the protesters like to think they have grouped themselves on the side of the oaks and history of England. They draw a distinction between love of one's country and love of one's political state, and they love their country with exactly the same fierceness as they hate their state. They enjoy the irony that to fell the tree, the "army" of the state must also fell the emblem of the country. (Griffiths and Vidal 1996, 25)

Finally, precisely because many direct activists were not local people, they were free from accusations of NIMBYism. Their commitment to protection of the land was not tainted by implications of narrow self-interest. They were not defending their personal property or their own immediate environment. Instead they were defending a whole range of things: natural beauty, the tranquillity of the countryside, the rights of nonhuman life to live undisturbed, the rights of local people and the British public to have their personal and communal histories unviolated. Certainly, they became deeply attached to the locations they sought to protect; as Strang (1997) has shown, the fact that engagement with a particular place is temporary does not mean that ties to that location will necessarily be weak. But the direct activists were driven by broader concerns: "At first it's a matter of prin-ciple. Then you fall in love with the place. Everything is unique. Everything has its own shape. Everything is different" (protester quoted in Griffiths 1995). And the uniqueness of everything became, itself, a quality to be defended. Diversity is pre-cious, and it is threatened by those who seek to bury the land under stretches of tarmac and concrete. The protesters' willingness to defend other people's back yards was evidence of their commitment to these broader concerns, which is why it meant something to be a veteran of several protests, to have made one's stand at Twyford, and Solsbury Hill, and Newbury. The credibility of direct activists is comparable with that of conscientious objectors in wartime, whose refusal to fight is ennobled by freedom from self-interest, driven not by a desire to save their own skins but by a belief that violence in general is wrong.

To return, briefly, to Robertson's concept of globalization, I am suggesting that its two component processes, compression of the world (in terms of social connections) and an increasing sense of the world as a single place, are reflected, at a national level, in the events described in this chapter. The movements of pro-testers around the country forged connections among sites whose common de-nominator was the threat of damage or destruction through development. One of the consequences of this was an increased sense of the country as a whole, or at least of rural Britain, as a place under threat and worth defending. Accompanying this shift in the practice and culture of British environmentalism was a growing understanding that one no longer needed to have local connections in order legit-imately to oppose local development proposals. It is important to stress that the expanding sense of place did not entail a detachment from the local. What was local was still considered precious, unique, sacred to individual memories and communal histories. But the new, national environmental conscience recognized the uniqueness of all localities; everywhere is worth protecting because everywhere is special and meaningful.

It is worth commenting that, as the direct action movement in the U.K. ap-peared to be coming to an end, following a change of government and changes in policy, a new wave of global protest has emerged. Since the late 1990s, the meet-ings and conferences of international economic and political institutions, such as the World Trade Organization, the World Bank, the International Monetary Fund, the European Union, and the G8 nations, have been accompanied by demonstra-tions against the damaging effects of global capitalism on human rights and wel-fare and the environment. Many thousands have taken part in these demonstrations and their venues—Seattle, Vienna, Prague, Melbourne, Genoa, Gothenburg—are becoming legendary, just as the sites of antiroads protests have become legendary within the U.K. (see Bircham and Charlton 2001). The peripatetic protester has be-come a global phenomenon. This is neither the time nor the place to consider the cultural consequences of this development, but there are some interesting continuities and parallels with the direct action movement in Britain.

Paul Kingsnorth (2000), himself a former direct activist, has noted that some of the participants in antiroads protests in the U.K. have now moved on to participate in the global anticapitalism movement, and that they have done so because they are recognizing the significance of the bigger picture. Environmentally damaging developments in Britain and everywhere else, as well as poverty and human rights abuses, are recognized as products of the global economic system. This realization has taken environmental protest out of the national arena and onto the global stage. It is ironic that, in order to oppose globalism, the protest movement has had to globalize itself, but this reflects what happened at the national level in the U.K. and, no doubt, in other countries as well. It was not until the direct activists made the connections, through their activities and by thinking and speaking of the country as a single place, that environmental protest had an impact on national development policies. Whether the global protest movement will meet with similar success remains to be seen.

Conclusion

This chapter has described a short episode in the history of environmental discourse in the U.K., an episode characterized by a particular style of protest that, temporarily at least, constituted rural Britain as a single place in need of protection. Paradoxically, it also highlighted the uniqueness of each locality by treating it as worthy of protection. Every tree, every pond and ditch became, potentially, a "site of struggle" (Seidel 1985, 1989), a point at which a battle or an argument could be won or lost. It would be unwise, I think, to suggest that these cultural consequences of the rise in direct action mark a change in the ways in which either the local or the national, or indeed the global, are understood. Instead, I would assume that people's understandings of place are continually fluid and variable, and that particular understandings crystallize around, or are brought into focus by, particular events and circumstances. There will be times when the whole planet appears as, or is best represented as, a single place, and times when a village or a small island appears fragmented. And the two are not mutually exclusive, but coexisting and complementary components of an infinite array of ideas through which we understand our surroundings. I agree with Robertson (1992) that globalizing and deglobalizing processes operate continually. One might wish to observe that a particular direction is becoming clear, but events can easily make a mockery of such pronouncements. My purpose in this chapter has been to describe a moment in environmental discourse at which globalizing tendencies appeared to dominate, creating an understanding of unity at the national level, and to show that this understanding was, in fact, dependent on an awareness of particularity and uniqueness at the local level.

I feel on safer ground suggesting, as a final comment, that direct action has had a significant impact on another aspect of environmental discourse, the relationship between the personal and the public, between an individual's experiences and motivations and their public expression in action. In his introduction to this volume, Carrier discusses the problem of how concerned individuals translate their personal desires into public action. He points out that personal motivations are often inappropriate for winning public arguments, and that they have to be transformed into an officially sanctioned, universalizing language in order to become acceptable in a public arena. So, for instance, particular activists might want to save a woodland because it is part of their personal history and identity, somewhere they used to play, explore, and make love. But invoking these personal memories in public debate, though it might elicit sympathy, would not win any arguments. So, as Carrier expresses it, the activist "must silence the personal to speak to the public." Personal attachments and desires are translated into arguments about the importance of biodiversity to future generations.

I would suggest that direct action is a means of participating in public discourse without silencing the personal. Through direct action, individuals emphasize and celebrate the personal by placing themselves, their own personal safety and comfort, on the front line. Direct action asserts that a particular tree, woodland, or landscape matters because it has helped to shape personal histories and identities, and, through direct action, is continuing to do so. Trees become homes, and the act of felling a tree becomes an act against the person, a personal violation. As mentioned above, there is nothing new in this style of protest, either within or outside the environmental movement. But there was something new about the extent to which it captured public attention and sympathy in Britain during the 1990s. In a sense, it raised the intensity of environmental activism to the level of industrial activism in the preceding decades, when the arguments were quite explicitly about "our" jobs and "our" community. Direct action was a way for individuals to declare their personal love for a particular locality, unashamedly, in a public discourse, and their personal hatred of the system that permits and promotes the destruction of much-loved places. Of course, the officially sanctioned language of that discourse still cannot admit such declarations, and this is likely to ensure that direct action will remain in the environmentalists' repertoire for the foreseeable future.

Notes

1. The events referred to here were given extensive coverage in the British national press. I have drawn mainly on reports in *The Guardian*, whose coverage was more detailed than that of other newspapers.

2. For a detailed and personal account of this case by one of the main protagonists, see McIntosh (2001).

3. For a comparison of the two cases, see Milton (2002, 139 ff.). These cases are not merely comparable; they are also connected, through the involvement of a Mi'kmaq chief in the Harris campaign (see McIntosh 2001, 196 ff.).

4. For instance, "The Ballad of Twyford Down: A Tribute to the Donga Tribe," by Jo Peacock, available on the Internet (www. nowhere.net/~raster/bicyclist/ballad_twyford .html).

5. Legal avenues for opposition do sometimes remain, particularly if it can be argued that the proposed development infringes European legislation. The campaigners against the Twyford Down cutting formally complained to the European Commission, in 1990, that the project infringed the environmental assessment Directive 85/337. Work began on the site in early 1992, but the Commission did not make a final ruling on the complaint until July of that year (see Kunzlik 1996 for a detailed analysis of this process).

6. The symbolism of the ancient past was strikingly invoked in a 1994 protest against plans to build a dual carriageway through the Sussex Downs. The cartoonist Steve Bell, landscape artist Simon English, and Friends of the Earth (FoE) laid out a 500-foot caricature of Prime Minister John Major. The figure evoked the Cerne Abbas Giant, a prehistoric figure cut into the chalk on a Dorset hillside. The "Grey Man of Ditchling," as the cartoon was called, held surveyors' poles, wore a traffic cone on his head and, unlike the ancient Giant, had his genitals discreetly hidden by a pair of briefs (*The Guardian*, 8 July 1994, 7).

References

Bellos, A., and G. Gibbs. 1996. First blood to the bailiffs in latest bypass battle. *The Guardian*, 28 December, 3.

Bircham, E., and J. Charlton, eds. 2001. *Anti capitalism: A guide to the movement*. London: Bookmarks Publications.

Bryant, B. 1996. *Twyford Down: Roads, campaigning and environmental law*. London: E. and F. N. Spon.

Conklin, B. A. 1997. Body paint, feathers, and VCRs: Aesthetics and authenticity in Amazonian activism. *American Ethnologist* 24: 711–37.

Dominy, M. 2000. *Calling the station home: Place and identity in New Zealand's High Country*. Lanham, Md.: Rowman & Littlefield.

Giddens, A. 1990. *The consequences of modernity*. Cambridge: Polity Press.

Griffiths, J. 1995. Frozen, fragile peace in the snow. *The Guardian*, 13 December, Society supplement, 4.

Griffiths, J., and J. Vidal. 1996. Battle of the lone pine. *The Guardian Weekend*, 6 April, 23–26.

Hornborg, A. 1994. Environmentalism, ethnicity and sacred places: Reflections on modernity, discourse and power. *Canadian Review of Sociology and Anthropology* 31: 245–67.

Kingsnorth, P. 2000. If it's Tuesday, it must be Seattle. *The Ecologist*, 22 February (from *The Ecologist* online archive, www. theecologist.org/archive_article. html).

Kunzlik, P. 1996. The legal battle: "An astonishing intervention." In *Twyford Down: Roads, campaigning and environmental law*, ed. B. Bryant, 225–94. London: E. and F. N. Spon.

McIntosh, A. 2001. *Soil and soul*. London: Aurum Press.

Milton, K. 1990. *Our countryside our concern: The policy and practice of conservation in Northern Ireland*. Belfast: Northern Ireland Environment Link.

———. 1996. *Environmentalism and cultural theory: Exploring the role of anthropology in environmental discourse*. London: Routledge.

———. 2002. *Loving nature: Towards an ecology of emotion*. London: Routledge.

Monbiot, G. 1996. What did you do in the battle? *The Guardian*, 7 February, Society supplement, 4.

Plows, A. 1995. Eco-philosophy and popular protest: The significance and implications of the ideology and actions of the Donga Tribe. In *Alternative futures and popular protest*, ed. C. Barker, P. Kennedy, and M. Tyldesley. Vol. 1, n.p. Manchester: Manchester Metropolitan University.

Porritt, J. 1996. The environmentalist's conclusions. In *Twyford Down: Roads, campaigning and environmental law*, ed. B. Bryant, 295–309. London: E. and F. N. Spon.

Robertson, R. 1992. *Globalization: Social theory and global culture*. London: Sage.

Satterfield, T. 2002. *Anatomy of a conflict: Identity, knowledge and emotion in old-growth forests*. Vancouver: University of British Columbia Press.

Seidel, G. 1985. Political discourse analysis. In *Handbook of discourse analysis*, ed. T. A. van Dijk, Vol. 4, 43–60. London: Academic Press.

———. 1989. We condemn apartheid, BUT . . . a discursive analysis of the European Parliamentary debate on sanctions. In *Social anthropology and the politics of language*. Sociological Review Monograph 36, ed. R. Grillo, 222–49. London: Routledge.

Strang, V. 1997. *Uncommon ground: Cultural landscapes and environmental values*. Oxford: Berg.

Vidal, J. 1992. Last ditch stand on Cobbett's patch. *The Guardian*, 20 March, 31.

———. 1993. That dying fall. *The Guardian 2*, 10 December, 16–17.

Wall, D. 1999. *Earth First! and the anti-roads movement*. London: Routledge.

Ward, D. 1994. Mway protest causes logjam in battle for Cinder Path Wood. *The Guardian*, 14 June, 3.

Weale, S. 1993. Bark and the bite. *The Guardian 2*, 24 September, 15.

Conclusion: Understandings Matter

JOSIAH HEYMAN

THE CHAPTERS IN THIS BOOK join a long tradition of anthropological attention to people and environments, a lineage that is intellectually admirable and vital for the contemporary world. Interest in culturally relevant plants, animals, soils, and geographic features has characterized anthropology from the beginning; one hopes that scholars, students, and activists never lose their interest in the sheer materiality of everyday life (e.g., Forde 1934). Explicit models of the relationship between culture, society, and environment emerged from the 1940s through the 1960s. At first the idea was that superorganic culture adapted to the environment, especially through food production (Steward 1955, 1977), but later work followed the lead of biological ecology in looking at people as local populations (sets of individuals) interacting with systems of energy and nutrient flows (Rappaport 1968). Culture and social relations in this view mediated and regulated these interactions. Profound work came out of these approaches, and it may seem begrudging to mention their limitations, but two points come to mind (see Orlove 1980). One was an excessive neatness, an emphasis on whole systems or adaptations and on stability and success. The other was a resolute traditionalizing of the ethnographic material, a search for apparently authentic ways of living in the environment before industry and modernity.

It is because of these assumptions, I think, that ecological anthropology lost its vibrancy and audience in the 1970s and 1980s, just as environmental awareness and activism took off. One substitute has been serious but inhuman science, such as ecological biology and earth systems; another has been a romantic longing for imagined environmental authenticity, on behalf of which anthropology is uncomfortably recruited. These tendencies sometimes merge into a scientifically knowledgeable but anthropologically naive rejection of human activity in the world. I thus find the revival of environmental anthropology heartening, and not just for the sake of the discipline. To science that is profound in every regard but the human, it insists on an equal awareness of human practices and ideas, while to dreams of timeless, traditional cultures, it insists on examining human-environment interactions in particular times and places, especially paying attention to the dilemmas of the present day. If our scholarship on environmental issues is to speak effectively to public concerns and movements (see Bodley 2001; Donahue and Johnston 1998; Johnston 1994, 1997), we need to use and deepen these qualities. This collection certainly does that.

While I see general agreement in environmental anthropology around the themes just stated, I also see two contrasting styles in response: a critical view of the present by means of grand contrasts, and detailed attention to specific processes and settings. It will not surprise the reader to hear that we need a bit of both, and that the present book takes some of the first approach and applies it to the second task. The grand schemes include Tim Ingold's (1993) contrast of sphere and globe and Arturo Escobar's (1999) regimes of nature (organic, capitalist, and technonature), as discussed in Carrier's introduction. I would add to his list Roy Rappaport's (1979, 1999) work on rituals, ultimate values, and the maladaptive character of the present, and Alf Hornborg's (2001) remarkable synthesis of thermodynamics, global unequal exchange, technology, and the semiotics of fetishism. Such authors (and here I generalize grossly) take patterns of environmental thought or practice as archetypes, contrast the archetypes rather than seeing them as interacting themes within a given situation, engage history and power but in general ways rather than as specific histories of power projects, and are normative in the sense of implying a strong preference for one archetype over another; but they face difficulties in delineating actual, messy conflicts. Though it may seem that I am toting up flaws, this is not the case, for strong generalizations are absolutely required if we are to confront strong problems and engage in strong debates.

The number of scholars emphasizing interplay and specificity is, not surprisingly, much greater, and it is hardly possible to do justice to them. I highlight Kay Milton's (1996) line of inquiry about variation in cultural ideas about environments found in different societies, and related ethnographies whose notable feature is their sensitivity to local environmental culture (e.g., Croll and Parkin 1992; Orlove 2002). Milton (1993) also brings a particular interest in cultures of environmentalism. Though quite different (emphasizing social relations rather than culture), so-called "political ecology" also bears mentioning, for it places environmental processes and problems in the contexts of international and national commodity economies, regional social formations, and specific contests over resources (e.g., Blaikie 1985; Bryant and Bailey 1997; Greenberg and Park 1994;

and the online *Journal of Political Ecology*).[1] The authors in the present book combine the culturalist and political ecology streams of thought. Understandings of the environment, we learn, are shaped by and respond to recent historical changes in politics and economics. Power relations matter, both local and impinging from other places, and indeed, styles of understanding embody specific power projects. Yet this book does not treat economic and political interests as if they were obvious and efficacious outside of cultural frameworks.

It is within this intellectual history, then, that we can understand the progress made by the scholars herein represented. Three recognitions are particularly important. First, while we might usefully contrast abstract versus personal (or contextual) understandings of the environment, these modes of understanding are not the exclusive possession of determinate social groups (locals versus outsiders, for example) but rather are used, cultivated, combined, or segregated by people of various social backgrounds. Carrier's study of personal motivations among expatriate environmental activists in Jamaica, and the way they disguise such personal qualities when working with funding organizations, captures complex realities by deft use of potentially rigid archetypes. Second, power is implicated in environmental discourses and forms of knowledge, but not as power/knowledge monoliths: rather, we see it in ongoing struggles, polarizations, compromises, victories, and losses among discernible actors whose stances and agendas constitute a mutable flow of environmental understandings. The ongoing debate over forests in Finland described by Berglund tracks just such a power/knowledge process. Third, contemporary international environmentalism and environmental destruction are studied together, certainly not as identical, but as sharing, forms of understanding and acting on the world. Many chapters in this book exemplify this; in MacDonald's particularly striking example, erstwhile species conservation combines with commoditized hunting tourism. A problem in this book, however, is slippage from these well-taken points to an overly simple reification and contrast of global and local.

Global and local, rather than being terms that cover a small set of definite characteristics, actually gloss complicated tendencies, actors, and processes, which are quite variable in whether and how they appear. The use of these two highly abstract words, while convenient (for me as much as for the other authors here), hides from us substantive details about these actors and processes. But it is from such specificity that the interesting analyses of environmental understandings derive. In the interest of breaking open "global" and "local," then, I will rattle off some possible components of each, concentrating on the ones most relevant to the chapters here. Turning first to contemporary "globalizing" processes and actors, we note that the accumulation and intensification of capitalism continues apace, so that there are fewer basic extractive industries and agricultural zones compared to the recent past, but those which continue are immensely large and efficient, such as the superquarry Milton mentions or the remaining Finnish forest sector in Berglund's study. Tourism and services have grown in connection with increased inter- and intranational inequality, population growth of the globally rich, and rapid communication and transportation. A number of the chapters revolve around commoditized tourism, including those by Macleod, Theodossopoulos, MacDonald, and Carrier. Cities continue to grow, expanding the already vast material flows (water, sewage, energy, food, trash, etc.) and human movement routes (roads, railroads, airports, etc.) required for them. We see this with British roadways (Milton) and Japanese trash compactors (Kirby). Finally, a massive scientific system achieves a myriad of small triumphs of technical knowledge, mostly in the pay of short-run interests. It has produced important knowledge about global-systemic processes, but the instrumentalism and technicism that works so well in small increments obstructs integrative understanding of people and nature seen together.

Each of these globalizing processes demands subsidiary investments—property reallocation or seizure, police and military security, expert management, and disposal or dispersal of waste—support activities which are often performed by collective (governmental and quasi-governmental) entities. These activities, however, challenge the finances and political legitimacy of local entities in rich nations as well as governments of all levels in poor ones. The decline of redistributive governmental taxation and spending means that support resources come through other mechanisms, including reliance on profits supposedly to be made by turning collective processes over to markets, funding by loans and grants from the wealthiest central governments of the world, and charitable foundations that draw on donations by and thus understandings of global wealthy people. Each of these agendas, from garbage disposal to global-change science, is a power project of a specific network of actors operating in social-political fields from very local to quite international. Some power projects (like transnational finance) are largely invisible, but many of them require mobilizing support and blunting opposition. Manipulation colors most of the cases in this volume, which frankly I find disturbing. Globalist environmental understanding, then, flows into, through, and out of such processes.[2]

The term "local" needs unpacking even more. In this, we should keep in mind both Eric Wolf's (1982) world historical anthropology, viewing mutable localities as nodes in an endlessly transforming global web, and James Ferguson and Akhil Gupta's (1997) concern with the political-discursive making of the local on which ethnographers have so naively relied. Localities, in this view, are not places where time has stopped and people have a special quality of direct sensuous relationship to each other and the environment. The localities in these chapters have undergone significant recent historical changes, and in this context the spatial and temporal local traditions are political causes and symbolic identifications constructed by specific leaders and their coalitions. For example, we notice rapid commercial transformation of localities in a number of chapters, especially in conjunction with the tourist industry. In the chapters by Theodossopoulos and Macleod, tourist booms undergirded the influence of key leaders who mobilized symbols of localism (e.g., the Brito kindred). Likewise, we see significant demographic changes (migration and population growth) that challenge established patterns of resource access and governance, as seen in Carrier's chapter about booming resort communities in Jamaica that attracted in-migrant fishermen. Although the time depth of industrial forestry in Finland (and perhaps for Kuusamo) is greater, the sentiments connecting regional identity with commercial lumbering still have a specific history of organizational development and symbolic elaboration.

To summarize, then, most localities in the contemporary world have undergone dramatic social, cultural, economic, and political changes on time scales of a generation or less. It behooves us to be more concrete in placing our current ethnographies of environmental understanding in these contexts. The fact that localities are malleable and caught up in the same changes as so-called global actors does not, in itself, obviate their (and our) concern with self-determination in environmental issues. But we should be careful about assuming a direct, sensuous, and personal understanding of the "local" without attention to exactly which moment within constant transformations this understanding encompasses, who are its promoters and opponents, and what are the sources of key symbols around which it coalesces.

We can then combine specific and dynamic components of the "global" with those of the "local" to give order to the variability of the chapters, in which global and local understandings seem to be all over the map, proenvironmentalist, antienvironmentalist, and flat-out contradictory. In a number of cases described here, extralocal actors or organizations initiate conflict and change by intruding on local resource use; their motivations are partly described in the "global" paragraphs just above. These impingements set up Carrier's central concern, a demanded translation of one kind of environmental understanding, essentially personal, into another kind, essentially bureaucratic. Local rejection of environmentalist initiatives seems to happen when such initiatives threaten an established local or regional extractive economy, to the defense of which local elites then rise (the time depth of this established economy does not have to be particularly long). The tourist economy on Zakynthos, described by Theodossopoulos, exemplifies this pattern. Such cases involve translation of tacit personal and local experiences into specifically economic abstractions rather than ones about "nature." On the other hand, translation into abstract environmentalist language apparently comes about when the economic initiative comes from the outside, threatening to impose new or highly intensified uses of biophysical resources against established local patterns. The lagoons in Belfast created by past industrial dredging summoned up environmentalist-localist loyalty when threatened by a larger-scale harbor plan as described by Milton. The capital and resource-intensive trash compactor studied by Kirby in Tokyo not only induced resistance, but actually resulted in interesting changes in environmental understanding that perhaps go beyond translation. Perhaps, then, local political coalitions view environmental activists as friends when globalizers push increased or novel resource use and extraction, and locals regard environmentalists as enemies when an established economy of resource extraction and use within a national and world economy is threatened by a conservation agenda.

This scheme is crude and undoubtedly misses many important phenomena, but it usefully emphasizes the need to adopt a dynamic, political view of the interplay among environmental understandings. Indeed, I have come close to questioning the usefulness of broad categorizations of understandings as global and local at all. I have treated them as highly fungible and conflictual (though I exaggerated these qualities to make my point), and the other authors show many times how apparently global actors wield localistic understandings, and vice versa. I do think that the distinction is useful, however, in terms of access to power, kinds of authorized versus unauthorized rhetoric, and long-term personal engagement with specific places. To sort these issues out, we might engage in a brief thought experiment. One analytical ideal type is that all thought is local thought, just placed in different social worlds: harbor planners, globetrotting environmental protestors, expatriate tourist dive-shop operators, displaced fishermen. The contrasting ideal type is a rigid contrast between unreflective localism and abstract globalism. On the one extreme, everyone is a local, whether rich or poor, cosmopolitan or backlander, and what we have is simply a clash of cultures; on the other extreme, global modes of understanding are radically different from local ones, and there are no sensuous, emotional, personal-contextual qualities to global thought.

What we see in these chapters is a midpoint between those two analytical extremes. Local understandings draw on particularistic experiences within mostly shallow historical contexts, but contexts enduring enough to seem true and permanent to the person experiencing them. And local understandings are not devoid of abstraction, especially when given help by crucial local leaders. Meanwhile, people playing roles in the various processes listed as "globalism," above, use certain kinds of abstraction more often, because in bureaucratic settings they are trained and rewarded for doing so, but they also bring to their worldview personal, often nonverbal, understandings of their surroundings, including important forms of social, gender, and regional prejudice. Hence, most understandings of globalizers differ from most local thought, but each has elements comparable to the other. More importantly, access to these modes of understanding and to speech and writing based on it is unequally distributed, with more of the power-related tools of abstraction in some people's hands than others. We see not a stark dichotomy in modes of thought but a tilted playing field: that is, inequalities.

The tilt comes from the advantage of some implicit understandings over others due to their bearers' ability to command abstractions of a specific kind during social struggles. Carrier (2001) has traced modern kinds of abstraction to the rise of capitalism, notably the creation and management of a division of labor. I consider it likely that other kinds of abstraction were crucial tools of power in past social orders, such as religious, ritual, and hierarchical abstractions. So my point is that abstraction (the culture trait) is not so much a characteristic of globalism as abstraction (the move in struggles) is a tool of globalizers. This means viewing understandings not so much as characteristics of people, but as practices that emerge and are codified in action. This is, I think, a crucial finding of this book, expressed particularly in its treatment of translation events not as horizontal transfers from one framework of meaning to another, but rather as forced changes in the register of public conversation and knowledge. I will return shortly to the critical point that these are *public* meanings, but first let us ask what aspects of the human-nonhuman relationship are at stake.

In the introduction, Carrier points out that the category "nature" is a human construction, and that specifically it partakes of the processes of abstraction and globalization diagnosed in this book. The assumption being criticized is that nature is one coherent thing, harmed or protected by external human activity. This does not match the weblike character of combined natural-human processes. The introduction makes a ritual bow toward the actual existence of biophysical "stuff" even if we view nature as a cultural construction, but we need to go further, in my opinion. Let us envision a variety of material and energy stocks and flows, interacting with a complex and evolving web of living things, not the least of which are humans. Let us try to avoid excessive implications of unity, while maintaining some willingness to generalize. Finally, let us assume that our interest is essentially human-centered; that is, environmentalism addresses how human changes in biophysical processes may in turn affect, in many cases harm, human adaptation on earth. Of course, this position is heavily debated and there is not room to argue for it on abstract grounds; instead, I hope the logic of my choice comes out in the discussion of human-biophysical issues that follows.

Massive nuclear war, with subsequent nuclear winter, certainly threatens all life, including humans, and must be considered the most global and profound environmental threat. Next to that in scale is global warming. Increased average temperature and other climate alterations caused by anthropogenic change to the composition of the atmosphere threaten contemporary human adaptations by coastal flooding, disruption of crops that are mainstays of our food system, increased frequency of hurricanes, and so forth. While global warming is immensely disruptive also to many organisms that are not directly used by humans, earth history shows that given time to adapt, life as a whole is resilient in the face of large fluctuations in temperature and humidity. Global warming has one other peculiarity: anthropogenic warming gases have definitely located sources (e.g., U.S. coal- and oil-fired electricity plants), but they largely mix in the atmosphere and their effects are distributed throughout the world according to extremely complex climate dynamics. The word "global" in this instance is thus appropriate. A telling contrast is with other atmospheric issues. Acid rain, for example, typically involves transport from coal-fired power plant to mountain forest, over distances that are interregional rather than global. Other kinds of air pollution ("smog") are essentially metropolitan.

The effort to maintain fresh water is complex in scale: sometimes a local question (such as drawing down nonrecharging or slowly recharging aquifers), but often one involving regional to interregional relationships around uses of rivers, lakes, large aquifers, and the like. And again, fresh water reduction or contamination will affect specific nonhuman organisms, but it is largely a concern because of human drinking, agriculture, and industry. Land degradation and toxic pollutants in land have mostly spatially limited proximate causes and effects, which is not surprising given the relative immobility of land, though there are some transport effects, and political ecologists have shown underlying distant causes. Again, the greatest concerns have to do with agriculture and pastoralism, rather than the existence of land itself. Finally, there is species loss. The relationship of spatial scale to species loss is complex, depending on habitat dynamics, migration, and species demographics, but in general the species most at risk are highly specialized and localized ones, having evolved in finely tuned ways to particular habitats and niches that are readily disrupted. Contemporary species conservation efforts often focus on marginal or isolated lands occupied by poor and culturally distinctive peoples, both because dominant cultures have already drastically reshaped habitats by intensive land use and because narrowly distributed species correlate with peculiar or isolated geographic zones (Orlove and Brush 1996). Furthermore, species conservation is ostensibly the least human-centered and the most non-human-centered thrust in environmentalism, yet it is based on a very human appreciation of species diversity, especially with preserving the present as we know it, since no one reasonably suggests that present species loss is halting the ongoing process of evolutionary species change and creation (a useful if slightly dated reference for the last two paragraphs is Turner et al. 1991).

This list is by no means complete; it involves gross generalizations and it is contingent on the never-ending development of new knowledge about the world.

In other words, I do not claim to have The True Scientific Facts. But it suffices to make two important points. First, "nature" or "environment" may be highly fetishized constructs, and all statements we make will indeed be constructs of some sort, but thinking in terms of complex and interwoven energy and material stocks and flows, of an evolutionary-ecology view of living beings, and of the deep history of the human occupation of the earth will get us past some of "nature's" worst reifications and mystifications while retaining a dialogue with sciences that are not so much concerned with the constructedness of concepts. And, as Hornborg (2001) has shown, taking this step enables us more effectively to critique the semiotics of such concepts and the work that they do in the world. Second, my list rests on a rough distinction between scale and abstraction, best understood by illustration. Global atmospheric composition, because of efficient mixing, is global in scale but not in the least abstract: it is a quite real unitary stock of gases. Our own personal sensory scales, however, lead us to understand anything global as abstract. On the other hand, reduction in global biodiversity is a human abstraction. The scale of species loss is largely local or regional, and specific to the species or set of interrelated species—a turtle variety in Zykanthos, a coral reef fish in Jamaica—as are the proximate causes of such losses.[3]

The latter example is significant, for at least four chapters in this book (Carrier, Macleod, Theodossopoulos, MacDonald), and arguably a fifth one (Berglund), involve the politics of species conservation. Concretely, they involve nonlocal organizations, in some cases allied with in-migrated environmentalists, funding the removal of habitat from local hunting, fishing, boating, and other uses, often in conjunction with their commoditization for tourism (diving, species viewing, trophy hunting). These five cases are also the ones where, allowing for complications, environmentalist initiatives were opposed by many local people and were seen as imposed from outside. (The other two chapters, by Milton and Kirby, are ones where locals or local-outside activist coalitions used environmentalist language to resist major infrastructure projects that came from outside.) Yet as we have noted, species and habitat conservation is more or less small and local in biophysical scale. Hence, in each instance, grandiose abstract understandings of environmentalism did not match localistic biophysical scale, and furthermore they framed issues in such a way as to take away responsibility and decision-making power from people who do live roughly coterminous with that biophysical scale.

The understandings at stake in this book, then, help establish *political scale*: the bounded arenas of conflict and consensus, and the struggles that occur within them or that redefine them (see Swartz, Turner, and Tuden 1966). A crucial example is Berglund's chapter on understandings of the Finnish nation. She is sceptical about the slippage between people's multivalent loyalty to Finland and single-valence definitions of the nation as a unit of economic interest. I share this scepticism, but I remain impressed with how Finland retains a sense of shared national involvement in the fate of its forests in an era when the political and fiscal autonomy of nations is eroding in favor of financial markets, trade blocs, and more powerful states. To make the point more broadly, this book describes a series of struggles, some open and some quiet and covert, over just which understandings will become public, will be shared or at least acknowledged in their power, and will thus set the boundaries for debating particular topics, in this case involving biophysical stocks and flows. Some understandings define the relevant arena of debate and decision as local traditions, others as national interest, yet others as world conservation.

In these struggles, certain actors have coercive technological, financial, and discursive power to establish their abstractions as the framework into which other understandings have to be translated. In the contemporary world this favors the carriers of projects (infrastructure, supply flows, financial capital accumulation, etc.) that I described above under the topic of globalization. There is, however, room for avoidance, subterfuge, and the like. Furthermore, powerholders often fail to obtain what they intend to, due to the complexity and sheer orneriness of the world (see Heyman 1999). One reason such power triumphs in the short run but frequently fails in the long run is that powerholders' favored abstractions may be maladaptive (in Rappaport's terms) insofar as they fail to construct a human political scale of involvement and responsibility that effectively corresponds with biophysical scales.

A disturbing quality of this book is the lack of effective and fair involvement, which I will call "democracy" (acknowledging the culturally grounded history of that concept and also the U.S. government's shameful use of it as a tool in authoritarian projects). A number of the chapters reveal incredible lies: the hiding and distortion of scientific evidence about the trash compactor described by Kirby, or the imaginary rhetoric of participation in planning described by MacDonald. Others involve outrageous resource grabs by means of barely disguised or even open force (Macleod's description of armed guards on the Dominican beach that was taken away from villagers for tourist hotels is alternately amazing and infuriating). The secret management of a "participatory" Jamaican environmental program by USAID is likewise deplorable, undermining nationality but even more importantly undermining honesty and accountability. In my own work on consumption and environmental policy, I have questioned price incentives and moral suasion as being both ineffective and favoring manipulation rather than involvement and responsibility (Heyman 2001). Reading these chapters brings me to ask what might be done differently. Readers may not share my inclination to moral evaluation and imaginative social speculation (see Heyman 1998, 2000, 2003), and those preferring analysis of strictly that which is, rather than that which could be, may want to break off here.

Put in simple terms (and this simplicity should not be pressed too far) we can envision political arenas that match biophysical scales, what Elinor Ostrom (1998,

2000) identifies as various levels of the commons. For example, this book shows that international environmental politics treats species and habitat conservation as a matter of global scale but that the relevant human hunters, fishers, users, and caretakers of the land are in small regions or localities. Communities are then coerced, or at best bribed, into protecting species, or more likely, they sneak around the laws and subvert the conservationist goals (see Vásquez-León 1999). Clearly, maintaining habitat and species survival needs to take place in a local commons, in which understanding, public debate, decisions, and responsibility for action align closely together. The local or regional decisions might kill off a lot of species, or they might not, but they are species whose survival or loss matters most to the people who live with them. On the other hand, global warming has global effects, and clearly merits a global understanding and decision-making arena, in which residents of the Nile delta and Pacific atolls, and poor consumers of imperiled basic grains, can hold the major producers of carbon dioxide, methane, and the rest responsible (fossil fuel power plants, notably in the U.S., users of gasoline-powered transportation, and large-scale cattle ranchers in tropical forests come to mind). Of course, the Kyoto pact is ostensibly global, but nations like the U.S. substantially ignore it, and part of the reason they can do so is, I think, an absence of truly global understandings (both global in extent and global in content) on this issue. I am thus envisioning a nested hierarchy of governance arenas based on shared understandings of environmental topics; a bit of this has been emerging as densely settled city-farm areas begin to forge shared knowledge and debates around scarce fresh water supplies, often cutting across traditional jurisdictions (e.g., Ingram, Laney, and Gillilan 1995).

A paralyzing failure of the social sciences, especially anthropology, in recent decades has been the divide between those who concern themselves with patterns of thought and speech, and those who concern themselves with patterns of biophysical objects and social action. It has vitiated our ability to speak effectively to crucial issues of our time, including environmental trends that threaten local, regional, and worldwide human adaptations. Carrier and his fellow authors are to be commended for bridging this canyon, for placing environmental understandings in the context of life histories, specific political struggles, and major inequalities of resources and power. Their work shows to us a crucial fact: the way that we understand our surroundings really does matter.

Notes

1. The journal is at http://dizzy.library.arizona.edu/ej/jpe.

2. Another component of globalization is the emergence of a globalized counterculture, as illustrated by international direct action environmentalists in British roadway protests (Milton) and First-World "drop out" environmentalists in Jamaica (Carrier).

Each social pattern creates its own characteristic internal dissenters, who simultaneously emphatically defy some dominant assumptions and use others; we should not be surprised to encounter similar understandings and modes of action among globalizing dissenters and "organization men."

3. In his chapter, MacDonald refers to the construction of scale, such as the global scale (also see Smith 1984). I also see people constructing political scales of action (I will call them "arenas") through key understandings. Indeed, my use of scale in this section as an "objective" nonhuman measure precisely contrasts with such constructed human scales, and is a way of furthering their analysis.

References

Blaikie, P. M. 1985. *The political economy of soil erosion in developing countries*. London: Longman.

Bodley, J. H. 2001. *Anthropology and contemporary human problems*. 4th ed. Mountain View, Calif.: Mayfield.

Bryant, R. L., and S. Bailey. 1997. *Third World political ecology*. London: Routledge.

Carrier, J. G. 2001. Social aspects of abstraction. *Social Analysis* 9: 239–52.

Croll, E. J., and D. J. Parkin, eds. 1992. *Bush base: Forest farm: Culture, environment and development*. London: Routledge.

Donahue, J. M., and B. R. Johnston, eds. 1998. *Water, culture, and power: Local struggles in a global context*. Washington, D.C.: Island Press.

Escobar, A. 1999. After nature: Steps to an antiessentialist political ecology. *Current Anthropology* 40: 1–30.

Forde, C. D. 1934. *Habitat, economy and society: A geographical introduction to ethnology*. London: Methuen.

Greenberg, J. B., and T. K. Park. 1994. Political ecology. *Journal of Political Ecology* 1: 1–11.

Gupta, A., and J. Ferguson, eds. 1997. *Anthropological locations: Boundaries and grounds of a field science*. Berkeley: University of California Press.

Heyman, J. McC. 1998. *Finding a moral heart for U.S. immigration policy: An anthropological perspective*. Washington, D.C.: American Anthropological Association.

———. 2000. Respect for outsiders? Respect for the law? The moral evaluation of high-scale issues by US immigration officers. *Journal of the Royal Anthropological Institute* (N.S.) 6: 635–52.

———. 2001. Working for beans and refrigerators: Learning about environmental policy from Mexican northern-border consumers. In *Exploring sustainable consumption: Environmental policy and the social sciences*, ed. M. J. Cohen and J. Murphy, 137–55. Amsterdam: Pergamon.

———. 2003. The inverse of power. *Anthropological Theory* 3: 139–56.

———, ed. 1999. *States and illegal practices*. Oxford: Berg.

Hornborg, A. 2001. *The power of the machine: Global inequalities of economy, technology, and environment*. Walnut Creek, Calif.: AltaMira.

Ingold, T. 1993. Globes and spheres: The topology of environmentalism. In *Environmentalism: The view from anthropology*, ed. K. Milton, 31–42. London: Routledge.

Ingram, H. M., N. R. Laney, and D. M. Gillilan. 1995. *Divided waters: Bridging the U.S.-Mexico border.* Tucson: University of Arizona Press.

Johnston, B. R., ed. 1994. *Who pays the price? The sociocultural context of environmental crisis.* Washington, D.C.: Island Press.

———, ed. 1997. *Life and death matters: Human rights and the environment at the end of the millennium.* Walnut Creek, Calif.: AltaMira.

Milton, K., 1996. *Environmentalism and cultural theory: Exploring the role of anthropology in environmental discourse.* London: Routledge.

———, ed. 1993. *Environmentalism: The view from anthropology.* London: Routledge.

Orlove, B. S. 1980. Ecological anthropology. *Annual Review of Anthropology* 9: 235–73.

———. 2002. *Lines in the water: Nature and culture at Lake Titicaca.* Berkeley: University of California Press.

Orlove, B. S., and S. B. Brush. 1996. Anthropology and the conservation of biodiversity. *Annual Review of Anthropology* 25: 329–52.

Ostrom, E. 1998. Scales, polycentricity, and incentives: Designing complexity to govern complexity. In *Protection of global biodiversity: Converging strategies,* ed. L. D. Guruswamy and J. A. McNeely, 149–67. Durham, N.C.: Duke University Press.

Ostrom, E., C. Gibson, and T. K. Ahn. 2000. The concept of scale and the human dimensions of global change: A survey. *Ecological Economics* 32: 217–39.

Rappaport, R. A. 1968. *Pigs for the ancestors.* New Haven, Conn.: Yale University Press.

———. 1979. *Ecology, meaning, and religion.* Richmond, Calif.: North Atlantic Books.

———. 1999. *Ritual and religion in the making of humanity.* Cambridge: Cambridge University Press.

Smith, N. 1984. *Uneven development: Nature, capital, and the production of space.* Oxford: Blackwell.

Steward, J. H. 1955. *The theory of culture change: The methodology of multilinear evolution.* Urbana: University of Illinois Press.

———. 1977. *Evolution and ecology: Essays on social transformation.* Urbana: University of Illinois Press.

Swartz, M. J., V. W. Turner, and A. Tuden, eds. 1966. *Political anthropology.* Chicago: Aldine.

Turner II, B. L., W. C. Clark, R. W. Kates, J. F. Richards, J. T. Mathews, and W. B. Meyer, eds. 1991. *The earth as transformed by human action: Global and regional changes in the biosphere over the past 300 years.* Cambridge: Cambridge University Press.

Vásquez-León, M. 1999. Neoliberalism, environmentalism, and scientific knowledge. In *States and illegal practices,* ed. J. McC. Heyman, 233–60. Oxford: Berg.

Wolf, E. R. 1982. *Europe and the people without history.* Berkeley: University of California Press.

About the Contributors

Eeva Berglund's research interests include environmental activism, technoscience, tourism, natural resource management, and the role of these in regional politics. She was lecturer in anthropology at Goldsmiths' College from 1998 to 2002. She has written on German environmentalism, *Knowing Nature, Knowing Science* (1998), and with David G. Anderson is coeditor of *Ethnographies of Conservation: Environmentalism and the Distribution of Privilege* (2002).

James G. Carrier has taught at the Universities of Papua New Guinea, Virginia, Durham, and Edinburgh, and currently holds research affiliations at the University of Indiana and Oxford Brookes University. He has written extensively on economy and political economy, including two edited collections, *Meanings of the Market* (1997) and *Virtualism: A New Political Economy* (1998, with Daniel Miller).

Josiah Heyman is professor of anthropology and chair of the sociology and anthropology department at the University of Texas at El Paso. He has written or edited three books and numerous journal articles, focusing on state power, migration, class formation, and transnational relations across the U.S.-Mexico border. He also has studied consumption, addressing energy, material use, and environmental policy from anthropological perspectives.

Peter Wynn Kirby teaches the anthropology of the environment and cities as an assistant professor at Asia Pacific University in Beppu, Japan. He is also affiliate lecturer in global environmentalism in the Faculty of Social and Political Sciences, University of Cambridge. In addition to several published articles and essays, he is coediting two collected volumes on space and power and is currently reshaping his Ph.D. dissertation—on the politics of waste in Japan—into a book.

Kenneth Iain MacDonald teaches in the department of geography and the interdisciplinary program in international development studies at the University of Toronto. He has conducted research in northern Pakistan over the past sixteen years. His work has been published in a number of journals including *Comparative Studies in Society and History* and *Society and Space*. Currently he is conducting work on the cultural politics of conservation, with a particular focus on the material and discursive interactions between international conservation NGOs and small-scale communities.

Donald Macleod is a research fellow at the University of Glasgow and director of the Crichton Tourism Research Centre. He has a doctorate in social anthropology from the University of Oxford and has undertaken fieldwork in the Canary Islands, the Dominican Republic, and Scotland. He has published on tourism, globalization, power, identity, environmental, and development issues.

Kay Milton is a reader in social anthropology at Queen's University, Belfast. Her main research interests are environmental and ecological anthropology and the anthropology of emotion. Her many publications in the former field include *Environmentalism: The View from Anthropology* (an edited volume, 1993) and *Environmentalism and Cultural Theory* (1996). Her most recent book, *Loving Nature* (2002), develops an ecological approach to the study of emotion.

Dimitrios Theodossopoulos is a lecturer in anthropology at the University of Bristol and a senior research fellow at St. Peter's College, Oxford. He is author of *Troubles with Turtles: Cultural Understandings of the Environment in a Greek Island* (2000) and coeditor (with Allen Abramson) of *Mythical Lands, Legal Boundaries: Land, Law and Environment* (2000). He is currently teaching and writing on a variety of themes, ranging from environmental politics to the ethnography of conflict and nationalism in the Balkans.